# *Shadal*
## ON LEVITICUS

Samuel David Luzzatto's
Interpretation of
the Book of *Vayikra*

translated and edited by
## Daniel A. Klein

KODESH PRESS

Published & Distributed by
Kodesh Press L.L.C.
New York, NY
kodeshpress@gmail.com

To Nancy Isaacs Klein
געלא רחל בת משה עמו״ש
mia carissima mamma

and to the memory of
Sidney Benjamin Klein
שמחה בנימין בן אלעזר הכהן ז"ל
mio carissimo papà

שמחו את ירושלם וגילו בה

# CONTENTS

# PREFACE

Leviticus is usually put into a kind of glass cabinet: it can be looked at, respected, and wondered at, but the real heart of the religion is presumed to be found in other parts of the Bible, especially Genesis, Exodus, and Deuteronomy, and the writings of the psalmists and prophets. [Such a] tradition does Leviticus wrong... The religion of Leviticus turns out to be not very different from that of the prophets which demanded humble and contrite hearts, or from the psalmists' love of the house of god.[1]

When I undertook to translate the writings of Samuel David Luzzatto (Shadal) on the Five Books of Moses 44 years ago,[2] I knew that I would eventually have to take the third book out of its glass cabinet. The prospect was daunting. For one thing, I wondered whether there would be much of an audience for this work, with its lack of stirring narratives and its emphasis on the details of animal sacrifices, ancient real estate law, and various skin disorders. But as I progressed through Leviticus (*Vayikra*), I was pleasantly surprised to discover that I was genuinely enjoying the process. Once again I have found that Shadal's interpretive approach simply makes sense, and makes sense simply.

---

1. Mary Douglas, *Leviticus as Literature*, p. 1.
2. With the following results up to now: *The Book of Genesis: A Commentary by Shadal (S. D. Luzzatto)*, Jason Aronson, 1998, and its second edition, *Shadal on Genesis: Samuel David Luzzatto's Interpretation of the Book of Bereshit*, Kodesh Press, 2019; and *Shadal on Exodus: Samuel David Luzzatto's Interpretation of the Book of Shemot*, Kodesh Press, 2015.

# Shadal on Leviticus

My daughter Liora, when preparing a series of women's classes on Leviticus, recently came to the startling realization that in the course of her many years of Jewish education, she had never once studied the book in school. Except for a brief foray into the laws of *tsara'at* (the so-called "leprosy") as a college undergraduate, I can essentially say the same thing. So, I imagine, can most readers of this new edition, despite the old idea of starting a child's Bible education with *Vayikra*, or at least its first chapter—"let the pure begin their studies with the pure," as the Midrash puts it. We would all be well advised to make up for lost time, and Shadal can serve as our guide. His insights into the purposes and benefits of the book's manifold rules and regulations, and his clear explanations of the book's sometimes difficult language, can help to open up Leviticus to those who have regarded it as a closed or overly challenging tome.

Once again the time has come for me to acknowledge the help, encouragement, and support of a circle of friends and Shadal enthusiasts, including Mitchell First, Shimon Steinmetz, Meylekh Viswanath, Ari Kinsberg, and Rabbi Aryeh Sklar. To these names I am pleased to add Malka Margolies, the daughter of Shadal's late biographer, Rabbi Morris B. Margolies, and a dedicated keeper of her father's flame.

Kudos to Rabbi Hillel Novetsky, whose website AlHaTorah.org has been a particularly valuable resource in my work, and who has kindly provided me with access to material from important manuscripts. Through my librarian daughter Aviva's online connections, I have become acquainted with Michelle (Hadassah) Chesner, the Norman E. Alexander Librarian for Jewish Studies at Columbia University, who has also been generous with the manuscript resources at her disposal. For additional research assistance, my thanks go to Rabbi Jerry Schwarzbard and Havva Zellner at the library of the Jewish Theological Seminary of America.

*Todah rabbah* to my dear friend and "brother from another mother," Dr. Shalom Rackovsky, for keeping me supplied with books that I needed from the Cornell University library. And for saving me untold time and effort in the wake of a computer crash, I give heartfelt thanks to my tech-savvy daughter Yehudit ("DD"), who secured the assistance of experts who magically retrieved several years' worth of Leviticus files from a deep, dark hole.

# Shadal on Leviticus

As always, I am grateful to Rabbi Alec Goldstein of Kodesh Press for believing in the Shadal project and seeing it to fruition with his scholarship, professional expertise, and aesthetic taste. With his help, and that of the *Santo Benedetto Signore*, I now go on to translate the remaining volumes of the *ḥumash* and, hopefully, even more of Shadal's Hebrew and Italian treasures as well.

Above all, I must express my thanks for the love and support of my dear family: my wife of 40-and-counting years, Bia; our son, Dr. Coby Klein, and our aforementioned daughters, Liora Wittlin, Aviva Rosenberg, and DD Klein; our fine children-in-law; and our amazing pack of grandchildren, *ken yirbu*. With sadness and fondness, I note the recent passing of my mother-in-law, Davida Hirsch. And I can never forget what I owe to my grandmother, Elizabeth Isaacs Gilbert of blessed memory, who changed my life on the day she first showed me an old book from her father's library, Volume 1 of Shadal's *Pentateuco*.

This book is lovingly dedicated to my mother, Nancy Isaacs Klein, who has reached the age of 90, *bli ayin ha-ra*, with the same vigor, humor, and common sense that I have always sought to emulate, and to my father of blessed memory, Sidney B. Klein, who thoroughly embodied his Hebrew name Simcha ("joy"), who encouraged each of his children to learn a new language and subtly steered me toward Italian, who cheerfully lent me Shadal research aid whenever asked, and who was proud and tickled to call me his "Italian son." *Grazie mille mamma e papà!*

Daniel Abraham Klein
Rochester, New York
October 17, 2020

# INTRODUCTION

Samuel David Luzzatto (1800-1865), known by his Hebrew acronym Shadal, has been described as a "multi-faceted genius."[3] A superb linguist, writer, educator, and religious thinker, Shadal devoted his talents above all to *parshanut ha-mikra*, the interpretation of the Jewish Scriptures. Though esteemed through the years in scholarly circles, Shadal long remained relatively unknown to the wider public, but the twenty-first century has seen an awakening interest in his work.[4] Hopefully, the publication of the present Leviticus volume will help further this trend.

Who was Shadal? It is surprisingly difficult to answer this question, because Luzzatto does not fit easily into any pigeonholes or conventional assumptions:

---

3. Israel Abrahams, "Samuel David Luzzatto as Exegete," *Jewish Quarterly Review* 57:83-100 (1966), p. 87.
4. See, for example, Robert Bonfil, Isaac Gottlieb, and Hannah Kasher, eds., *Samuel David Luzzatto: The Bi-Centennial of His Birth* (Jerusalem: Hebrew University Magnes Press, 2004); Shmuel Vargon, *S. D. Luzzatto: Moderate Criticism in Biblical Exegesis* (Ramat Gan: Bar-Ilan University Press, 2013); Ephraim Chamiel, *The Middle Way: The Emergence of Modern-Religious Trends in Nineteenth-Century Judaism Responses to Modernity in the Philosophy of Z. H. Chajes, S. R. Hirsch and S. D. Luzzatto* (Brighton, MA, Academic Studies Press, 2014); Marc Gopin, *Compassionate Judaism: The Life and Thought of Samuel David Luzzatto* (CreateSpace Independent Publishing Platform, 2017).

# Shadal on Leviticus

### 1. *Was Shadal Italian?*

Yes, insofar as he lived in a geographical region of Europe known as "Italy," was a native speaker of Italian, and was in many ways a product of the local culture. But he was never a resident or citizen of a unified, independent country called Italy. Throughout his lifetime, Shadal's native city of Trieste and longtime home city of Padua belonged (except for brief periods of Napoleonic rule) to the Austrian Empire. Padua became a part of the new Kingdom of Italy in 1866, the year after Shadal's death, while Trieste was annexed to Italy only at the end of World War I.

### 2. *Was Shadal's ancestry Sepharadi, Ashkenazi, or neither?*

According to family tradition, the Luzzatto family emigrated to what is now Italy in the mid-1500's from the eastern German province of Lausitz, or Lusatia. The Luzzattos were thus of Ashkenazi origin, and hence a small private synagogue in the Venice ghetto, the Scuola Luzzatto, observed the "German rite."[5] In other words, in the long history of Italian Jewry, the Luzzattos were relative newcomers to the peninsula, as opposed to the community's earliest elements, which trace their origins back to the time of the Roman Empire and are considered neither Ashkenazi nor Sepharadi. It also follows that attempts to identify Shadal as a neglected Sephardic scholar,[6] though well intentioned, are less than accurate.

### 3. *Was Shadal a rabbi?*

Strictly speaking, no. He declined an offer of *semikhah* from his main teacher, Abraham Eliezer Halevi, Chief Rabbi of Trieste,[7] and in an 1838

---

5. Cecil Roth, *Venice* (Philadelphia: Jewish Publication Society, 1930), p. 141.
6. See, for example, Henry Aharon Wudl, "On Republishing the Works of Sephardic Scholars," haSepharadi.com, Mar. 25, 2018, https://hasepharadi.com/2018/03/25/on-republishing-the-works-of-sephardic-scholars/.
7. Morris B. Margolies, *Samuel David Luzzatto: Traditionalist Scholar*, p. 30.

letter he insisted that he was neither a rabbi nor a decisor of Jewish law.[8] Earlier that year, however, he had in fact received what might be viewed as an honorary ordination. Rabbi Abraham Reggio, one of the leading Italian rabbis of the day, wrote Luzzatto a document describing him as "a reasoning thinker and intellectual... in Bible as well as in Mishnah and Gemara" and bestowing upon him the title of *Ma'alat he-Ḥakham* ("exalted scholar"), i.e., "Rabbi." Apparently this honor was conferred on Shadal at the behest of the Collegio Rabbinico of Padua, where he taught Bible, Hebrew, and Jewish history and religion for 36 years.[9] But it seems that he seldom if ever made personal use of this title, which is why he has always been known by the simple acronym "Shadal" and not, as one occasionally sees, "Rashdal."

### 4. *Was Shadal a participant in the Haskalah?*

The Haskalah or "Jewish Enlightenment" movement, which may be said to have started in the 1770's and lasted till about 1880, favored freedom of thought and inquiry, and had among its goals the renewal of Hebrew as a literary language. Shadal shared these interests, and to that extent he may be viewed as a "Maskil." However, he was sharply opposed to the tendencies of the movement's more radical wing to glorify European culture, encourage assimilation, and advocate religious reform.

Out of the Haskalah emerged a related movement, the *Wissenschaft des Judentums* ("the science of Judaism"), which sought to apply academic scholarly methods to Jewish studies. Although Shadal never attended a university and was largely self-taught in such disciplines as linguistics and philosophy, he became an important practitioner of the *Wissenschaft* approach, and he corresponded and cooperated with the movement's leading figures. On the other hand, he took many of these colleagues to task for engaging in Jewish scholarship "without regarding it as something precious in itself. After all, Goethe and Schiller are more precious in their eyes than all the prophets, the Tannaim, and the Amoraim. They study Israel's antiquities as others study the antiquities of Egypt, Assyria, Babylonia, and Persia, that is to say, for the love of

---

8. Letter to Hirsch B. Fassel (Sept. 18, 1838), *Iggerot Shadal*, p. 544.
9. *Il Corriere Israelitico*, 16 (August 1877), pp. 57-60.

science or the love of glory."[10] This critique is strikingly similar to one previously expressed by Rabbi Samson Raphael Hirsch, who was himself no friend of the *Wissenschaft* movement.[11]

## 5. Was Shadal Orthodox?

If we understand the term "Orthodox" in its literal Greek sense of "correct belief," then it can be said that Shadal fit the bill. It has been observed that Shadal firmly believed in *Torah min ha-shamayim* (the Divine origin of the Torah) as well as the Torah's unity and accurate transmittal by Moses,[12] and that he affirmed as "irreducibles" of Judaism the belief in Divine Providence, the immortality of the soul, the coming of the Messiah, and the resurrection of the dead.[13] Luzzatto was also convinced of the truth of the miracles recounted in the Bible: "If miraculous events are written in it, we have no proof with which to contradict its words, for our [empirical] investigation cannot grasp what is not in the ordinary way of the world."[14]

Yet it has been asserted that Shadal's commentary "occasionally deviates from Orthodox beliefs."[15] This concern has been raised— apparently even in his own time—in connection with his views on the development of the Oral Law (*Torah she-be-al peh*), which he regarded as a product, in part, of legislation by the Rabbis enacted under the authority granted to them by the Written Torah but often arising from the historic and sociological needs of their times. "Turning those laws

---

10. Letter to Solomon Judah Rapoport (June 5, 1860), *Iggerot Shir*, p. 1366, cited in Margolies, *Samuel David Luzzatto*, p. 157.
11. "Moses and Hesiod, David and Sappho... Isaiah and Homer, Delphi and Jerusalem... we pack them all peacefully together in our minds in the same box, they all rest peacefully in the same grave... The tears and sighs of our fathers fill no longer our breasts, but our libraries." ("Die Trauer des 9. Av" (1855), in *Judaism Eternal*, trans. I. Grunfeld, pp. 133-134.)
12. *Ha-Ensiklopediyah ha-Ivrit*, s.v. "Luzzatto, Shemuel David."
13. Margolies, *Samuel David Luzzatto*, p. 69.
14. S. D. Luzzatto, *Meḥkerei ha-Yahadut* I, part 2, p. 79.
15. Rabbi Gil Student, "Shadal and the Orthodox Canon," http://www.Torahmusings.com/2016/01/shadal-and-the-orthodox-canon/ (January 11, 2016).

into historical contingencies deprives them of all sanctity," it has been claimed.[16] Elsewhere I have discussed this issue at length, making the argument that in fact there is room within the Orthodox tent for Shadal's approach.[17]

If we understand "Orthodox" as a label for one who is a thoroughly observant Jew in practice (*shomer Torah u-mitsvot*), Shadal can be said to come within this criterion as well. "The observance of the commandments in all of their particulars," it has been noted, "was a matter which Luzzatto regarded as absolutely essential to the Jew, ethically and ethnically."[18] Moreover, Shadal was adamantly opposed to the nascent Reform movement of his time, maintaining that the very term "Reform" was a "specious" name that served to mask the movement's goal of "totally abolishing the Mosaic law."[19] There is, however, a single recorded indication suggesting that Shadal may have chosen not to follow one particular normative halakhic rule as a matter of personal practice; this issue will be treated separately and in depth below.

In any event, Shadal has been characterized as "Orthodox" by a number of writers. Specifically, he and Samson Raphael Hirsch have been linked as exponents of a "Neo-Orthodoxy," which comprised "an acceptance of the totality of Jewish law and practice within a framework of modernism," that is, an active participation in secular life and affairs.[20] Shadal himself once stated that he believed himself to be "Orthodox"—while remarking wryly that the majority of "kosher" Jews might not agree.[21] But on another occasion, he addressed himself to his traditionalist critics and implored, "You, my sincere and upright

16. Ibid.
17. See my introduction to *Shadal on Exodus*, pp. 19-31; see also my article, "Unconventional but Not Unorthodox: Shadal's Approach to the Oral Torah," *La Rassegna Mensile di Israel*, Vol. 84 Iss. 1-2, pp. 47-68 (2018).
18. Margolies, *Samuel David Luzzatto*, p. 78.
19. Letter to A. J. Fürst (Sept. 1, 1843), in *Epistolario italiano francese latino*, pp. 424-425.
20. David Rudavsky, "Samuel David Luzzatto and Neo-Orthodoxy," *Tradition*, vol. 7 no. 3 (Fall 1965), p. 23.
21. Letter to Abraham Geiger (March 2, 1851), in *Index raisonné des livres de correspondance de feu Samuel David Luzzatto* (Padua, 1878), pp. 100-101.

brothers, who sigh and moan over all the abominations that are being perpetrated among us, do not declare war against me, for I am with you, not with your enemies, Heaven forbid!"[22]

# Leviticus:
# Italian Translation, Hebrew Commentary

Equally at home in Italian and Hebrew, Shadal wore two hats in his contributions to Bible scholarship. He authored Italian translations of the Five Books of Moses, Isaiah, and Job,[23] and he wrote commentaries in Hebrew on the aforementioned books as well as on Jeremiah, Ezekiel, and Proverbs. In his Italian translation work, he strove to render the Bible "accessible to all," while preserving "the aspect, the color of the original."[24] In his commentaries, as a master of Hebrew grammar and usage, Shadal focused on the plain meaning (*peshat*) of the biblical text as he saw it. Although he was a devout believer in the divinity, unity, and antiquity of the Torah, Shadal approached the text in a remarkably free spirit of inquiry, drawing upon a wide variety of sources, ancient and contemporary, Jewish and non-Jewish. As a result, many of his interpretations may strike even the modern reader as fresh and novel.

Shadal's complete work on Leviticus, including both the Italian translation and the Hebrew commentary, was a posthumous assemblage that first appeared in 1874 as volume 3 of *Il Pentateuco volgarizzato e commentato (Hamishah Humshei Torah Meturgamim Italkit u-M'forashim Ivrit),* printed in Padua. His Italian translation—reprinted

---

22. Letter to Osias Schorr (1838), in *Mehkerei ha-Yahadut* I, part 2, pp. 248-249.

23. An Italian translation of the entire Jewish Bible (Tanakh), begun by Luzzatto and completed by some of his students ("continuatori") appeared after his death: *La Sacra Bibbia volgarizzata,* Rovigo, 1871. Besides Isaiah and Job, a number of the books (including Joshua and Judges) bear his name as sole translator; others (including the Psalms) were translated by him in part, and still others are credited solely to various students.

24. S. D. Luzzatto, *Il Pentateuco volgarizzato e commentato (Hamishah Humshei Torah Meturgamim Italkit u-M'forashim Ivrit),* vol. 1 (Padua, 1871), pp. xlv-xlvi.

# Shadal on Leviticus

from *Il Pentateuco colle Haftarot volgarizzato ad uso degl' Israeliti*, vol. 3 (Trieste, 1860)—is an important component of his treatment of the book, not only because any biblical translation is itself a form of commentary, but particularly because his actual commentary in Hebrew tends to be more sparse and sporadic for Leviticus than it is for Genesis and Exodus. Thus, there are many instances where the only indication of how Shadal understood a specific word or phrase comes from his Italian rendering, or from a bracketed explanation that he added to the translation. For example, the somewhat mysterious word *omer* (Lev. 23:10) is passed over in silence in the Hebrew commentary, but Shadal translates it as *manipolo* ("sheaf") and adds a statement in brackets, "according to the tradition: barley flour of the measure of an *omer*." It was only in this way that Rabbi David Zvi Hoffmann, in his own later Leviticus commentary, was able to understand and discuss Shadal's interpretation of the word *omer*.

The book's commentary component was apparently compiled after Shadal's death from transcripts of his lectures at the Collegio Rabbinico, faithfully recorded by his students. Manuscripts of such records (though not covering most of Leviticus) have been discovered by Yonatan Bassi, a descendant of one of these students.[25] Unfortunately, Shadal did not live to supervise a definitive edition of his *Pentateuco*, and one interesting result is that the Italian translation does not always agree with the Hebrew commentary.[26]

Occasionally, the commentary features an essay-length treatment of a particular topic, such as the significance of the sacrificial system (at Lev. 1:2) or of the regulations of purity and impurity (at Lev. 12:2). At other times, however, Shadal's comment on a given word or phrase is terse to the point of near incomprehensibility, or it offers a bare citation to a work that most readers would find unfamiliar or hard to trace. For instance, Shadal's entire comment on the word *shok* ("leg") in Lev. 7:32 reads as follows:

---

25. See Bassi's edition of the commentary, *Perush Shadal la-Torah* (Jerusalem: Carmel, 2015). Other manuscripts with sections of the commentary, some possibly in Shadal's own hand, reside in the libraries of Columbia University and the Jewish Theological Seminary in New York, and of the Schocken Institute in Jerusalem.
26. See, for example, Lev. 25:33 and my notes ad loc.

# Shadal on Leviticus

See *Sefer Mitsvot Gadol*, Positive Commandments 183; *Tosefot Yom Tov* on *Ḥullin*, end of ch. 10; and *Sefer ha-Zikkaron*.

It takes some heavy lifting in order to flesh out this comment for the benefit of the average modern reader—and that was my task as the editor of this volume (see my explanatory footnote *ad loc.*). It is not that Shadal was trying to be obtuse (as he sometimes accused the medieval commentator Ibn Ezra of being); rather, his commentary—as opposed to his translation—was never actually intended for a broad, popular audience, but was created for the use of his rabbinical students, who presumably would have been familiar with sources such as *Sefer ha-Zikkaron* and might have had access to them in the library of their Collegio.

If one pays close enough attention, little gems of subtle humor may be detected in Shadal's Leviticus commentary. Here are some examples:

- Lev. 2:2—expressing the view that the sacrificial term *azkaratah* means "its scent" (that is, those parts of an offering that are meant to emit a scent), Shadal explains that the word *zekhirah* ("remembering") has as its most basic meaning "to give off a scent," for remembering a past event is like detecting the scent of something after it passes from one's sight. Shadal observes that Moses Mendelssohn wrote to the contrary, that a scent is called *zekher* because it resembles the "memory" of something tangible. But Mendelssohn had it backwards, Shadal says, because he failed to keep in mind that words describing abstract things like "memory" are normally derived from words describing things that can be perceived by the senses, like "scent." This statement of Shadal contains a little joke: in the Hebrew, the phrase "he failed to keep in mind" is *hu lo zakhar*.

- Lev. 12:2—in discussing the laws of the *tsara'at* disease, Shadal says, "Many have thought that the reason for keeping the *metsora* ("leper") at a distance is because this disease is contagious through touch, but it seems to me that if the Torah had been concerned about contagion, how many other diseases are contagious—and yet the Torah did not prescribe any regulation for them. How is it that the

Torah did not command a thing concerning pestilence?" In Hebrew, this last sentence reads, *eikh lo tzivetah davar al devar ha-dever?* Surely it is no coincidence that this sentence contains three words in close succession that sound so similar and are, in fact, spelled the same way (דבר) in Hebrew. This is a good example of Shadal's fondness for plays on words.

- Lev. 21:7—explaining that the phrase *ve-ishah gerushah me-ishah* means a woman divorced *from* her husband, not *by* her husband, Shadal strongly disagrees with the notion that the *mem* prefix in words such as *me-ishah* and *mimmenni* means "by," and he points out that the early Hebrew grammarians "knew that if one were to say (as in *Kerem Ḥemed* vol. 7 [1843], p. 100) *ahuv mimmenni me'od*, the import of these words would be, 'He is loved much more than I am,'" and not "he is much loved by me." The average reader will be excused for failing to see the humor in this remark, but a little digging reveals that Shadal is in fact shooting a sarcastic barb at a colleague. The anonymous author of the cited article in *Kerem Ḥemed* has been identified as Rabbi Solomon Judah Leib Rapoport,[27] who (to use an apt slang term) was a "frenemy" of Shadal. In the article, Rapoport says, "Indeed Luzzatto is... *ahuv mimmenni me'od*, and is in fact deserving of being loved by any reader of his enlightened and beneficial books, but nevertheless he is a creature of clay like any other man..." In effect, Shadal is responding, "You may think you said, 'He is much loved by me,' but what you actually did was admit, 'He is loved much more than I am!'"

## Major Themes in Shadal's Leviticus

Three of the subjects that receive the closest attention in the Book of Leviticus are the workings of the sacrificial system, the signs and symptoms of *tsara'at*, and the prohibition of certain sexual relationships. In dealing with each of these subjects, Shadal not only follows his usual style of focusing on particular words and phrases, but also pulls back to provide a broad overview of these legal fields and the rationales behind

---

27. A hat tip to Shimon Steinmetz for pointing out this identification to me.

them. There is an unmistakable common thread that can be detected in all of these discussions: an emphasis on the social utility of the laws in question.

To the modern mind, bringing burnt offerings and other sacrifices may seem like an unnecessary or even barbaric way to worship God, but Shadal points out that this system yielded benefits to society. "The divine Torah," says Shadal in his comment to Lev. 1:2, "whose goal was not to teach the nation knowledge and wisdom, but rather to guide it on the paths of righteousness, did not abolish the custom of sacrifices, not that this would have been beyond its power, but because this custom is not evil in and of itself and does no harm to people or to the betterment of their ways; rather, it is beneficial to them. If the Torah had announced to the people that God has no desire for burnt offerings or sacrifices, the next day they would have said, 'What desire does God have that we be righteous, and what would it profit us to perfect our ways?' And because one of the basic principles of the Torah is the belief that God watches over the activities of humankind and that He loves doers of good and hates the wicked, it was necessary that God would not be described in the full exaltedness of His true position, but that His majesty would be slightly lowered, as it were, and He would be described in human thought as a great King Who knows all their activities, hears their cries, and accepts their gifts."

Would not other, more "refined" modes of worship have sufficed? Not at the time when the Torah was given, says Shadal. "If instead of sacrifices, God had commanded prayer, hymns, Torah reading, and preaching words of moral instruction, the greatness and fear of God would not have been impressed upon the hearts of the masses, for it would have seemed to them that the gods of the nations, whose worshippers presented them with various sacrifices, were greater and more glorious than our God, Whose worship consisted merely of intangible things."

Why require all of the sacrifices to take place in one central location? Again, Shadal invokes reasons of social utility. "As a result of having a single Sanctuary, the entire people would gather at a single place, their hearts would be bound together in a bond of affection, they would always form a single society, and each tribe and clan would not become a people unto itself."

# Shadal on Leviticus

Even the seemingly arbitrary rule requiring the meat of an individual's "sacrifice of contentment" to be entirely eaten within two days was a way of promoting social cohesion, according to Shadal. In his comment to Lev. 19:9, he explains that the reason for this rule "was that the offeror would be compelled to invite others to his sacrifice, so that they would eat it with him. If he were permitted to salt the meat of the sacrifice and preserve it for days or months, he alone would eat it with his household, but since the eating was forbidden later than the day after, he would be compelled to offer some of it to others, and this would bring about an act of charity and kindness."

Turning to the laws of *tsara'at*, Shadal once again discerns a socially useful underlying rationale, that of reinforcing the nation's religious belief. Commenting on Lev. 12:2, he says that "a change in the appearance of the skin was thought by the ancients to be a sign of God's reproach, and they considered the leper to be stricken with a plague of God as a punishment for some serious sin; for this reason they would keep apart from the leper as they would from one who was excommunicated by the Omnipresent. Similarly, a change in the appearance of a garment or a house was considered a sign of God's reproach, as if the stricken garment or house were despised by the Omnipresent by reason of some great sin that had been committed within them. *Because all of this supported a faith in Divine Providence and in God's reward and punishment,* the Torah upheld this belief and commanded that the leper be kept distant, the stricken garment burned, and the stricken house demolished, and that the [cured] house be ritually sprinkled" (emphasis mine).

It should be noted that in Shadal's view, it seems to make no difference whether the Lord actually needed or desired sacrifices, or whether physical disfigurements were actually triggered by sin. To him, the important point is that the common people were under such impressions, and that there was no reason to disabuse them of these beliefs. He thus seems to subscribe to the concept of "necessary beliefs," which are conducive to improving social order, regardless of whether they are literally true. This approach is seen elsewhere in Shadal's Torah commentaries, notably in connection with building of the Tabernacle, where he expresses the view that one of the purposes behind the collection of the silver half-shekel for the structure's bases was to diminish—but not to abolish—the people's fear of the "evil eye" (see his comment on Exod. 30:12). In addition, Shadal does not appear to have been concerned with exploring any deeper, hidden meanings that the sacrificial system might have entailed. This bothered Nehama Leibowitz, who asserted that his "simplistic explanation... divested the sacrifices of the halo of mystery and sanctity that surrounds them."[28] But here, once again, Shadal is following a consistent approach, having flatly declared elsewhere that Judaism is *una religione senza misteri*, "a religion without mysteries."[29]

As for the forbidden sexual unions (*arayot*), Shadal acknowledges that at least some of the prohibitions are aimed at furthering the wellbeing of the home and the perfection of an individual's virtuous traits, but he maintains that all of them are "for the benefit of society" (comment on Lev. 18:6). "The prohibition of relations with another's wife has an obvious purpose," he says, "which is to avoid the violence, rivalry, and murder that result from adultery. Even if a man were to consent to this and to offer his wife to a rich man, this practice would be forbidden because of the corruption that the resulting destruction of virtue would cause to the nation as a whole." He goes on to state that one of the purposes of the incest prohibitions is to further "the wellbeing of the state. The taking of one's mother, the wife of one's father, the father's sister, or the wife of the father's brother are acts against the honor of the father and mother, and the depreciation of parental honor would cause destruction of virtue and undermine the family regime."

Particularly interesting is Shadal's assertion that the prohibition of taking one's sister "seems to be based on the wellbeing of the state, for if taking a sister were permitted, most men would marry their sisters, each family would thus become a people unto itself, the families would not intermarry or mix with each other, and the nation would not become one people, but would turn into many peoples that would be distant from each other and not love one another."

Generally absent from Shadal's evaluation of these sexual prohibitions

---

28. *New Studies in Vayikra*, p. 17.
29. Letter to Giuseppe Almeda (Mar. 6, 1839), in *Epistolario italiano francese latino*, p. 289; for an English version of the letter, see the appendix to this volume, pp. 257-274.

is any consideration of their intrinsic wrongness or repugnance. This is surprising, because an act such as incest has traditionally been regarded by legal scholars as a *malum in se*, that is, one that is inherently and essentially evil or immoral.[30] In contrast, Shadal's analysis would seem to classify it as more akin to a *malum prohibitum*, that is, an act that is wrong simply because it is prohibited by law. But by emphasizing the harmful social results of the *arayot* offenses, perhaps Shadal is staking out a kind of middle approach.

It should also be pointed out that Shadal applies a similar social-utility focus to other Torah laws outside of Leviticus, even where such a focus might be unexpected. For example, he notes that the Second Commandment's prohibition of polytheistic worship has the beneficial effect of fostering universal brotherhood: "Polytheistic beliefs cause the hearts of the various peoples to be sundered, for the members of one nation, who worship a particular god, will despise the members of another nation who worship another god... Only those who believe in One God know that we all have one Father, that One God created us, and that all humankind is dear to Him" (comment on Exod. 20:3). Likewise, Shadal states that one of the key purposes of requiring a weekly Sabbath observance is that the people should rest not at random times, but all on the same day, "in order that they should be able to gather together to eat and drink and converse with one another, so that love might increase among them, and also that they should be able to assemble in houses of worship and hear Torah from the mouths of the Sages" (comment on Exod. 20:11).

# "I have accepted it for myself in practice": Shadal and Leviticus 19:27

In my Introduction to *Shadal on Genesis*, I dealt with criticisms that have been aimed at Samuel David Luzzatto from both the "right" and the "left" as to whether his approach to biblical interpretation was too modern or not modern enough. In my Introduction to *Shadal on Exodus*,

---

30. See, for example, Mark S. Davis, "Crimes Mala in Se: An Equity-Based Definition," 17 *Criminal Justice Policy Review* 270, 271, 273 (Sept. 2006).

# Shadal on Leviticus

I examined his novel understanding of the development of the Oral Law and whether it could be deemed "Orthodox." In the present Introduction, I find it appropriate to zero in on a controversy that has arisen over Shadal's understanding and practical application of one particular legal provision in the book of Leviticus.

In a lengthy letter to his colleague Rabbi Solomon Judah Leib Rapoport, dated March 25, 1833,[31] covering a wide variety of subjects, Shadal laments the fact that the two of them entertained quite different opinions about the medieval scholar Abraham Ibn Ezra. That is, Rapoport admired and defended Ibn Ezra, while Shadal accused him of hypocrisy. In particular, Shadal says that he objects not to Ibn Ezra's straying from the opinions of the Talmudic Sages in his biblical commentaries, but rather to his occasional effusive (and allegedly insincere) expressions of support for those same opinions.

Suddenly, mid-diatribe, Luzzatto veers off on a brief tangent, apparently wishing to make the point that his opposition to Ibn Ezra is not total or unreasonable. He says (p. 246), "And although I am not among his admirers, I have accepted his interpretation (against the Halakhah) of the verse 'Do not cut in a circle the extremities (of the hair) of your head' [*lo takifu pe'at roshkhem*, Lev. 19:27]—that this is only [as a sign of mourning] for a dead person—and I have accepted it for myself in practice, even though I do not instruct others accordingly, since I have nothing to do with [halakhic] instruction."

This brief and rather cryptic remark, published more than 16 years after Shadal's death, lay buried virtually unnoticed[32] in *Iggerot Shadal* for over a century, but it ultimately proved to be a ticking time bomb.

In 1993, Rabbi Dr. Marc B. Shapiro published an article, "Maimonides' Thirteen Principles: The Last Word in Jewish Theology?" in volume 4 (pp. 187-242) of *The Torah U-Madda Journal*, a publication of Yeshiva University. The article maintained that each of the Thirteen Principles had in fact met with opposition by authoritative Jewish figures

---

31. *Iggerot Shadal*, vol. 1, pp. 244-261.
32. But not entirely; the statement is paraphrased in the *Jewish Encyclopedia* (1906), s.v. "Beard" (Cyrus Adler, W. Max Muller, and Louis Ginzberg).

# Shadal on Leviticus

over the centuries. One of these figures, said Shapiro, was Samuel David Luzzatto, who objected to Maimonides' Third Principle, under which anyone who ascribed a bodily form to God was to be deemed a heretic (pp. 192-193).

Shapiro's article generated letters to the editor, which were published in the next volume of the *Journal*. Responding to these letters, Shapiro noted, "In my article I was careful to quote only authorities whom I believed to be acceptable to Orthodoxy."[33] Then he dropped a footnote:

> I should, however, point out that were I to publish the article today I would omit references to the idiosyncratic Samuel David Luzzatto. Despite his unquestioned piety and relentless struggle to cleanse Judaism from non-Jewish philosophical influences, I now see that in a private letter he admitted that, in practice, he did not accept a certain halakhah as set down in the Talmud, preferring instead Ibn Ezra's interpretation of the verse in question. See *Iggerot Shadal* (Cracow, 1882), 246. Presumably this fact was unknown to both *Mossad ha-Rav Kook*, which published his *Yesodei ha-Torah* (1947), and R. Shaul Yisraeli, who included Luzzatto in his *Perakim be-Mahshevet Yisrael* (Jerusalem, 1974).[34]

In other words, Shapiro understood Shadal's statement itself as tantamount to a confession of heresy. Seemingly surprised that no one had ever made an issue of it before, Shapiro apparently took the view that the statement was such a serious breach that it could single-handedly cancel the value of the entire remainder of Shadal's life work, at least in Orthodox eyes. As Rabbi Dr. B. Barry Levy observed a few years later, Shapiro's comment "effectively excommunicates Luzzatto, who, it seems, is now better left outside the canon of acceptable Orthodox writers, though it remains to be seen if this exclusion was necessitated more by the integrity of nineteenth-century Orthodox thinking or the

33. *Torah U-Madda Journal* 5 (1994), p. 185.
34. Ibid., n. 6, pp. 188-189.

expectations of its late twentieth-century followers."[35]

Let us take another look at the statement in question, try to figure out exactly what Shadal meant or did not mean, and place it in a broader context. First of all, it should be noted that he cited only the first half of Lev. 19:27, *lo takifu pe'at roshkhem*. His own Italian translation of this clause reads, *Non taglierete in circolo l'estremità (dei capelli) del vostro capo* ("Do not cut in a circle the extremities (of the hair) of your head"). In the letter to Rapoport, Shadal seems to say that (1) he understands the plain sense [*peshat*] of this prohibition to refer only to an act performed as a mourning custom, (2) he recognizes that the normative Halakhah is not so restricted but imposes a blanket prohibition, and (3) he nevertheless follows the *peshat* in his personal practice. The simplest implication would seem to be that Shadal used to cut the extremities of his hair in a circle (i.e., remove the hair from the sides of his head) as long as this was not for mourning purposes. There is one difficulty with this understanding: all the available portraits of Shadal show him with hair on his temples and sporting typical nineteenth-century sideburns (see, for example, the cover of this book).

What else could Shadal have been implying? Perhaps the answer lies in the second half of Lev. 19:27, *ve-lo tashḥit et pe'at zekanekha*, which he translates as *e non destruggerai l'estremità della tua barba* ("and do not destroy the extremities of your beard"). In his commentary on this clause, Shadal says that according to the *peshat*, all Israelites are forbidden to "destroy" their beards for purposes of mourning the dead. Further, he distinguishes this prohibition from a parallel provision in Lev. 21:5, forbidding priests to "shave" [*lo yegallehu*] the extremities of their beard, implying that "destroying" is a more complete removal than "shaving." Once again, however, normative Halakhah does not restrict the *lo tashḥit* prohibition to a mourning context, and it defines "destruction" as the use of a single-edged razor,[36] in other words, "shaving" as that term is commonly used. Thus, by admitting that his practice was to follow the *peshat*, Shadal may have been intimating that

---

35. B. Barry Levy, *Fixing God's Torah: The Accuracy of the Hebrew Bible Text in Jewish Law* (New York: Oxford University Press, 2001), n. 122, p. 193.

36. See, for example, *Makkot* 20a and *Shulḥan Arukh, Yoreh De'ah* 181.

# Shadal on Leviticus

he was in the habit of shaving with a razor.

Coming from a figure of Shadal's stature, such an admission would be frankly shocking. As Shmuel Vargon has observed, Shadal's statement "arouses astonishment, for Shadal did in fact recognize the importance of fulfilling the *mitsvot* that the Rabbis established," even if their halakhic norms departed from what he regarded as the *peshat* of the Torah's text. "It is hard to explain why, with respect to this particular *mitsvah*, Shadal permitted himself to practice the Halakhah in keeping with the *peshat* of the text as he saw it, especially during a period of time when he was teaching at the Collegio Rabbinico of Padua."[37]

Before condemning Shadal as a heretic or a hypocrite, however, it is important to scrutinize his actual words once again. Nowhere does he say that he shaves with a razor; nowhere does he admit to violating the normative Halakhah in any specific way at all; nowhere does he even claim that Ibn Ezra himself would have advocated shaving with a razor or otherwise violating the Halakhah.[38] What Shadal does say is merely that Ibn Ezra's understanding of the *peshat* of Lev. 19:27— that the prohibitions of that verse seem to be connected with mourning practices—is at variance with the Rabbis' authoritative interpretation, which does not limit these prohibitions to the mourning context. So far, so good; Ibn Ezra's exegetical method was in fact to examine the theoretical *peshat* of the Torah's legal texts while at the same time accepting the Rabbinic Halakhah in practice.[39] But then Shadal goes on to say that he does rely on Ibn Ezra's understanding of the *peshat* to

37. Shmuel Vargon, "Samuel David Luzzatto's Critique of Rabbinic Exegesis Which Contradicts the Plain Meaning of Scripture" (Hebrew). *Jewish Studies, an Internet Journal*, vol. 2 (2003), p. 99, n. 7.

38. The *Jewish Encyclopedia* (s.v. "Beard") is thus quite off the mark when it says, "In Italy the influence of the non-Jewish population was so strong that even so zealous a representative of rabbinical Judaism as Samuel David Luzzatto remarked in a private letter that he no longer concerned himself with the prohibition of shaving, because he thought the Bible intended it to apply only to priests."

39 ."...Ibn Ezra and other (Rabbanite) practitioners of the 'way of peshat' specifically avoided drawing halakhic implications from their philological exegesis." Mordechai Z. Cohen, "A Talmudist's Halakhic Hermeneutics: A New Understanding of Maimonides' Principle of Peshat Primacy," *JSIJ* 10 (2012), p. 260.

justify doing... something. The question is, what?

It is true that all depictions of Shadal show him as beardless. However, even before the invention of the electric shaver in the twentieth century, the traditional straight razor was not the only means of removing one's beard. Alternative methods included depilatory creams or powders, which received halakhic approval from some authorities[40] but not from others.[41] Many Italian Jews from the seventeenth century onward removed their beards by such means,[42] and Shadal himself may well have been one of them. But it is possible that in light of the less than unanimous support for this practice among halakhic authorities, Shadal may have chosen to fall back on what he regarded as the *peshat* of Lev. 19:27 to justify his beardlessness, at least in his own mind—after all, he was not removing his beard for mourning purposes. And so perhaps this was all that he meant to "confess" privately to his friend Rabbi Rapoport: not that he invoked the *peshat* to defend his shaving with a razor (an activity uniformly recognized as halakhically forbidden), but that he invoked the *peshat* merely to defend removing his beard by other means (an activity that was at least arguably permitted under normative Halakhah). Under such a cautious reading of his words, Shadal's only "sin" would have been to invoke the *peshat* to begin with, an approach that even he would not normally have followed in interpreting practical Halakhah.

Such a reading, it might be argued, is not only cautious but far-fetched. However, the alternative is no less difficult—to conclude that a traditionalist figure like Shadal rejected a clear rule of Halakhah. Given the cryptic and ambiguous nature of Shadal's statement, the record of his otherwise zealous advocacy of halakhic observance,[43] the apparent

---

40. See, for example, the responsum of R. Ezekiel Landau (1713-1793) in *Noda Bi-Y'hudah* II, *Yoreh De'ah* 81.

41. See, for example, the opinion of R. Joseph Fiametta (d. 1721) recorded in a responsum of his son-in-law, R. Samson Morpurgo (1681-1740), in *Shemesh Tsedakah, Yoreh De'ah* 61. It should be noted that Rabbi Morpurgo himself was beardless.

42. See *Jewish Encyclopedia*, s.v. "Beard."

43. As I have mentioned above, his biographer stated that the "observance of the commandments in all of their particulars was a matter which Luzzatto regarded as absolutely essential to the Jew" (Margolies, *Samuel David Luzzatto: Traditionalist Scholar*, p. 69).

# Shadal on Leviticus

dearth of evidence that his supposed transgression was ever denounced or even discussed by others during his lifetime, and the fact that no one, to my knowledge, has ever yet unearthed evidence of any other such personal lapses on his part, it seems only fair to give him the benefit of the doubt (*kaf zekhut*) and read his statement so as to minimize any fault-finding or controversy.[44] But even assuming for the sake of argument that the statement in question should be read in a more damning way—in a way that cannot be excused from a traditionalist point of view[45]—it would still seem that to give this one anomaly such weight as to blot out the totality of Shadal's achievements as a Jewish thinker and writer would amount to an extreme and unfair judgment. Those impressive achievements deserve to be evaluated on their own merits, regardless of the perplexing mystery of Shadal's grooming habits.

# Translating Shadal into English

Unless you are an Italian rabbi or rabbinical student, chances are that you will find the 1874 edition of Shadal's Leviticus less than user-friendly. The Hebrew commentary, though for the most part beautifully clear, is sometimes abbreviated and cryptic. The text translation fills in some of the gaps left by the commentary, but this part of the book is, after all, in Italian. For those who are more proficient in English than they are in Italian or Hebrew, a new edition with the following features would be necessary:

---

44. Similarly, Vargon (citing a suggestion by Prof. Moshe Ahrend) says that it might be assumed, "on the basis of information about his life style and his battle against the Reformers, that he made himself clean-shaven [*hitgalle'ah*] in a manner allowed by Halakhah, and that he distinguished between *hashhatah* and *gillu'ah*." (Vargon, "Samuel David Luzzatto's Critique," p. 100, n. 11.)
45. It should also be noted that such an admission of guilt would have been totally inadmissible as evidence in a halakhic court of law, under the principle of *ein adam mesim et atsmo rasha* ("one cannot inculpate oneself," *Sanhedrin* 9b).

31

- An English version of the text translation.
- An English version of the commentary.
- Explanatory notes, sometimes in-depth and extensive.

Until now, no version of Shadal's Leviticus has satisfied all of these needs. The 1965 Schlesinger edition, the first republication of the book's Hebrew portion since 1874, contained some useful footnotes, but it omitted the text translation, and it expurgated the commentary by deleting or abridging many of Shadal's references to non-Jewish sources.[46] The 2012 Munk edition translated only this expurgated version of the commentary into English, omitted the text translation, and provided no footnotes.[47] The 2015 Bassi edition, though restoring the full Hebrew commentary and enhancing it with material from significant manuscripts, once again omitted the text translation and provided no notes.[48]

The edition of Leviticus that you now have before you—based on the original, unabridged 1874 printing—is the first to contain an English version of the text translation, which appears verse by verse in boldface, interspersed with the translated comments on each verse. In other words, the boldface material is translated from Italian, and the non-boldface material is translated from Hebrew.

While translating Shadal's Italian rendering of the Torah text into English, I generally kept as close as I could to his wording and style, though at the same time keeping an eye on the Hebrew original. The standard American English system of quotation marks has been introduced. However, I have made no editorial insertions to this part of the work. Thus, within the text translation, any brackets or parentheses are those that appeared in the 1874 printing.

In translating the Hebrew commentary, my work was facilitated by Shadal's wonderfully lean, down-to-earth writing style, but a few modifications were in order. To accommodate the modern reader's eye, I have freely inserted new sentence and paragraph breaks. Also

---

46. *Perush Shadal al Ḥamishah Ḥumshei Torah*, ed. Pinhas Schlesinger (Tel Aviv: Dvir, 1965).

47. *Torah Commentary by Samuel David Luzzatto*, trans. Eliyahu Munk (Brooklyn: Lambda Publishers, 2012).

48. *Perush Shadal la-Torah*, ed. Yonatan Bassi (Jerusalem: Carmel, 2015).

included are editorial insertions and footnotes that serve to clarify or finish implied thoughts that might not be obvious to the reader, to identify obscure references, to supply materials that Shadal alluded to with a bare citation, and to supplement some of his comments in the light of more recent scholarship. Because the Leviticus commentary is leaner than the commentaries to the previous two books of the Torah, the reader may find these supplementary materials especially useful and interesting. See, for example, my note to Lev. 13:2, explaining why Shadal translates *tsara'at* as "leprosy" and how others have sought to identify this disease, and my notes to various verses in Lev. ch. 11 as to the identity and characteristics of certain birds and animals that are listed as kosher or non-kosher.

Two "witnesses" to the development of the Leviticus commentary over the course of Shadal's career are manuscripts known as Lutzki 672 (at the Jewish Theological Seminary) and Columbia X 893 L 9765 (at Columbia University). I have selectively incorporated references to these manuscripts where they provide interesting material that adds to or varies from the 1874 printing. The reader should be aware that the reason such material did not make it into that printing is, most likely, either that the compilers did not have access to it, or that it was not deemed to reflect Shadal's latest, most authoritative interpretation.

Within the translated commentary, any bracketed materials are my own editorial insertions, unless otherwise marked. Parenthesized materials are generally those that were so marked in the original, except for translations of individual Hebrew or other foreign words or phrases, which I have added. There were no footnotes in the original; all footnotes in the present work are my own.

In transliterating Hebrew words, I have generally followed a slightly modified version of the *Encyclopaedia Judaica*'s system, reflecting the popular Israeli "Sephardic" pronunciation. With regard to the translation of biblical verses that appear in cross-references, (1) any verses cited from within the book of Leviticus are, of course, translated as they appear in the present work; (2) verses from the other four books of the Torah are translated according to my English rendering of Shadal's Italian version of those verses; and (3) verses from the rest of the Bible (*Nevi'im* and *Ketuvim*) are translated, in general, as they appear either in the 1917

Jewish Publication Society version (as used in the Soncino Books of the Bible) or the 2004 Keter Crown Bible Chorev, with some exceptions, mainly the substitution of "you" for the archaic "thou" and "thee."

# In Conclusion: Engaging the Reader

In our time, an English translation of Shadal's Hebrew commentary seems necessary in order to bring his work into broad public notice. The fact that this holds true with respect not only to the general public, but also to much of the Jewish public, is one that the author himself would have found deeply disappointing. Shadal had a "burning zeal for the Hebrew language," holding that its revival was "essential to the preservation of the honor of the Jewish people," and considering it "vital to the understanding of the Bible to gain full mastery of the Hebrew idiom in all its phases."[49] Yet notwithstanding the remarkable renewal of Hebrew in the modern state of Israel, it has been observed that a "large majority of North American Jews lack any proficiency in the Hebrew language and don't seem particularly troubled by that fact."[50]

One suggested way to begin to address this problem is not to aim for "full-on fluency" in Hebrew where none exists, but to foster an "engagement" with the language, encouraging people to be curious about it, to interact with it, and to appreciate its connection with Jewish life and culture.[51] It is my hope that this *Vayikra* volume and my other Shadal translations can serve as tools to further such engagement. We owe Samuel David Luzzatto, and ourselves, at least that much.

---

49. Abrahams, "Samuel David Luzzatto as Exegete," p. 100.
50. Jeremy Benstein, *Hebrew Roots, Jewish Routes: A Tribal Language in a Global World* (Millburn, N.J.: Behrman House, 2019), p. xii.
51. Ibid., pp. xv ff.

# Vayikra

*Purposes of the sacrificial system • Burnt offerings •*
*Flour offerings • First fruits • Sacrifices of contentment •*
*Aspersion sacrifices • Repentance sacrifices*

**1:1. Having called Moses, the Lord spoke to him from the tent of congregation, saying:**

***Having called*** *(va-yikra el,* ויקר׳א אל*).* With respect to the small *alef* [at the end of the word *va-yikra*], see my comment on the phrase *katsti be-ḥayyai* (Gen. 27:46).[1]

**1:2. "Speak to the children of Israel and say to them: When someone among you wishes to offer a sacrifice to the Lord, from among the**

---

1. There, Shadal explains the small initial *kof* of the word *katsti* (which follows the final letter *kof* in the name Yitsḥak) by expressing the view that ancient scribes would delete one of two identical letters when a word began with the same letter as the final letter of the preceding word, and that later the missing letter would be added between the words, written small because the space was narrow. He cross-refers to the example of *va-yikra el* in the present verse, where the small final *alef* of *va-yikra* is followed by the initial *alef* in *el*.

**quadruped animals you may offer your sacrifice from the bovine species and from the ovine (or caprine).**

*from among the quadruped animals, etc.* This is a parenthetical phrase; the phrase "When someone among you wishes to offer" is connected to the phrase below, "If a burnt offering is the sacrifice" [next v.]. The parenthetical phrase is in second person plural, while the rest of the section ("When someone among you wishes to offer," "If a burnt offering is the sacrifice that he wishes to make") is entirely in third person singular.

Here I thought it appropriate to express my view in brief on the subject of sacrifices. Sacrifices did not originate from a Divine command, but rather from human will, for people voluntarily chose to give thanks to God for His kindnesses to them, or to bring a gift before Him to assuage His wrath, or to appease Him so that He might grant their requests. This was because it was unlikely for human beings to conduct themselves toward their God in any other way than that in which they would conduct themselves toward a flesh-and-blood king.

When they came to bring a gift to God, they found no better device than to burn it in fire, for by burning it they were removing it from their domain and from the domain of all other human beings, as well as the domain of the animals, beasts, and fowl. Moreover, by virtue of the fact that it was burned and its smoke ascended on high, it appeared to them as if it were going up to God. A thing that was burned for the honor of God was called *kodesh,* from the words *yekod esh* ("burning of fire"); later the term *kedushah* ("holiness") was transferred to describe other things.[2]

The divine Torah, whose goal was not to teach the nation knowledge and wisdom, but rather to guide it on the paths of righteousness, did not abolish the custom of sacrifices, not that this would have been beyond its power, but because this custom is not evil in and of itself and does no harm to people or to the betterment of their ways; rather, it is beneficial to them. If the Torah had announced to the people that God

---

2. Shadal's derivation of the word *kodesh* from *yekod esh* and the word's semantic development were treated at length in his article in *Bikkurei ha-Ittim ha-Ḥadashim,* 5606 (1845/46), pp. 35-37, and in Shadal's comment on the word *ba-kodesh* in Exod. 15:11.

has no desire for burnt offerings or sacrifices, the next day they would have said, "What desire does God have that we be righteous, and what would it profit us to perfect our ways?" And because one of the basic principles of the Torah is the belief that God watches over the activities of humankind and that He loves doers of good and hates the wicked, it was necessary that God would not be described in the full exaltedness of His true position, but that His majesty would be slightly lowered, as it were, and He would be described in human thought as a great King Who knows all their activities, hears their cries, and accepts their gifts. This necessity existed not only in that generation, but equally in every generation.

If instead of sacrifices, God had commanded prayer, hymns, Torah reading, and preaching words of moral instruction, the greatness and fear of God would not have been impressed upon the hearts of the masses, for it would have seemed to them that the gods of the nations, whose worshippers presented them with various sacrifices, were greater and more glorious than our God, Whose worship consisted merely of intangible things. This is characteristic of the masses in all generations, and not just the common people, but most of humankind: who is honored among them? One who honors himself and increases his own rank. In contrast, one who is forbearing and does not seek greatness for himself is not important in their eyes. Thus the true God, even though He has no need for the honor of humankind, was compelled for the sake of our benefit to convey His fear into our hearts so that we would not sin. And because in those days His fear could not have been conveyed into the hearts of the people by any means other than sacrifices, He commanded these.

The result of the sacrificial system that was maintained by the public in the Sanctuary was this: it was impressed on the hearts of the masses that a great God and King dwelled in their midst, that they were dear to Him, that He commanded them to perform services that would be favored by Him, and that by performing these services at His command, they would come into His favor every day and constantly draw His love upon themselves.

The Torah commanded that each individual should not build an altar for himself, but that the entire community should bring their sacrifices at a single location that God would choose. This was not, Heaven forbid, for the purpose of diminishing the practice of sacrifices (as was the opinion of Maimonides in *Guide for the Perplexed* 3:32), but was for the benefit and wellbeing of the nation, the perfection of its virtues, and the safeguarding of the religion. As a result of having a single Sanctuary, the entire people would gather at a single place, their hearts would be bound together in a bond of affection, they would always form a single society, and each tribe and clan would not become a people unto itself. If each person were to build an altar for himself, it would suffice for each one that God would favor him and accept his offerings, and his heart would not be troubled at all for the other members of his nation. In contrast, it was the Torah's intention that the benefit be a general one for the nation at large, and that all Israel should be responsible one for the other.

It would also have been possible that the service would become corrupted within one clan or tribe, which would change its laws; little by little they might come to follow the laws of other peoples and establish for themselves practices abhorrent to God, even sacrificing their own sons and daughters. However, having the service in only one location would render corruption less likely, for this process would then require the agreement of the entire people (see my comment at Num. 15:15).[3]

The purpose of public offerings was that Israel should have a tabernacle and a sanctuary for the worship of God, in order that it might be impressed upon their hearts that the Lord was in their midst, that He was their king and leader who kept watch over their deeds and gave them due recompense in accordance with their actions. This impression would not have been formed in the hearts of the masses without some tangible matter that would suggest it.[4] Thus it was necessary that the

---

3. There, on the phrase "You and the foreigner must be equal before the Lord," Shadal comments that the foreigner [*ger*] must follow the same laws as the Israelites with regard to sacrifices, so that foreigners do not introduce idolatrous customs into the land of Israel.

4. Nehama Leibowitz quotes at length from Shadal's comment up to this point (*New Studies in Vayikra*, pp. 15-16). She concludes with a criticism: "Rejecting Maimonides' 'depreciation' of the sacrifices, S.D. Luzzatto sought to elevate them in the eyes of the student. His simplistic explanation, however, divested the sacrifices of the halo of mystery and sanctity that surrounds them" (ibid., p. 17).

sanctuary assume the structure of a royal palace, that it contain a table and candelabrum, that on the table there be a display of bread and the vessels pertaining to the table, its plates and its bowls. Given that it was customary to present deities with an offering of edible things, it was appropriate for us to bring before our King various kinds of food and drink, with the sacrifices corresponding to food and the libations corresponding to drink.

It was likewise necessary for the King to have attendants to serve in His house and stand before Him, and these were the priests. One of them was to see the King's face and occupy the first rank in the kingdom, and this was the high priest. The Sanctuary and its vessels, the priests and their garments had to be splendid and magnificent so as to impress upon the people the greatness of the King Who dwelled in the house, that His fear be upon them so that they would not sin.

Though at first, when each individual built an altar for himself, the service was given over to anyone or to the firstborns, now that offerings were to be brought in one place only, the service had to be put in the hands of a single clan that would serve in the name of the entire people. It would be fitting for this clan, which was dedicated to the service of God, to be free of any other occupation or employment, and since their service was in the house of God in the name of the entire people, it would be fitting for their sustenance to be provided by the nation.

However, it would not have been proper for every priest and Levite to receive a fixed stipend, with the righteous sharing equally with the wicked. Rather, the Torah left it up to each individual Israelite to give his gifts to any priest or Levite of his choice, and as a result the priests and Levites would strive to be accepted by the public for their probity and honest behavior.

The sacrifices offered by individuals were for the individual's benefit, throughout all the events that would befall him. If something good would come to him, he would give thanks to God and bring his sacrifice, and it would thereby be impressed on his heart that the good that befell him was from God, and he would trust in Him and improve his ways so as to always draw upon himself His love and compassion. If he was in distress, he would pray to God and make a vow that if He would relieve him, he would present Him with a sacrifice; and when relief and salvation arose for him, he would fulfill his vow, and it would be impressed upon his heart that God had saved him.

If he sinned unintentionally, he would bring a sacrifice, and it would be impressed on his heart that his God had forgiven him and he was in His favor as before. If there had been no atonement [available] for an unintentional sinner, he would have said in his heart, "Who will save me from this harsh God? For I sinned without meaning to do so, and He was angry with me and cast me from His presence, and I have no hope of assuaging His wrath. If so, why should I continue to guard myself from sinning from this day forward?" In contrast, the intentional sinner would not bring a sacrifice, so as not to have it impressed on his heart, in keeping with the thought of the ancient peoples, that God would accept a bribe from sinners and forgive their iniquities.

Yet another benefit arose from the individual's sacrifices: apart from the portion that they contributed to the priests, even that which was left to the owners had to be eaten by them in companionship with others, for they were not permitted to leave any of it over till the next day or the day after, or even to salt the meat of the offering and bring it back to their houses outside of Jerusalem and eat it with the members of their household. One who fulfilled his vow to God for a kindness that He bestowed upon him would be obligated to have others rejoice with him, and as a result he would come to be bonded in affection with people that he had not known previously, or at least he would cause the poor and destitute to benefit from his festive meal; see below at Lev. 19:9.

**1:3. "If a burnt offering[5] is the sacrifice that he wishes to make, (this is) of the bovine species; he will present it (consisting of) an immaculate male. At the entrance of the tent of congregation he will present it, so that it may be accepted for him before the Lord.**

*so that it may be accepted for him (li-r'tsono).* As the Targum [Onkelos] translates, *le-ra'ava leih,* i.e., that the sacrifice be acceptable before God,

---

5. Heb. *olah*; Shadal's Italian translation is *olocausto.* Although "holocaust" (from the Greek for "wholly burned") is an accurate rendering of *olah,* its unfortunate connotation in post-World War II English makes it an undesirable choice for translation here.

for the benefit of the one who brings it. The word *ratson* in the Torah and other ancient books does not mean *voluntas* ("will"), nor does the verb *ratsah* mean *velle* ("to wish"); so too Mendelssohn commented here.

**1:4. "He will place his hand on the head of the burnt offering, and it will be accepted for him, to expiate for him.**

*to expiate for him.* The sacrifice does not atone for an intentional sin [*avon*], but only for an unintentional sin (except for some of the sacrifices of repentance [*ashamot*]). The burnt offering is not brought for a sin, but rather as a gift to make oneself acceptable to the Lord, to "expiate" [*le-khapper*] for himself, i.e., to cover over his faults that he was not aware of, or to seek mercy from Him when he fears that an unknown sin will cause his request to be rejected.

**1:5. "He will slaughter the bullock before the Lord, and the sons of Aaron, priests, will present its blood, and they will scatter it round about upon the altar that is at the entrance of the tent of congregation.**

*He will slaughter (ve-shaḥat).* Similar to the verbs [in the next v.] *ve-hifshit* ("and he will skin") and *ve-nittaḥ* ("and he will cut"), this refers back to the owner of the sacrifice, who would do this himself or through someone else of his choosing. Likewise, the phrase "The entrails and the legs he will wash in water" (below, v. 9) refers to the owner (see *Netivot ha-Shalom* there). Everything that the priest [himself] had to do is so designated expressly in the text.

**1:6. "And he will skin the burnt offering, and he will cut it into its quarters.**

**1:7. "And the sons of Aaron the priest will place fire upon the altar, and they will arrange firewood upon the fire.**

**1:8. "The priests, sons of Aaron, will arrange the quarters, the head, and the fat on the firewood that is on the fire upon the altar.**

# Shadal on Leviticus

**1:9.** "The entrails and the legs he will wash in water, and the priest will burn the whole on the altar. It is a burnt offering, a sacrifice to be burned, a propitiatory aroma, to the Lord.

*The entrails and the legs he will wash in water.* To remove their filth in honor of the Exalted One (Abravanel).

**1:10.** "If the sacrifice that he wishes to offer as a burnt offering is of the small cattle, that is, of the lambs or of the kids, he will present it (consisting of) an immaculate male.

**1:11.** "He will slaughter it on the north side of the altar before the Lord; and the sons of Aaron, priests, will scatter its blood round about upon the altar.

**1:12.** "And he will cut it into its quarters, and (he will cut) its head and the fat; and the priest will arrange them on the firewood that is on the fire upon the altar.

*its head.* He would not "dissect" [*menatte'aḥ*] the head or the fat [as he would the body of the animal; the Hebrew verb in the phrase "And he will cut it into its quarters" is *ve-nittaḥ*]; rather, he would sever the head (for in the act of slaughtering, the head is not separated from the body), and he would cut the fat with a knife. These two actions, though not precisely *nittu'aḥ* ("dissection"), involve severing and cutting with a knife and so are included within the verb *ve-nittaḥ*.

**1:13.** "The entrails and the legs he will wash in water, and the priest will present the whole and will burn it on the altar. It is a burnt offering, a sacrifice to be burned, a propitiatory aroma to the Lord.

**1:14.** "And if of the flying creatures he wishes to offer a burnt offering to the Lord, he will present his sacrifice of the turtledoves, or of the young doves.

**1:15.** "The priest will present it to the altar, and he will cut its head

**and burn it on the altar; and he will cause its blood to drip on the wall of the altar.**

*and he will cut its head (u-malak et rosho).* He will sever the head from the neck. Here, he was to cut off the head completely and burn it separately, while below, in the case of the aspersion [sprinkle] offering [*hattat*], he was not to sever the head (Lev. 5:8). The blood of the fowl was of limited quantity, and there was not enough of it to collect it in a vessel and scatter it round about upon the altar. For this reason, the owner was commanded to cause its blood to drip on the wall of the altar, and similarly in the case of the aspersion offering of a fowl, it says, "And he will sprinkle some of the blood of the sacrifice of aspersion" (Lev. 5:9), which was not to be collected in a vessel. It was also for this reason that the cutting of the head was to be done on top of the altar, so that none of the blood would be lost (Abravanel).

*and he will cause its blood to drip (ve-nimtsah).* Before burning it, but there is no need to understand the Heb. as meaning "and he will have already caused its blood to drip." Rather, the burning is mentioned first, since it is the principal action, and then the text goes back to caution that when cutting the head, he should cause the blood to drip on the wall of the altar. Wessely wrote that the *vav* [in *ve-nimtsah*] does not convert the verb from the past tense to the future, but this is erroneous.

**1:16. "He will remove the crop, with its feathers, and he will throw it near the altar, to the east, to the place allotted for the ashes.**

*the crop (mur'ato).* Mur'ah is related to the word *meri* ("fatted ox") and denotes the place into which [a bird's] feed is inserted.

**1:17. "He will split it, with the wings (attached), without dividing (the body in two); and the priest will burn it on the altar, on the firewood that is on the fire. It is a burnt offering, a sacrifice to be burned, a propitiatory aroma, to the Lord."**

# Shadal on Leviticus

**2:1. "When someone wishes to present to the Lord a flour offering, his offering will consist of fine flour, and he will drip some oil upon it, and he will place some incense upon it.**

*a flour offering (minḥah).* Derived from the root *nu'aḥ* ("to be pleasant"), as in *re'aḥ niḥo'aḥ* (propitiatory or pleasant aroma), although the [noun prefix] *mem* was later taken as if it were part of the root; *minḥah* was pronounced with a quiescent *nun,* and the plural was pronounced *menaḥot* [rather than the proper *minḥot*], on the model of *semaḥot* [the plural of *simḥah,* in which the initial letter is part of the root].[6]

**2:2. "He will bring it to the sons of Aaron, priests; and the priest will take of it a fistful of the fine flour and of the oil, together with all the incense, and he will burn on the altar its scent [that is, those parts of the offering that were meant to emit a scent]. It is a sacrifice to be burned to the Lord, a propitiatory aroma.**

*will take of it a fistful (ve-kamats).* Undoubtedly it was the priest who took the fistful [though "the priest" does not appear here in the Hebrew text], for otherwise the text would have had to add, "And he [i.e., the owner of the sacrifice] will place it on the palms of the priest." The reason why it is not written that "the priest" would take the fistful is the juxtaposition of the phrase with [the preceding word] "priests"; moreover, the text says *ve-kamats... ve-hiktir ha-kohen* [i.e., in the Hebrew, the subject "the priest" appears after the second verb *ve-hiktir,* "and he will burn"] as if the two actions were one, for immediately after he took the fistful, he burned its scent on the altar.

*its scent (azkaratah).* The Hebrew is derived from the concept of smell, as in, "Its scent [*zikhro*] shall be as the wine of Lebanon" (Hosea 14:8). The entire term *zekhirah* ("remembering") has as its most basic meaning "to give off a scent," and was transferred to denote remembrance, for

---

6. See Shadal's comment on the word *minḥah* at Gen. 4:3, where he additionally notes that the word is related to *naḥat* ("satisfaction") and signifies "that which an inferior gives to a superior to appease him and set his mind at rest if there is a possibility that the inferior has offended him."

remembering a past event is like detecting the scent of something after it passes from one's sight. Mendelssohn wrote to the contrary, that a scent is called *zekher* because it resembles the "memory" that preserves the impressions of things after they disappear from the senses. He failed to keep in mind (*hu lo zakhar*), however, that all the words that denote mental activities and anything that is not perceived by the senses are transferred words, all of which were taken from their original meanings that referred to tangible matters.[7] The word that indicates "smell" must necessarily have preceded the word that indicates "memory."

**2:3. "And the remainder of the flour offering (belongs) to Aaron and to his sons; it is a most holy thing [see Lev. 6:9-11], (a portion assigned to them) from the things to be burned to the Lord.**

**2:4. "And when you wish to present a flour offering to be baked in an oven, it will be of fine flour, unleavened cakes kneaded with oil, and cakes of soft dough anointed with oil.**

**2:5. "And if that which you wish to present is a flour offering to be fried in a pan, it will be of fine flour kneaded with oil, unleavened.**

**2:6. "You will break it in pieces, and you will drip oil upon it; it is a flour offering.**

---

7. This linguistic theory, a key component of Shadal's commentary—see, for example, his derivation of the word *kodesh* from *yekod esh* ("a burning of fire") at Ex. 15:11—is supported by modern scholarship. According to the Israeli linguist Guy Deutscher, in *The Unfolding of Language* (New York: Henry Holt and Co., 2006), "The only way we have of expanding our expressive range to encompass abstract concepts is to draw on concrete terms" (p. 128). "The truth of the matter is that we simply have no choice but to use concrete-to-abstract metaphors. And when one stops to think about it, this is not even so surprising, since after all, if not from the physical world, where else could terms for abstract concepts come from?... The mind cannot just manufacture words for abstract concepts out of thin air — all it can do is adapt what is already available. And what's at hand are simple physical concepts" (p. 127).

**2:7. "And if that which you wish to present is a flour offering to be made in a baking pan, it will be made of fine flour (kneaded) in oil.**

*a baking pan (marḥeshet).* A deep utensil, unlike the *maḥavat* ("frying pan") [as in v. 5 above]; see Rashi [who also comments that the *marḥeshet* was deep]. The proof of this is found in the phrase, "or made *in* [*va-*] the *marḥeshet* or *on* [*al*] the *maḥavat*" (below, 7:9) (Wessely).

**2:8. "You will be able to bring to the Lord a flour offering to be made in any of these (ways). He [the offeror] will present it to the priest, who will bring it to the altar.**

*to be made (ye'aseh) in any of these (ways).* Perhaps the Hebrew should be read as *ya'aseh* ("he will make"), that is, [with the subject being] "the offeror," who is the [implied] subject of the subsequent phrase, "He will present it to the priest."

**2:9. "The priest will take from the flour offering its sweet scent [that is, the portion mentioned in v. 2] and will burn it on the altar. It is a sacrifice to be burned to the Lord, a propitiatory aroma.**

**2:10. "And the remainder of the flour offering (belongs) to Aaron and to his sons; it is a most holy thing, (assigned to them) from the things to be burned to the Lord.**

**2:11. "Any flour offering that you present to the Lord will not be made of leavened bread, for of no leavening, nor of any honey, must you burn a sacrifice to be burned to the Lord.**

**2:12. "In an offering of first fruits you will present them to the Lord, but on the altar they will not ascend for a propitiatory aroma.**

**2:13. "And any flour offering that you present, you will salt it with salt, and you will not omit salt, (a symbol) of reconciliation with your God, from your flour offering. Over any sacrifice of yours you will present some salt.**

*salt, (a symbol) of reconciliation with your God (melaḥ berit Elohekha).*
To this day, Arab princes, when establishing a covenant [*berit*], present
a vessel of salt and together they eat bread with salt (Rosenmueller). It
was a well known custom in ancient times in the lands of the east that
a covenant was established with salt. Because every sacrifice is in fact
intended to placate and appease God and to bring him into a *berit* with
us, He commanded that salt be placed in every sacrifice, and He called
it *melaḥ berit Elohekha,* for by means of that salt you establish a *berit*
with your God.

**2:14. "And if you present to the Lord an offering of first fruits, of
almost ripe grain, toasted with fire, (then) crushed as fresh grain is
crushed, will you present your offering of first fruits.**

*an offering of first fruits (minḥat bikkurim).* According to the plain
meaning, this is an individual's offering brought voluntarily (as per
Ibn Ezra), not a public offering, and the [introductory] word *im* is to
be understood in its ordinary sense [to mean "if," not "when," *contra*
Rashi, who maintains that this offering is the obligatory public *omer*
offering]. In a manuscript version of Rashi [the comment on the word
*geres* ("crushed") reads] *leshon shevirah u-teḥinah gasah* ("a term
meaning a coarse breaking and grinding"), not *gorsah* ("he grinds it"),
and this is correct.[8]

**2:15. "You will put oil on it, and you will place some incense upon
it; it is a flour offering.**

**2:16. "The priest will burn the sweet scent, (a portion, that is) of its
crushed grain and of its oil, together with all of its incense. It is a
sacrifice to be burned to the Lord."**

**3:1. "And if his sacrifice is a sacrifice of contentment [of rendering
thanks and payment of a vow], if he wishes to present it of the bovine**

---

8. In the Chavel edition, the word *gorsah/gasah* does not appear at all.

species, whether male or female, he will present it immaculate before the Lord.

*a sacrifice of contentment (zevaḥ shelamim).* As in, "Sacrifices of *shelamim* were due from me; this day I have paid [*shillamti*] my vows" (Prov. 7:14). This is a sacrifice of rejoicing that is eaten collectively in order to increase joy and peace [*shalom*] in the world. Perhaps its name derives from [the fact that this sacrifice is brought when one's] desire and hope is fulfilled [*nishlemah*].

**3:2.** "He will place his hand on the head of his sacrifice, and he will slaughter it at the entrance of the tent of congregation; and the sons of Aaron, priests, will scatter its blood upon the altar round about.

**3:3.** "Of the sacrifices of contentment he will offer as a sacrifice to be burned to the Lord the tallow that covers the entrails, and all the tallow that is on the entrails.

**3:4.** "And the two kidneys, and the tallow that is upon them, which is (that is) on the flanks, and the omentum that is on the liver, which he will remove together with the kidneys.

**3:5.** "The sons of Aaron will burn it [the tallow] on the altar, together with the burnt offerings that are on the firewood that is upon the fire. It is a sacrifice to be burned to the Lord, a propitiatory aroma.

**3:6.** "And if the sacrifice that he makes to the Lord for a sacrifice of contentment is of small cattle, male or female, immaculate he will present it.

**3:7.** "If he offers his sacrifice of the ovine species, he will present it before the Lord.

**3:8.** "And he will place his hand on the head of his sacrifice, and he will slaughter it in front of the tent of congregation, and the sons of Aaron will scatter its blood upon the altar round about.

**3:9.** "Of the sacrifice of contentment he will offer in a sacrifice to be burned to the Lord the tallow, the entire tail, which he will remove near the spine, and the tallow that covers the entrails, and the tallow that is on the entrails.

*the spine (he-atseh).* So called because it resembles an *ets* ("tree") from which branches come out (Wessely).

**3:10.** "And the two kidneys, and the tallow that is on them, which is (that is) on the flanks; and the omentum that is on the liver, which he will remove together with the kidneys.

**3:11.** "The priest will burn it on the altar; it is food, a sacrifice (that is) to be burned, to the Lord.

**3:12.** "And if his sacrifice is of the caprine species, he will present it before the Lord.

**3:13.** "And he will place his hand on its head, and he will slaughter it in front of the tent of congregation, and the sons of Aaron will scatter its blood upon the altar round about.

**3:14.** "And he will offer of it in a sacrifice, (that is) to be burned to the Lord, the tallow that covers the entrails, and all the tallow that is on the entrails.

*And he will offer of it in a sacrifice (mimmennu korbano).* Mendelssohn translated *mimmennu korbano* as "from that sacrifice," but this is incorrect.

**3:15.** "And the two kidneys, and the tallow that is on them, which is (that is) on the flanks, and the omentum that is on the liver, which he will remove together with the kidneys.

**3:16.** "And the priest will burn it on the altar; it is food, a sacrifice (that is) to be burned for a propitiatory aroma. Every tallow belongs to the Lord.

# Shadal on Leviticus

**3:17.** **"A perpetual statue for all the ages to come, in all of your residences; any tallow and any blood you shall not eat."**

**4:1. And the Lord spoke to Moses, saying:**

**4:2.** **"Speak to the children of Israel, saying: A person who transgresses in error against one of all the precepts of the Lord that are prescribed not to do, and he acts against one of them –**

*against one of all the precepts… against one of them* (mi-kol mitsvot… me-aḥat). [The prefix *mem* signifies] "against" one, as in:

- "And I have not acted wickedly against my God [*me-Elohai*]" (II Sam. 22:22);
- "And sins in error against the things consecrated to the Lord [*mi-kodshei YHVH*]" (Lev. 5:15);
- "And the amount of his sacrilege [*asher ḥata min ha-kodesh,* lit. 'that which he sinned against a consecrated thing'] he will pay" (Lev. 5:16).

**4:3.** **"If it is the anointed priest who sins, so that the people would become guilty of it, he will present to the Lord, for the sin committed by him, a young bull, immaculate, in a sacrifice of aspersion.**

*so that the people would become guilty of it* (le-ashmat ha-am, lit. "to the guilt of the people"). For the nation bears the guilt of its leaders and is punished because of them, an idea expressed in the phrase, "Would You kill a nation, although innocent?" [Gen. 20:4, where Abimelech fears that his entire nation will be penalized for his taking of Sarah]. In truth, a leader's corruption causes many disasters for his people, but the ancients believed that the nation was punished directly for the sin of the leader. It is also likely, as per Rashi, that [the people bear responsibility for the priest's sin because] they depend on him to effect atonement for them; this requires further study.

*a sacrifice of aspersion (ḥattat).* This itself is the "guilt offering" [*asham*], but it is called *ḥattat* because it involves aspersion [i.e., sprinkling of blood] upon the prominences of the altar, and since aspersion is called *ḥittui,* as in the expression "Sprinkle me [*teḥatte'eni*] with hyssop [and I will be pure]" (Ps. 51:9), this sacrifice is called *ḥattat,* not because it comes [to atone] for "sin" [*ḥet*]. Accordingly, Onkelos (below, Lev. 6:19) translates the phrase *ha-kohen ha-meḥattei otah* ("that priest who makes the aspersions for it") as *kahana di-mekhapper be-demah* ("the priest who atones *with its blood*"), mentioning the blood that was to be sprinkled.

Only in the case of the variable sacrifice [*oleh ve-yored*], where a poor person brings a tenth of an *ephah* of flour for a *ḥattat,* is there no *ḥittui* because there is no blood.   Nevertheless, this sacrifice is called *ḥattat* because it is offered as a substitute for the ewe-lamb or the two turtledoves [below, Lev. 5:11].

**4:4. "He will bring the bull to the entrance of the tent of congregation, before the Lord, and he will place his hand on the head of the bull, and he will slaughter the bull before the Lord.**

**4:5. "The anointed priest will take from the blood of the bull, and he will bring it into the tent of congregation.**

**4:6. "The priest will dip his finger in the blood, and he will sprinkle of that blood seven times before the Lord, toward the door-curtain of the Sanctuary.**

**4:7. "The priest will put some of that blood on the prominences of the altar of the aromatic incense, which is before the Lord, in the tent of congregation; and all the (remainder of the) blood of the bull he will pour out at (the site called) the foundation of the altar of the burnt offerings, which is at the entrance of the tent of congregation.**

**4:8. "And all of the tallow of the bull of the aspersion sacrifice he will raise of it in tribute, the tallow that coves the entrails, and all the tallow that is on the entrails.**

# Shadal on Leviticus

**4:9.** "And the two kidneys, and the tallow that is on them, which is (that is) on the flanks, and the omentum that is on the liver, which he will remove together with the kidneys –

**4:10.** "Just as (the tallow) will be removed in tribute from the bull of the contentment sacrifice; and the priest will burn them on the altar of the burnt offerings.

**4:11.** "The skin of the bull, then, and all of its flesh, together with its head and its legs, and its entrails and its dung –

*The skin of the bull.* [This verse] is connected to what follows.

**4:12.** "The entire bull (in sum) he will bring out of the camp, to a pure place, where the ash is poured out, and he will burn it over the firewood; upon the place of the pouring out of the ash will it be burned.

**4:13.** "And if all the assembly of Israel errs, some one thing remaining unknown to the body of the nation, so that they do one of those things that the Lord has commanded not to be done, and (then) they recognize themselves culpable[9] –

*all the assembly of Israel (kol adat Yisrael).* To be understood literally, "all the community." This would not occur only as a result of an error by the leaders or the judges, for the text does not mention the Sanhedrin, nor does it refer at all to any order of a court. According to the plain meaning, it would make no difference if the error resulted from a court order or an instruction of the high priest or the king, or if it occurred without any instructor.[10]

---

9. Hebrew *ve-ashemu.* This verb, used repeatedly throughout this chapter, is discussed by Shadal in his comment on the phrase "But we are culpable [*ashemim*]" in Gen. 42:21. There he explains that the term *asham* has the basic meaning of "recognizing sin," and that in the verse in question, Joseph's brothers meant to say, "We are deserving of punishment for what we did to him."

10. *Contra* Rashi, who maintained, citing the *Sifra*, that *adat Yisrael*

**4:14.** "The offense into which they have fallen having become known, the body of the nation will present a young bull in a sacrifice of aspersion, and they will bring it before the tent of congregation.

**4:15.** "The elders of the congregation will place their hands on the head of the bull before the Lord, and the bull will be slaughtered before the Lord.

**4:16.** "And the anointed priest will bring some of the blood of the bull in the tent of congregation.

**4:17.** "The priest will wet his finger from the blood, and he will sprinkle seven times before the Lord, against the door-curtain.

*will wet... from the blood (ve-taval min ha-dam*, lit. "will dip... from the blood"). See Wessely's comment at Lev. 14:16.[11]

**4:18.** "And some of that blood he will put on the prominences of the altar situated before the Lord, which is (that is) in the tent of congregation; and all the (rest of the) blood he will pour out at the foundation of the altar of the burnt offerings, which is at the entrance of the tent of congregation.

**4:19.** "And all of its tallow he will raise in tribute and he will burn it on the altar.

**4:20.** "He will do with this bull as he did [that is, as he would do] with (his own) bull of aspersion sacrifice, just so [as in vv. 3-12 above] he

---

meant "the Sanhedrin," whose error in instruction caused "the body of the nation" [*ha-kahal*] to commit an offense.

11. There, on the phrase *ve-taval... min ha-shemen* (lit. "will dip... from the oil"), Wessely (in *Netivot ha-Shalom*) notes that the verb *taval* is usually followed by the preposition *be-* ("in"), but in these two instances it is followed by *min* ("from"), indicating the source from which something is wetted. In both the present verse and in Lev. 14:16, Shadal translates *ve-taval* as *bagnerà,* which can be understood either as "he will dip" or "he will wet."

**will do with it. So the priest will propitiate for them, and they will be pardoned.**

**4:21. "He will take the bull out of the camp, and he will burn it as he burned [that is, would burn] the preceding bull. This is the aspersion sacrifice of the body of the nation.**

**4:22. "If it happens that a prince [in other words, the political head of the nation] sins, and does in error one of those things that the Lord his God has commanded that they not be done, and (then) he recognizes himself culpable –**

**4:23. "Or he is made to know the deficiency in which he has fallen, he will bring his sacrifice, (that is) a kid, male, immaculate.**

*Or he is made to know (o hoda).* Either he recognizes his culpability on his own [*ashem*], or he is made to know it [*hoda*] by others (Rashbam). So that we should not think that one who failed to recognize his sin until it was made known to him by others would need greater expiation than one who recognized and confessed it on his own, the phrase "or he is made to know" is added, in order to say that one law applies to them both (A. H. Mainster). However, this is not mentioned with regard to the high priest, for due to his great holiness, it was not to be suspected that his sin would be hidden from his eyes, or that he would sin intentionally but claim, "I acted unintentionally" (Mainster).

With respect to "the body of the nation" [*ha-kahal*], it does not say "*or* they are made to know," for it cannot be otherwise—it would be impossible for every single individual in the nation to recognize the sin on his own; rather, of necessity some of them would open the eyes of their fellows and make the sin known to them. Where it says, with regard to the body of the nation, *ve-nod'ah ha-ḥattat* (lit. "*and* the offense having become known") [above, v. 14], the meaning is, "Then, when the offense becomes known to them, they will do such and such."

**4:24. "And he will place his hand on the head of the kid, and he will slaughter it before the Lord, in the place where the burnt offerings are sacrificed. It is a sacrifice of aspersion.**

**4:25.** "And the priest will take with his finger from the blood of the sacrifice of aspersion, and he will put it on the prominences of the altar of the burnt offerings, and the (rest of its) blood he will pour out on the base of the altar of the burnt offerings.

**4:26.** "And all of its tallow he will burn on the altar, like the tallow of the sacrifice of contentment. Thus the priest will propitiate for him with regard to his sin, and it will be pardoned for him.

**4:27.** "And if one of the people sins in error, doing one of those things that the Lord has commanded that they not be done, and (then) he recognizes himself culpable—

**4:28.** "Or the deficiency committed by him becomes known to him, he will bring his sacrifice, (that is) a kid, immaculate, female, for the sin that he committed.

**4:29.** "And he will place his hand on the head of the sacrifice of aspersion, and he will slaughter the sacrifice of aspersion, in the place of the burnt offerings.

**4:30.** "And the priest will take from its blood with his finger, and he will put it on the prominences of the altar of the burnt offerings, and all (the rest of) its blood he will pour out at the base of the altar.

**4:31.** "And all of the tallow he will remove from it, as the tallow of the sacrifice of contentment is removed, and the priest will burn it on the altar, in a propitiatory aroma to the Lord. Thus the priest will propitiate for him, and it will be pardoned for him.

*in a propitiatory aroma to the Lord.* Since these sacrifices are occasioned by sin, this expression was added to make it known that they are as agreeable and pleasing to Him, rising before Him in a propitiatory aroma, as any of the other sacrifices.

**4:32.** "And if of the ovine species he will bring his offering for a sacrifice of aspersion, he will bring it (consisting of) an immaculate female.

**4:33.** "And he will place his hand on the head of the sacrifice of aspersion, and he will slaughter it for a sacrifice of aspersion, in the place where the burnt offerings are slaughtered.

**4:34.** "And the priest will take with his finger from the blood of the sacrifice of aspersion, and he will put it on the prominences of the altar of the burnt offerings, and all (the rest of) its blood he will pour out at the base of the altar.

**4:35.** "And all of its tallow he will remove, as the tallow of the lamb of the sacrifice of contentment is removed; and the priest will burn it on the altar, above the (other) things to be burned to the Lord. Thus the priest will propitiate for him with regard to the sin that he committed, and it will be pardoned for him.

***above the (other) things to be burned to the Lord.*** He will burn these tallows on top of the daily burnt offering [*olat tamid*] and the other things to be burned to the Lord that are found on the altar, so that the priest should not think it improper for the tallows of the aspersion sacrifice to be placed above the burnt offering. However, the two expressions "in a propitiatory aroma to the Lord" and "above the things to be burned to the Lord" are used [only] here and not above [in the parallel passages in Lev. 4:5, 19, and 26] so that we should not think that this [sacrifice] is meant for the exaltation of the sinner (i.e., the high priest, the assembly of Israel, or the prince), and therefore this is mentioned only where the sinner is "one of the people."

**5:1.** "If, then, a person sins, hearing an adjuration [with which one entreats those present to give testimony in court as to that which they know in his favor], when he was a witness (of the thing in question), having seen (the deed), or having known of it, in which case, if he does not testify, he falls into sin –

**hearing an adjuration** *(ve-shame'ah kol alah),* etc. This is the equivalent of saying that he has sworn falsely [that he knew nothing of the matter]. The expression "hearing" is used because such was the custom, i.e., he [the witness] himself would not pronounce the oath [*alah*] and the curse [for giving false testimony]; rather, others would administer the oath to him and he would answer "Amen," as in the case of the *sotah* [suspected wife, see Num. 5:22]. In contrast, an oath that was unaccompanied by a curse would come from his own mouth and was known as a *shevu'at bittui* ("an oath of obligation"), the purpose of which was to do himself ill or good [see below, Lev. 5:4].

This case alone [of those discussed in this chapter] deals with a person who acts intentionally, while the ones below pertain to those who act unintentionally. This case is included with the others because the person who hears the adjuration may think himself justified [in declining to testify], saying to himself, "Why should I be obligated to become involved in a dispute that is not my own and to testify on behalf of this person? And why should I cause harm to his opponent?"

According to Wessely, besides [having to offer] the sacrifice, he does not attain propitiation if he does not placate his neighbor, in the event that his refraining from testifying on his behalf causes him harm.

**5:2. "Or if a person has touched any impure thing, whether the corpse of some impure wild beast, or the corpse of some impure domestic animal, or the corpse of some impure swarming thing [a small quadruped, see 11:29], and this was unknown to him, and he became impure [and ate a sacred thing or entered the Temple], and (then) he recognizes himself culpable –**

*and this was unknown to him, and he became impure.* And then he ate a sacred thing or entered the Sanctuary (Rashi), or he touched other persons and did not warn them that he was impure (A. H. Mainster).

**5:3. "Or if he has touched some human impurity, any uncleanness by which one can become impure, and this was unknown to him, [and he became impure and ate a sacred thing or entered the Temple,] and (then) he recognizes himself culpable –**

*and this was unknown to him, etc.* Rashi's comment should read *ve-ne'elam ve-hu yada* (not *ve-lo yada*); that is, Rashi is asking how, if it was unknown to him, he "knew"; and he is answering that at first he knew but then he forgot. See *Sefer ha-Zikkaron* and *Siftei Ḥakhamim.*[12]

**5:4. "Or if a person has sworn, obligating himself with his own lips, to do ill [to himself, that is, to subject himself to some privation] or good [to some other person], in sum, to anything to which the man can obligate himself with an oath, and this becomes unknown to him [that is, if he forgets it, and he violates the obligation that he had assumed]; then he comes to know it, and he recognizes himself culpable for any of these things.**

*to anything to which the man can obligate himself.* Including even those things that do not involve doing ill or good (Wessely), and perhaps excluding those things that a person is not permitted to take upon himself, as for example to injure himself, and all the more so his neighbor.

*and this becomes unknown to him.* He forgets his oath, and as a result he violates it.

**5:5. "Now, when he feels himself culpable for any of these things, he will confess the sin in which he has fallen.**

---

12. The phraseology in this verse is *ve-ne'elam mimmennu ve-hu yada,* lit. "and this was hidden from him and he knew." As Chavel notes (p. 330), the reading of Rashi's comment as *ve-ne'elam ve-hu yada* means that the person knew of his impurity at first, then forgot about it and became culpable by eating a sacred thing or entering the Sanctuary, and finally "knew" (i.e., became aware) that he had forgotten. Chavel further notes that *ve-hu yada* was the reading favored by *Sefer ha-Zikkaron,* but that the alternative reading *ve-lo yada* ("and he did not know") was supported by other authorities and would refer to the person's interim period of forgetting. To Rosenbaum and Silbermann (p. 148), it was "obvious" that the reading *ve-lo yada* was a misprint. *Siftei Ḥakhamim* likewise supports the reading *ve-hu yada.*

***he will confess.*** This is a verbal confession over a sacrifice, when he places his hand upon it if the sacrifice is an animal, or without placing the hand if he brings a bird or a flour offering. For this reason it is first stated that he will confess, and afterwards it is specified that his sacrifice will be *oleh ve-yored* [a variable or "sliding scale" offering].[13]

**5:6. "And he will bring his sacrifice of repentance to the Lord, for the sin that he committed, (that is) a female of the small cattle, a ewe or she-goat, in a sacrifice of aspersion, and the priest will propitiate for him with regard to his sin.**

**5:7. "If, however, his resources do not reach so far as (to be able to bring) a small animal, he will bring for his sacrifice of repentance to the Lord, for the sin committed, two turtledoves, or two young doves, one in a sacrifice of aspersion, and one in a burnt offering.**

***one in a sacrifice of aspersion, and one in a burnt offering.*** So that a portion of them will be for the priests and a portion for Heaven, for the one that will be an aspersion sacrifice will be partly eaten by the priests, and the one that will be a burnt offering will be entirely for Heaven (Abravanel; so also seems to be Ibn Ezra's view).

**5:8. "He will bring them to the priest, who will first present the one destined for the sacrifice of aspersion, and he will cut its head near the neck, but without detaching the head (from the body).**

---

13. In an earlier version of his comment on this verse (found in the Lutzki 672 manuscript), Shadal takes the view that the confession here is not a verbal one, since no particular addressee is identified, and it would have been unlikely for the confession to be addressed to the general public. Rather, this "confession" is merely the person's realization, before bringing the sacrifice, that he is deserving of punishment. Shadal goes on to say that in the case of Aaron's Yom Kippur sacrifice on behalf of the nation, where it states that "he will confess *over it* all the sins of the children of Israel" (Lev. 16:21), the confession is indeed verbal, because it is made during the act of the sacrifice.

*who will first present the one destined for the sacrifice of aspersion.*
So that first of all [the offeror's] sin will be propitiated, and afterwards
he will bring the burnt offering to become reconciled with his Lord and
cleave to Him (Abravanel; Rashi alluded to this as well).[14]

*and he will cut its head.* See above at Lev. 1:15.

5:9. "And he will sprinkle some of the blood of the sacrifice of
aspersion on the wall of the altar, and the remainder of the blood
will be made to drain at the foundation of the altar. It is a sacrifice
of aspersion.

5:10. "Of the second one, then, he will make a burnt offering
according to the rite. Thus the priest will propitiate for him with
regard to the sin that he committed, and it will be pardoned for him.

5:11. "And if his resources do not reach two turtledoves or two
young doves, he will bring in an offering for the sin committed a
tenth of an *ephah* of fine flour, for [that is, in place of] a sacrifice of
aspersion. He will not put oil upon it, and he will not place incense
upon it, for it is [that is, it represents] a sacrifice of aspersion.

5:12. "He will bring it to the priest, and the priest will take from
it a fistful of its scent [that is, a portion of the flour, destined to be
burned], and he will burn it on the altar, together with the sacrifices
to be burned to the Lord. It is [that is, it represents] a sacrifice of
aspersion.

5:13. "Thus the priest will propitiate for him, with regard to the sin
committed by him for one of these (aforementioned) things, and it
will be pardoned for him. And it (the offering) will be the priest's,
like every other flour offering."

14. Rashi, citing *Zevaḥim* 7b, likens the aspersion sacrifice to an
    advocate who enters first to obtain pardon, and the burnt offering to
    a gift that is brought in afterward.

# *Vayikra*

**5:14. And the Lord spoke to Moses, saying:**

**5:15. "If a person commits a sacrilege, and he sins in error against the things consecrated to the Lord, he will bring for his sacrifice of repentance to the Lord from the small cattle an immaculate ram, of the value of (two) silver shekels, according to the weight of the Temple, for a sacrifice of repentance.**

*of the value of (be-erkekha,* בערכך*).* The final *khaf* is not a pronominal suffix [i.e., the word *erkekha* does not mean "your value"]; rather, such is the structure of this noun, with the final letter of the root [ערך] doubled [כך].[15] In vv. 18 and 25 below, the expression *be-erkekha le-asham* is to be understood as per Rashi, "the value mentioned above in connection with the sacrifice of repentance."

In all three instances of the sacrifice of repentance [*asham*], the value is fixed according to the severity of the offense, which constitutes disrespect toward Heaven, whether the person ate a consecrated thing [vv. 15, 16], or did not know one of the laws of God [vv. 17-19], or swore falsely [vv. 20-26]; accordingly, a severe penalty was imposed with the value set at two shekels (A. H. Mainster). Not only was the value not made to vary (as in the cases above [vv. 1-13]) according to the offeror's wealth or poverty, but the offering always consisted of an immaculate ram.

*shekels (shekalim,* שְׁקָלִים*).* Perhaps the proper reading would have been שְׁקָלַיִם [*shekalayim,* in the dual form rather than the regular plural].

In Rashi's comment that the term *me'ilah* ("sacrilege," "misappropriation") always denotes *shinnui* ("change")—taken from *Torat Kohanim* [i.e., *Sifra,* the halakhic midrash on Leviticus]—[the word *shinnui*] is similar in meaning to *shikkur* ("lying," "falsification"). Likewise, in the saying, "It is permissible *le-shannot* [lit. "to change"] for the sake of peace" (*Yevamot* 65b), the meaning is "to lie," for anyone who lies is "changing" a thing from what it truly is. So also, a wife who acts faithlessly [*mo'elet*] toward her husband is lying and pretending to love him but actually loves another.

---

15. See also Shadal's comment on the word *erkekha* at Lev. 27:2.

**5:16.** "The amount of his sacrilege [that is, of the sacred thing that has been appropriated] he will pay, and he will add to it a fifth, and he will give all of this to the priest, and the priest will propitiate for him with the ram of the sacrifice of repentance, and it will be pardoned for him.

**5:17.** "And if someone who has sinned and done one of all those things that the Lord has commanded not to be done, and not knowing this (that he sinned), he (later) recognizes himself culpable, he will bear his sin [that is, he is guilty until he brings a sacrifice].

**5:18.** "He will then bring to the priest from the small cattle an immaculate ram, of the (aforementioned) value, for a sacrifice of repentance, and the priest will propitiate for him with regard to the error committed while he did not know (that he sinned); and it will be pardoned for him.

*for a sacrifice of repentance.* According to the Sages, this is an *asham talui* [a repentance sacrifice for doubtful guilt], for the offeror is in doubt and does not know whether he has sinned or not. A. H. Mainster objects that this is not the meaning of the expression "who has sinned and done one of all those things," or the expression "with regard to the error committed while he did not know." He maintains that above (throughout chapter 4) it speaks of an erroneous action (that one did not know that [the food he was eating] was tallow, or that the woman [with whom he was having intercourse] was a menstruant) (i.e., ignorance of fact), while here it speaks of ignorance of the law. He cites as support the expression "with regard to the error committed while he did not know." Perhaps this is what Ibn Ezra meant when he said [in his comment on this verse], "and he did not know if it was forbidden." However, the rest of Ibn Ezra's comment is obscure and confused, and it is impossible to understand what he truly thought.[16]

---

16 The portion of the comment in question may be translated as follows: "Many are of the opinion that this is an *asham talui*—he does not know whether he committed the act or not, while the *ḥattat* (sacrifice of aspersion) is brought if at first he did not know but then he knew. In the case of the *ḥattat*, he did not know that his act was

# Vayikra

**5:19.** "It is a sacrifice of repentance: that person feels himself culpable toward the Lord."

**5:20.** And the Lord spoke to Moses, saying:

**5:21.** "When someone sins and commits an infidelity toward the Lord, disavowing to his neighbor a deposit, or laying hands (upon the goods of others), or committing a robbery, or defrauding his neighbor—

*and commits an infidelity (u-ma'alah ma'al) toward the Lord.* This refers to one who swears falsely.

*or laying hands.* This phrase is connected to "when someone sins and commits an infidelity toward the Lord," not to "disavowing." The expression "laying hands" [*tesumet yad*] is similar to "putting forth one's hand" [*shelihut yad*] (Exod. 22:10).

*defrauding (ashak).* See below, Lev. 19:13.

**5:22.** "Or if he has found a lost thing and denies it, and swears falsely; (if he sins, in sum) through one of those actions that a man can commit sinning [to the harm of another's property]:

**5:23.** "When (I say) he will have sinned, and he feels himself culpable, he will restore that which he has robbed, or that which he has obtained by fraud, or the deposit that was entrusted to him, or the lost object that he found—

**5:24:** "Or whatever thing for which he swore falsely; he will pay for it (that is) entirely, and he will add to it a fifth. All of this he will give, when he feels himself culpable, to the one to whom the thing belonged.

---

forbidden but he later became aware of it, while in the case of the *asham,* he knew that it was forbidden but later forgot, and then he remembered, or it is an *asham talui.*"

63

# Shadal on Leviticus

**5:25: "And he will bring (in addition) his sacrifice of repentance to the Lord: (he will bring, that is) to the priest, from the small cattle, an immaculate ram of the (aforementioned) value, for a sacrifice of repentance.**

*And... his sacrifice of repentance.* The sacrifice is besides his return of the robbed object; it does not propitiate for the sin between man and his fellow, but rather for the one between man and God.

**5:26:  "And the priest will propitiate for him before the Lord, and there will be pardoned for him whatever thing that he will have done, and for which he feels culpable."**

# *Tsav*

*Role and rights of the priests • Rejected offerings •*
*Tallow and blood prohibitions • Installation of the priests*

**6:1.  The Lord spoke to Moses, saying:**

**6:2.  "Command Aaron and his sons as follows: This is the law regulating the burnt offering.  This sacrifice, called *olah* [because it is destined to be wholly burnt and to go up in flame], will be on the fire upon the altar all night, until morning, and (during all this time) the fire will be kept lit upon the altar.**

*Command Aaron and his sons.*   At the beginning of the book [Lev. 1:2], God said, "Speak to the children of Israel," while here He said, "Command Aaron and his sons."  Nachmanides wrote that there, God was commanding the bringing of sacrifices, and it was Israel that would be bringing them, but here He said "Command Aaron" because He was speaking about [the procedures for] making the sacrifices, and the priests would be making them.

My student Rabbi Judah Aryeh Osimo adds that the main intent of the *parashah* of *Vayikra* [above, chapters 1-5] is to relate matters regarding the sacrifices insofar as they concern the owners, and incidentally it refers to a small portion of that which concerns the priests. In the *parashah* of *Tsav*, on the other hand, the main point is to relate that which concerns the priests, both that which is assigned to them to do and that which is allotted to them to receive in exchange for their service, as well as that which is assigned to them to instruct [the people], such as the length of time in which the sacrifices may be eaten, the prohibition of eating them while in a state of impurity, and the prohibition of consuming the tallow and blood.

***This sacrifice, called* olah.** The Hebrew [derived from the root *alah*, "to ascend"] denotes setting alight and burning, as in *be-ha'alotekha et ha-nerot* ("when you light the lamps") [Num. 8:2]. The verse means to say, "This sacrifice, which is called *olah* because it is wholly burnt, will be on the fire on the altar all night, and in the morning its ashes will be removed." So seems to be Ibn Ezra's opinion as well.

***This sacrifice, called* olah, *will be on the fire upon the altar all night, until morning.*** The main point of this section is to issue the command regarding the removal of the ashes, and therefore it says that the sacrifice was to be burned throughout (the day as well as) the night until the morning, but not afterward, for the ashes were to be removed in the morning (R. Judah Aryeh Osimo).

**6:3. "Then the priest will put on his linen garment, and he will dress himself with linen trousers upon his flesh, and he will remove the ashes to which the fire will have reduced the burnt offering over the altar, and he will place them beside the altar.**

*his linen garment.* The one who comes to remove the ashes will wear his priestly garments, in order to indicate that this is a [holy] service that requires such garments (Wessely); only the bringing of the ashes outside the camp is not such a service, and [for this] he wears other garments.

*the ashes to which the fire will have reduced the burnt offering* (*ha-deshen asher tokhal ha-esh,* lit. "the ashes that the fire will have consumed"). [This is to be understood] as if it said "that which the fire will have turned to ashes in consuming the burnt offering."

**6:4. "He will then take off his vestments, and he will put on other garments, and he will bring the ashes outside the camp, in a pure place.**

**6:5. "And the fire (that is) on the altar will be kept lit there; it will not be allowed to be extinguished; and the priest will kindle wood there from morning to morning, and he will arrange over it the burnt offerings, and he will burn over it the tallow of the sacrifices of contentment.**

**6:6. "Fire will be made to burn unceasingly on the altar; it will never be allowed to be extinguished.**

**6:7. "And this is the law regarding the flour offering: the sons of Aaron will present it before the Lord, (that is) in front of the altar.**

**6:8. "(The priest) will remove with his fist some of the fine flour of the offering and some of its oil, and all of the incense that is on the offering, and he will burn this scent of it on the altar to the Lord, a propitiatory aroma.**

**6:9. "And the remainder of it Aaron and his sons will eat; it will be eaten in unleavened loaves, in a sacred place; in the courtyard of the tent of congregation they will eat it.**

**6:10. "It must not be baked as leavened bread; it is that [i.e., one of those things] which I have assigned for them as a portion of the sacrifices to be burned to Me; it is a most holy thing, like the sacrifice of aspersion and like the sacrifice of repentance.**

**6:11. "Any male of the children of Aaron will be able to eat it, a perpetual right for all the ages to come, (to be collected) from the**

sacrifices to be burned to the Lord; anything that touches these
things will become holy."

*will become holy.* See Exod. 29:37.[1]

**6:12. And the Lord spoke to Moses, saying:**

**6:13. "This is the offering of Aaron and of his sons, which they will
present to the Lord (each one in his time), at the time when one of
them is anointed: a tenth of an *ephah* of fine flour, a flour offering,
daily, half in the morning and half in the evening.**

*of Aaron and of his sons.* According to the plain meaning, this refers
only to the high priest, who would bring a flour offering of fried cakes
[*minḥat ḥavitin*] on the day of his anointing and, from then on, a daily
flour offering for the rest of his life. The meaning of "and of his sons,"
according to Ibn Ezra and Rashbam, is whichever of his sons who would
succeed him as high priest, as is specified in v. 15. However, the Rabbis
interpreted this to mean that an ordinary priest, when performing his
first service, would have to be initiated by bringing a flour offering.
Apparently this was the custom among the priests, even though it was
not [actually] a commandment from the Torah.

**6:14. "It will be made on a pan, in oil; you will present it fried;
cooked in the manner of the flour offerings [which are fried after
being cooked, and then broken] in pieces [2:6] you will present it to
the Lord, a propitiatory aroma.**

---

1. There, on the phrase "everything that touches the altar will become
holy," Shadal comments that according to the Rabbis, followed
by Rashi, the outer altar and the sacred utensils made holy any
object that touched them, but only if that object was appropriate for
holiness. However, Shadal expressed agreement with Ibn Ezra's
view that even an object that was not appropriate for holiness, once
it touched a sacred utensil, became one from which a "stranger" (not
of the priestly family) was forbidden to derive benefit.

*fried (murbekhet).* Ibn Ezra wrote that this word has no "brother," but R. Moses Landau and the *Me'ammer* criticized him, noting that *murbekhet* appears again below, in Lev. 7:12, and also in 1 Chron. 23:29. But their criticism is null and void, for from those two sources nothing at all can be learned about the meaning of *murbekhet,* and it is indeed like one who has no brother.

**6:15. "And the priest who, from among his sons, will be anointed in his place, will make it [this offering]. It is a perpetual law. Completely whole it will be burned to the Lord.**

**6:16. "And any flour offering of a priest will be completely burned; it will not be eaten."**

**6:17. The Lord spoke to Moses, saying:**

**6:18. "Speak to Aaron and to his sons, saying: This is the law with respect to the sacrifice of aspersion: in the place where the burnt offering is slaughtered the sacrifice of aspersion will be slaughtered, before the Lord; it is a most holy thing.**

**6:19. "That priest who will make its aspersions will eat it; in a holy place it will be eaten, in the courtyard of the tent of congregation.**

***That priest who will make its aspersions*** *(ha-kohen ha-meḥattei otah)* ***will eat it.*** Similar provisions are found below in Lev. 7:7-9. This is how matters were from the time of Moses to that of David; then the 24 priestly watches were instituted [see 1 Chron. ch. 24], and all those who served on a particular day (who were referred to as a *beit av,* "household") would share the meat of the aspersion and repentance sacrifices that were brought that day. [In keeping with these later conditions, and against the *peshat* or plain meaning,] the Sages were constrained to interpret *ha-kohen ha-meḥattei otah* as excluding [only] a priest who was in a state of impurity at the time of the service (see Rashi's comment here and below at Lev. 7:7-9). When will the eyes of the foolish be opened, those who say that the Torah was written in the era of the Monarchy?[2]

**6:20. "Anything that touches its flesh will become sacred; and if some of its blood is sprinkled on a garment, that part on which it was sprinkled you shall wash in a sacred place.**

*is sprinkled (yizzeh).* The Hebrew is in the [imperfect] *kal* conjugation of the root *nazah,* which signifies "leaping," i.e., "if some of its blood leaps onto a garment." In the *hif'il* conjugation [*yazzeh*], the word means that one "throws" a liquid in such a way that it leaps from one place to another.

**6:21. "And the earthenware vessel in which it is cooked shall be broken; and if it was cooked in a copper vessel, this will have to be cleansed and rinsed.**

*cleansed and rinsed (u-morak ve-shuttaf ba-mayim,* lit. "and cleansed and rinsed in water"). It seems to me that the word *u-morak* should be accented with a [disjunctive] *tipha* [rather than the conjunctive *merha* that appears], for the rinsing is with water, but the cleansing is not with water but with sand or some other matter. Even if some water were mixed with the sand, the water would not be the main thing, but the sand. See below at Lev. 12:2 [where cleansing a copper vessel with sand is mentioned toward the end of the comment].

**6:22. "Any male of the priests will be able to eat it; it is a most holy thing.**

---

2.   Rashi expresses the view, in keeping with the Talmud in *Zevaḥim* 99a and *Sifra*, that any of the priests who are fit to offer the sacrifice may eat of it, not only the particular priest who offers it. Shadal's comment implies not only that this reading departs from the *peshat*, but also that the *peshat* itself is an indication of the Torah text's antiquity, reflecting as it does the conditions that obtained when the sacrificial system was first instituted by Moses, not those of the Monarchical period when the number of priests had increased to the point where it was necessary to divide them into 24 shifts.

*Any male of the priests will be able to eat it.* The priest who makes its aspersions is permitted to give of its meat to anyone he wishes, as long as that person is a priest and a male (Wessely, in keeping with the plain meaning of v. 19 above).

6:23. "But every sacrifice of aspersion, the blood of which must be brought to the tent of congregation, in order to propitiate [make the aspersions] in the Sanctuary, will not be eaten but will be burned."

7:1. "And this is the law regarding the sacrifice of repentance; that is a most holy thing.

7:2. "In the place where the burnt offering is slaughtered will be slaughtered the sacrifice of repentance, and its blood he (the priest) will scatter on the altar round about.

7:3. "And he will offer from it all of its tallow: the tail and the tallow that covers the entrails.

7:4. "And the two kidneys, and the tallow that is upon them, which is (that is) on the flanks, and the omentum that is on the liver, which he will remove together with the kidneys.

7:5. "And the priest will burn all of this on the altar, in a sacrifice to be burned to the Lord. It is a sacrifice of repentance.

7:6. "Every male among the priests will be able to eat it; in a sacred place it will be eaten, it is a most holy thing.

7:7. "The sacrifice of aspersion and that of repentance have one same law; both the one and the other belong to that priest who will have performed their respective propitiatory functions.

7:8. "And the priest who will offer the burnt offering of any person— the skin of the burnt offering will belong to the same priest.

# Shadal on Leviticus

**7:9.** "And every flour offering, whether cooked in an oven or made in a baking pan or on a frying pan, will belong to the priest who will have offered it.

**7:10.** "And every flour offering kneaded with oil, or dry, will belong to all the sons of Aaron, to the one and the other alike.

*will belong to all the sons of Aaron (le-khol benei Aharon tihyeh).* To all of them, literally, as long as they were few in number, as in the time of Moses, or to all who were present in the Temple on that day, after they had proliferated and multiplied. A matter for study is the question of why these offerings were different from the ones in the previous verse. Nachmanides said that with the ones mentioned above, the priest was involved in their baking, but Wessely refuted his view and interpreted the phrase "to all the sons of Aaron" in accordance with his own approach (above at Lev. 6:22), that the one who made the offering was permitted to give of his portion to any of the other priests. It seems to me, however, that this is not the meaning of *le-khol benei Aharon tihyeh,* for in that case it should have said *kol benei Aharon yokheluha* ("all the sons of Aaron will eat it"), similar to the statement above [in v. 6, "Every male among the priests will be able to eat it"]. Rather, *le-khol benei Aharon tihyeh* is an expression that is equivalent to *la-kohen ha-makriv otah lo tihyeh* ("will belong to the priest who will have offered it") [in v. 9 above].

**7:11.** "And this is the law of the sacrifice of contentment, which one will present to the Lord.

**7:12.** "If he offers it for thanksgiving, he will present together with the sacrifice of thanksgiving unleavened cakes kneaded with oil, and cakes of soft dough anointed with oil, and fried fine flour, (made into) cakes kneaded with oil.

**7:13.** "Accompanied with cakes of leavened bread he will present his offering, together with his sacrifice of contentment made for thanksgiving.

**7:14.** "He will offer in tribute to the Lord a loaf of each of these various forms of offering, which will belong to the priest who will have scattered the blood of the sacrifice of contentment.

**7:15.** "Then the meat of his sacrifice of contentment made for thanksgiving will be eaten on the same day on which he makes the sacrifice; he must not leave of it until the next day.

**7:16.** "If, however, the sacrifice (of contentment) offered by him is a vow, or a spontaneous gift, it will be eaten on the day on which he will present his sacrifice, and also on the next day that which is left over of it will be able to be eaten.

*a vow (neder).* [Established by the offeror's statement,] "I hereby obligate myself [to bring an offering]." [In contrast, the obligation to present] a *nedavah* ("spontaneous gift") [is established by the statement,] "This one [i.e., this particular animal] is hereby [designated as an offering]."[3]

**7:17.** "But that which (still) is left over of the meat of the sacrifice must on the third day be burned.

**7:18.** "And if some of the meat of his sacrifice of contentment is eaten on the third day, (the sacrifice) will not be accepted, it will not be counted in favor of the one who presents it; rather, it will be rejected, and the person that eats of it will incur a sin.

*And if some of the meat of his sacrifice of contentment is eaten on the third day.* If the offeror leaves over some of the meat of the sacrifice until the third day and does not burn it, but eats of it or allows others to eat of it on the third day, then his sacrifice will not be counted in his favor; rather, it will be a rejected thing [*piggul*], and anyone that eats of its meat *even within the proper time* (on the first or second day) will

---

3. See *Kinnim* 1:2. There, the Mishnah explains that if an animal that is to be brought in fulfillment of a *neder* dies or is stolen, the offeror must bring another one in its place, while if an animal that has been designated as a *nedavah* dies or is stolen, the offeror is under no obligation to replace it with another.

incur a sin. This is the [plain] meaning of the text, but this is indeed a great stringency, for one who eats of the meat of the sacrifice within the proper time would incur a sin as if he ate *piggul*; because the leftover portion was not burned afterward, he would be like one who eats of it on the third day. Over this R. Eliezer expressed his astonishment (*Zevaḥim* 29a): after the sacrifice has been deemed valid, can it be invalidated retroactively? For this reason, the Rabbis were constrained to remove this text from its plain meaning and to explain that the sacrifice is not invalidated by eating on the third day unless it was the offeror's intention at the time of the offering to eat it on the third day. Thus they interpreted the phrase *ha-makriv oto lo yeḥashev lo* (lit. "it will not be counted in favor of the one who presents it") as a warning to offerors that they should not have the intention [*yeḥashevu*] at the time of the offering to eat of its meat on the third day, and anyone who eats of it then (if, before eating, he was aware of the offeror's intention) will incur a sin.

After having been astonished for a number of years as to why the Rabbis (in the words of Rashbam) "uprooted" this text from its plain meaning,[4] today (Purim 5607 [1847]) I merited to understand "that which they had seen concerning this matter."[5] And similarly, in every instance in which the Rabbis turned away from the plain meaning of the Scriptures, where the statement is not an individual's opinion but is agreed to without dissent, it is not a mistake that they made, but rather

4. As Nehama Leibowitz points out (*Gilyonot Nehama, Parashat Tsav*, 5703 [1943]), Shadal's approach differs from that of Wessely in the *Biur*, according to which the Rabbis' interpretation of this verse does not "uproot" the plain meaning but actually follows it. Wessely maintains that the phrase *im he'akhol ye'akhel ba-yom ha-shelishi* should not be interpreted to mean "and if it is eaten on the third day," but should be understood as if it said *le-he'akhel*, i.e., "if it is brought in order to be eaten on the third day." However, Shadal was aware of Wessely's approach and rejected it, agreeing with the *Me'ammer* (see the Lutzki 672 manuscript), who said that it was forced and ungrammatical.
5. Hebrew *mah ra'u al kakhah*, a phrase taken from Esther 9:26. As Martin Lockshin notes ("*Peshat* vs. *Halakha* Dilemma: Shadal and Tradition," http://thetorah.com/peshat-vs-halakha-dilemma-shadal-and-tradition/, n. 19), this was "an appropriate verse for Shadal to allude to on Purim."

a *takkanah* ("regulation," "ordinance") that they instituted, according to the needs of the generations—and who is a *Reformator* like they were? But their *takkanot* were made with deep wisdom, fear of God, and love of humankind, not for their own benefit or honor, and not in order to find favor in the eyes of flesh and blood.[6]

**7:19. "And the meat (of the sacrifice) that has touched any impure thing will not be eaten, but will be burned. (So also) with regard to the meat, every pure person will be able to eat the meat (of the sacrifice).**

**7:20. "But the person who eats of the meat of a sacrifice of contentment offered to the Lord, having upon him some impurity, that person will be cut off from the midst of his nation.**

**7:21. "And a person who has touched any impure thing, some human impurity, or some impure domestic animal [that is, one that has died of itself], or some abhorrent [forbidden to be eaten] impure [dead of itself] animal, and then eats of the meat of a sacrifice of contentment offered to the Lord, that person (I say) will be cut off from the midst of his nation."**

*some abhorrent... animal (shekets).* Meaning a creeping thing or fish or bird that is forbidden to be eaten. *Shekets tamei* ("an abhorrent impure animal") means one of the creeping things [etc.] that cause impurity with their death.

**7:22. The Lord spoke to Moses, saying:**

---

6. This bold statement is one of Shadal's most important formulations of his theory as to the origin and development of the Oral Law, *Torah she-be-al peh.* See my discussion of this subject in the Introduction to *Shadal on Exodus: Samuel David Luzzatto's Interpretation of the Book of* Shemot, pp. 19-31; see also my article, "Unconventional but Not Unorthodox: Shadal's Approach to the Oral Torah," *La Rassegna Mensile di Israel,* Vol. 84 Iss. 1-2 (2018), pp. 47-68.

**7:23.** "Speak to the children of Israel as follows: any bovine, ovine, or caprine tallow you shall not eat.

**7:24.** "The tallow of an animal dead of itself, or torn to pieces (by some wild beast), may be used for any labor, but you shall not eat it. [The law applies equally to the tallow of slaughtered animals, but these are not mentioned here because the Israelites of the Mosaic times, living in the desert, were not permitted to slaughter any domestic animal without making a sacrifice of it and burning its tallow and blood on the altar; see ch. 17].

*The tallow of an animal dead of itself, or torn to pieces.* This was said with regard to the generation of the desert, which ate no meat other than the sacrifices of contentment and did not have any permitted tallow other than that of an animal dead of itself [*nevelah*] or torn to pieces [*terefah*] (and therefore it subsequently says with respect to blood, "in any place of your residence" [below, v. 26], that is, whether in this generation or when you are settled in your land). Since it says that the tallow was permitted for labor, it mentions [once again] the prohibition of eating it, even though this did not [strictly speaking] need to be said (this was the opinion of the Targum ascribed to Jonathan ben Uzziel; see *Netivot ha-Shalom*).[7] For future generations, this verse teaches that tallow [although prohibited for eating] does not have the impurity of *nevelah*. This verse,

---

7.   The so-called Targum Jonathan on this verse concludes, "But the tallow of a kosher animal will be offered on the altar, and you shall not eat it." Mendelssohn's commentary in *Netivot ha-Shalom* expresses the view that the general prohibition of eating tallow had to be repeated here so that the desert generation would not be misled into thinking that the prohibition applied only to the tallow of sacrifices, and that once they entered the land of Israel and were allowed to eat non-sacrificial meat, the tallow of such meat would be permitted. Mendelssohn goes on to say that for this reason, the law of the tallow of *nevelah* and *terefah* was added here, for even though such meat was not used for sacrifice, even during the desert period, its tallow was not allowed to be eaten, and from this prohibition one could infer that it would be forbidden to eat the tallow of non-sacrificial meat in future generations.

too, serves as proof that the Torah was written during the generation of the desert.[8]

**7:25. "For anyone who eats the tallow of a (quadruped) animal of which there may be made a sacrifice to be burned to the Lord, that person (I say) who eats of it will be cut off from the midst of his nation.**

*of a (quadruped) animal of which there may be made a sacrifice.* That is, a sacrifice may be brought from that species.

**7:26. "And any blood you shall not eat, in any place of your residence, neither of flying creatures nor of quadrupeds.**

*And any blood... neither of flying creatures nor of quadrupeds.* So that we should not think that the prohibition of blood is merely like the prohibition of tallow, which pertains only to species that may be brought as a sacrifice, the phrase "neither of flying creatures nor of quadrupeds" is added. Wild beasts [*hayyah*] are included in the term "quadrupeds" [*behemah*] (Wessely).

**7:27. "Any person who eats any blood, that person will be cut off from the midst of his nation."**

**7:28. The Lord spoke to Moses, saying:**

**7:29. "Speak to the children of Israel, saying: One who wishes to offer to the Lord his sacrifice of contentment will bring from his sacrifice of contentment (the portion of) his offering to the Lord.**

**7:30. "With his hands he will bring the parts to be burned to the Lord; he will bring (that is) the tallow upon the breast, the breast (however) to make of it a waving before the Lord [not so that it may be burned].**

---

8. See Shadal's comment on Lev. 6:19 and the footnote thereon.

**7:31.** "And the priest will burn the tallow on the altar, and the breast will belong to Aaron and to his sons.

**7:32.** "And the right leg you will give in tribute to the priest from your sacrifices of contentment.

*leg (shok).* See *Sefer Mitsvot Gadol*, Positive Commandments 183; *Tosefot Yom Tov* on [Mishnah] *Ḥullin*, end of ch. 10; and *Sefer ha-Zikkaron.*[9]

**7:33.** "The one among the sons of Aaron who will offer (on the altar) the blood and the tallow of the sacrifice of contentment will have for his portion the right leg.

**7:34.** "For the breast of waving and the leg of tribute I accept from the children of Israel, from their sacrifices of contentment, and I give them to Aaron the priest and to his sons as a perpetual right (to receive) from the children of Israel.

*the leg of tribute.* It is not called "the leg of waving" because it was not waved; rather, it is called "the leg of tribute" [*shok ha-terumah*] because it was contributed [*muram,* lit. "raised"] to the Most High, that is, to the priest (see Exod. 29:24).[10]

---

9.  *Sefer Mitsvot Gadol* (R. Moses of Coucy) cites Rashi's definition of *shok* (in his comment on this verse) as that portion of the hind leg from the knee joint to the middle joint that is called the *sovekh shel regel*, but R. Moses observes that Rashi failed to spell out [*lo dikdek*] that this definition is the one given by R. Judah [in *Ḥullin* 10:4], and that the Rabbis' majority opinion defines *shok* as extending from the knee joint all the way up to the socket of the hip bone. Both *Tosefot Yom Tov* (R. Yom Tov Lipmann Heller) and *Sefer ha-Zikkaron* (R. Abraham Bukarat) express surprise that Rashi seemingly adopted R. Judah's opinion and not the Rabbis' majority opinion, and both of them refer to R. Moses' comment in *Sefer Mitsvot Gadol*.

10. In his comment there, Shadal says that "the breast of waving" served as an object on which to spread the tallows that had to be waved— that is, lifted up and moved about in order to symbolize their transfer from the offeror's domain to that of Heaven—and then it was left

**7:35.** "This is the right connected with the dignity of Aaron and with the dignity of his sons, (to receive) from the sacrifices to be burned to the Lord, as soon as they are brought near [that is, qualified] to exercise the functions of priests of the Lord—

**7:36.** "That which, that is, the Lord has commanded that they be given by the children of Israel, as soon as they are anointed, (and this) as a perpetual right, for all the ages to come."

**7:37.** This is the law for the burnt offering, for the flour offering, and for the sacrifice of aspersion, and for the sacrifice of repentance, and for the sacrifice of installation, and for the sacrifice of contentment—

**7:38.** That the Lord commanded to Moses on Mount Sinai, when He commanded the children of Israel to present their sacrifices to the Lord in the desert of Sinai.

**8:1.** The Lord spoke to Moses, saying:

**8:2.** "Take Aaron, and with him his sons, and the vestments, and the oil of anointing, and the bull destined for a sacrifice of aspersion, and the two rams and the basket of the unleavened breads.

**8:3.** "And gather all the assembly at the entrance of the tent of congregation."

*And gather all the assembly (ha-edah).* Rashi wrote that "the lesser comprised the greater" [i.e., that the small area accommodated the entire people]; this is because he thought that the *edah* was the [whole] "community" [*kahal*], but this is not so.

---

to the priest, like the basket in which the first fruits were placed. In contrast, he says, the right leg was a tribute to God, Who in turn granted it to the priest.

**8:4.  And Moses carried out all that the Lord commanded him, and the assembly gathered at the entrance of the tent of congregation.**

**8:5.  And Moses said to the assembly, "This is the thing [that is, all that you see me do] that the Lord has commanded to be carried out."**

**8:6.  Moses had Aaron and his sons present themselves and bathe themselves in water.**

**8:7.  Then he put the tunic on him, and he girded him with the belt, and he had him put on the mantle, and he put the dorsal on him, and he girded him with the band of the dorsal, and with that he adorned him [with all these vestments].**

**8:8.  And he put the pectoral on him, and he placed in the pectoral the Urim and the Tummim.**

***and he placed in the pectoral the Urim and the Tummim.***  Moses placed them in the pectoral [*ḥoshen*] at the time of dressing; thus, they were not fixed in the pectoral, but the priest would make use of them on occasion [as an oracle] and take them out of the pectoral.  Perhaps they consisted of 22 letters engraved on 22 small pieces of wood or metal, and the priest would remove one letter and then another, and God's Providence would bring about for him the proper answer for his question.  Each of these letters would have been called by a special name; the *alef* would have been called *ur* ("illumination") and the *tav* would have been called *tom* ("perfection," "purity"), and their aggregation from *alef* to *tav* would have been called Urim and Tummim.  From this was derived the Rabbinic tradition that from the letters of the names of the tribes they would understand the answer.[11]

---

11.  In *Yoma* 73b, it is said that the messages of the Urim and Tummim were composed of letters contained in the names of the tribes that were inscribed in the twelve gemstones on the pectoral; according to R. Yohanan, the appropriate letters would protrude, while according to Resh Lakish, they would come together to form words.  Shadal's own description is in some ways more closely paralleled by Thomas Kelly Cheyne and John Sutherland Black in the *Encyclopaedia*

**8:9.** And he put the mitre on his head; and he put on the mitre, on the front part, the plate of gold, sacred diadem, as the Lord commanded Moses.

**8:10.** And Moses took the oil of anointing, and he anointed the tabernacle and all that was in it, and (thus) he consecrated them.

**8:11.** And he sprinkled of it on the altar seven times, and he anointed the altar and all of its furnishings, and the basin and its pedestal, to consecrate them.

**8:12.** And he dripped of the oil of anointing on the head of Aaron, and he anointed him to consecrate him.

**8:13.** Then Moses had the sons of Aaron present themselves, and he had them put on tunics, and he girded them with belts, and he wrapped them turbans, as the Lord commanded Moses.

**8:14.** And he had the bull destined for the sacrifice of aspersion brought near, and Aaron and his sons placed their hands on the head of the bull of the sacrifice of aspersion.

**8:15.** Then, having slaughtered it, Moses took the blood, and he placed some of it with his finger on the prominences of the altar round about, thus purging the altar [see Exod. 29:36][12]; and the (rest of the) blood he dripped at the base of the altar, and thus he consecrated it, so that the expiations might then be made upon it.

---

*Biblica* (1903), s.v. "Urim and Thummim"; they suggest that the Urim and Tummim were kept inside the priest's garment and drawn or thrown from it, and that "we should imagine them as small flat objects, perhaps tablets of wood or bone." However, Cheyne and Black express the view that these objects were only two in number.

12. In his translation of Exod. 29:36, which mentions the sprinkling of blood on the altar to make expiation for the altar, Shadal adds the bracketed phrase "[that is, to purify it of every fault that might have been committed during its construction, or in the offering of its materials]."

# Shadal on Leviticus

**8:16.** Then he took all the tallow that is on the entrails, and the omentum of the liver, and the two kidneys, and their tallow, and Moses burned them on the altar.

**8:17.** And the bull, and its skin and its meat and its waste, he burned outside the camp, as the Lord commanded Moses.

**8:18.** And he caused to be brought near the ram destined for a burnt offering, and Aaron and his sons placed their hands on the head of the ram.

**8:19.** And having slaughtered it, Moses scattered the blood on the altar round about.

**8:20.** Then Moses cut the ram into its quarters, and he burned the head and the quarters and the fat.

**8:21.** And the entrails and the legs he washed in the water, and Moses burned all of the ram on the altar. It is a burnt offering, for a propitiatory aroma; it is a sacrifice to be burnt to the Lord, as the Lord commanded Moses.

**8:22.** Then he caused to be brought near the other ram, the ram destined for the sacrifice of installation, and Aaron and his sons placed their hands on the head of the ram.

*the ram destined for the sacrifice of installation (eil ha-millu'im).* See *Netivot ha-Shalom.*[13]

---

13. N. H. Wessely's comment on this verse in *Netivot ha-Shalom* cites Rashi's view that *eil ha-millu'im* is synonymous with *eil ha-shelamim* ("the ram of the sacrifice of contentment") and Nachmanides' view that this second ram was a "sacrifice of contentment" because the newly installed priests were giving thanks for having been assigned their role in God's house. However, Wessely expresses his own view that *eil ha-millu'im* should be understood in the literal sense as "the ram of installation" (*Einsetzungswidder* in Mendelssohn's German translation) because it was different in several respects from the *shelamim*.

8:23. And having slaughtered it, Moses took from its blood, and he placed some of it on the top of Aaron's right ear, on the thumb of his right hand, and on the big toe of his right foot.

8:24. Then he caused to be brought near the sons of Aaron, and Moses placed some of that blood on the top of their right ear, and on the thumb of their right hand, and on the big toe of their right foot; then Moses scattered the (rest of the) blood on the altar round about.

8:25. Then he took the tallow and the tail and all the tallow that is on the entrails, and the omentum of the liver, and the two kidneys, and their tallow, and the right leg.

8:26. And from the basket of the unleavened breads that was before the Lord, he took a cake of unleavened bread, and one of oiled bread, and one of soft dough, and he placed them on top of the tallows and on top of the right leg.

8:27. And he placed all of it on Aaron's palms and on the palms of his sons, and he made of them a waving before the Lord.

8:28. Then Moses took those things from upon their palms, and he burned them on the altar with the burnt offering. They are a sacrifice of installation, for a propitiatory aroma; it is a sacrifice to be burned to the Lord.

8:29. Then Moses took the breast, and he made of it a waving before the Lord. From the ram of installation it [the breast] belonged to Moses, as the Lord commanded Moses.

8:30. And Moses took from the oil of anointing and from the blood that was on the altar, and he sprinkled some of it upon Aaron, and on his garments, and with him (also) upon his sons, and on his sons' garments; and thus he consecrated Aaron and his vestments, and with him (also) his sons and his sons' vestments.

**8:31.** And Moses said to Aaron and to his sons, "Cook the meat at the entrance of the tent of congregation, and there you will eat it, as well as the bread that is in the basket of installation, as I have prescribed, saying, 'Aaron and his sons will eat it.'

**8:32.** "And that which will be left over of the meat and of the bread, you will burn.

**8:33.** "And from the entrance of the tent of congregation you will not go forth for seven days, until (that is) the days of your installation are completed, because for seven days your installation will be celebrated.

**8:34.** "As has been done on this day, (the same) the Lord has commanded to be done (for six more days), to propitiate for you.

**8:35.** "And at the entrance of the tent of congregation you will remain day and night, for seven days, and you will observe the prescription of the Lord, otherwise you will die; for so I was commanded."

**8:36.** And Aaron and his sons carried out all the things that the Lord commanded through Moses.

# Shemini

*Installation of the priests, continued • Nadab and Abihu and the "strange fire" • "These are the animals that you may eat" • "These, however, you shall not eat"*

**9:1. Now on the eighth day, Moses called Aaron and his sons, and the elders of Israel.**

***Now on the eighth day.*** Of the installation and of the month of Nisan, as per Ibn Ezra. See *Netivot ha-Shalom* on Exod. 40:2, citing R. Elijah Mizrahi, who in turn cites the *Sifrei* [on Num. 9:6] as saying that this was the opinion of R. Akiva; however, according to the printed version this is not so.[1]

---

1. In *Sifrei* on Num. 9:6, there is a dispute as to the identity of the men who were impure because of contact with the dead and who were thus unable to bring the paschal sacrifice at the proper time. R. Ishmael says that they were the bearers of Joseph's bones, while R. Akiva says that they were Mishael and Elzaphan, who were assigned to remove the bodies of their cousins Nadab and Abihu from the camp (Lev. 10:4-5). Mizrahi, as cited by *Netivot ha-Shalom*, elaborates on R. Akiva's opinion, adding language that does not appear in the printed *Sifrei*: although Mishael and Elzaphan could not bring the

# Shadal on Leviticus

**9:2. And he said to Aaron, "Take for yourself a young calf for a sacrifice of aspersion and a ram for a burnt offering, immaculate, and present them before the Lord.**

**9:3. "And to the children of Israel you shall speak, saying, 'Take a kid for a sacrifice of aspersion and a calf and a lamb born within a year, immaculate, for a burnt offering.**

**9:4. "'And an ox and a ram for a sacrifice of contentment, to sacrifice before the Lord, and a flour offering kneaded with oil, for today the Lord will show Himself to you.'"**

*will show Himself (nir'ah).* The [feminine-indicating vowel] *kamats* in the word *nir'ah* [נִרְאָה] presents a difficulty, for the word is a masculine participle and would properly have been vocalized with a *segol* [*nir'eh*, נִרְאֶה]. The phrase "for today the Lord will show Himself to you" refers to the descent of the fire from heaven to consume the sacrifices (Rashbam, Ibn Ezra), for indeed any open and obvious miracle is a manifestation of God's glory; cf. "And tomorrow morning you will see the majesty of the Lord" (Exod. 16:7), which refers only to the descent of the manna. So perhaps the word *nir'ah* was intentionally vocalized in the feminine style in order to indicate that [the subject] is to be understood as "the fire [*esh* (f.)] of the Lord" and not God Himself.[2]

---

paschal sacrifice "on that day" (Num. 9:6), they could have brought it on the next day (i.e., on the 15th of Nisan), after their seven days of impurity, which indicates that the start of their impurity—Nadab and Abihu's death—occurred on the eighth of Nisan. Since that day was the eighth day of the installation, it follows that the installation itself began on the first of Nisan.

2. Nehama Leibowitz observes that the phrase "today the Lord will show Himself to you" presents two problems: (1) what "appearance" of the Lord are mortals able to perceive, and (2) why is the word *nir'ah* vocalized as it is? She then cites Shadal's comment and concludes, "This solves the theological as well as grammatical problem" (*New Studies in Vayikra*, pp. 98-99). It should further be noted that in Shadal's translation of Exod. 24:10, the phrase "And they saw the God of Israel" is followed by the bracketed phrase "[that is, the fire in which He appeared]."

**9:5. They brought before the tent of congregation that which Moses commanded, and all of the assembly came near and stood before the Lord.**

*They brought before (va-yik'ḥu... el penei,* lit. "they took before"). An elliptical phrase, meaning that "they took that which Moses commanded and they brought it before the tent of congregation"—on the model of *kaḥem na elai* ("Bring them here to me," lit. "Take them to me") (Gen. 48:9).

**9:6. And Moses said, "This is that which the Lord has commanded that you do [that is, that you should bring these sacrifices], so that the majesty of the Lord may be shown to you."**

**9:7. Then Moses said to Aaron, "Draw near to the altar, and make your sacrifice of aspersion and your burnt offering, and propitiate for you and for the people, and make the people's sacrifice and propitiate for them, as the Lord has commanded."**

**9:8. Aaron drew near to the altar, and he slaughtered his calf destined for the sacrifice of aspersion.**

**9:9. The sons of Aaron presented its blood to him, and he dipped his finger in the blood, and he placed some of it on the prominences of the altar, and the (rest of the) blood he poured at the base of the altar.**

**9:10. And the tallow and the kidneys and the omentum (removed) from the liver, of the sacrifice of aspersion, he caused to be burned on the altar, as the Lord commanded Moses.**

*he caused to be burned (hiktir) on the altar.* He placed them on the altar, and when the fire of Heaven descended, they were burned (Rashbam).

**9:11. And the meat and the skin he burned outside the camp.**

9:12. And he slaughtered the burnt offering, and the sons of Aaron presented him with its blood, and he scattered it on the altar round about.

9:13. And the burnt offering they presented to him piece by piece, and the head, and he burned it on the altar.

9:14. And he washed the entrails and the legs, and he burned them on the altar, with (the remainder of) the burnt offering.

9:15. Then he caused to be brought near the sacrifice of the people, and he took the kid destined for the sacrifice of aspersion, for the people's sake; he slaughtered it and he made aspersions of it, as (he had made) of the previous one.

9:16. And he caused to be brought near (the animals destined for) the burnt offering, and he made it according to the rite.

9:17. And he caused to be brought near the flour offering, and he filled his hand with it, and he burned it on the altar, besides the (flour offering of the) burnt offering of the morning.

9:18. Then he slaughtered the ox and the ram, destined for the sacrifice of contentment for the people's sake, and the sons of Aaron presented him with its blood, which he scattered on the altar round about.

9:19. Likewise (they presented him with) the tallows (taken) from the ox, and from the ram the tail, and that (tallow) which covers (the entrails), and the kidneys, and the omentum of the liver.

9:20. They placed the tallows upon the breasts, and he burned the tallows on the altar.

9:21. And of the breasts and of the right leg Aaron made a waving before the Lord, as He commanded Moses.

**9:22. Then Aaron raised his hands toward the people, and he blessed them; then he came down, after having made the sacrifice of aspersion and the burnt offering and the sacrifice of contentment.**

**9:23. And Moses and Aaron entered into the tent of congregation, and they came out of it, and they blessed the people, and the majesty of the Lord appeared to all the people.**

*And Moses and Aaron entered, etc.* After Aaron performed his service, Moses went in with him, as if to present him before the King and to beseech Him to favor him, or to hear whether he was in favor before Him. Then it was announced that he was [indeed] in favor before Him, and he was given permission to bless the people; then they went out and blessed the people, and at once the majesty of the Lord appeared.

**9:24. And there went forth a fire from before the Lord [that is, from the most holy place], and it consumed [instantaneously] upon the altar the burnt offerings and the tallows; and all the people, having seen this, raised a cry, and they threw themselves on their faces.**

**10:1. Then Nadab and Abihu, sons of Aaron, each took a fire shovel, and they put fire on them, and they placed some incense upon it, thus presenting before the Lord a strange fire, which He had not commanded them.**

*thus presenting before the Lord a strange fire (esh zarah).* Their intention was not to burn the [regular] morning incense (as Rashbam held, and as I believed for twenty years; see *Bikkurei ha-Ittim* 5588 [1829], p. 145), for if this were the case, what place would there have been for the two fire shovels? (See the *Biur* for additional proofs.[3]) Rather, they

---

3. The *Biur* (i.e., the commentary by Wessely in Mendelssohn's *Netivot ha-Shalom*) to this verse raises the following points as arguments against the idea that Nadab and Abihu were offering the regular morning incense: (1) the morning incense would already have been brought at the time in question; (2) there was only one offering of morning incense, not two; (3) the morning incense was offered on the

presented an offering of incense that God had not commanded, and their sin was on account of pride, for it was not enough for them to be their father's attendants: "and the sons of Aaron presented him with its blood" [above, 9:12]. They sought to show that they, too, were priests of God like Aaron, and since Moses had not commanded them to perform any service of their own, they chose for themselves a prestigious service, and they presented before the Lord a strange fire. It does not say "a strange incense," for in fact the incense was not a "strange" one (see the *Biur*[4]), but the fire was "strange." If this incense offering had been at the command of Moses, he would have instructed them not to take [their own] fire, for the fire was to come from God, just as it came to consume the burnt offering. However, they acted on their own initiative, and since they were unsure whether God's fire would come forth to consume the incense offering that He had not commanded, they were compelled to bring a "strange fire."[5]

**10:2. And a fire from before the Lord came forth, and it consumed them, and they died before the Lord.**

*And a fire... came forth.* A different fire, not the fire that consumed the burnt offering (as Rashbam held), for if it were so, the text should have said, "And *the* fire came forth"; see Wessely's comment [in the *Biur*] on the preceding verse.

---

altar, not on fire shovels; and (4) if Nadab and Abihu were offering the morning incense inside the tent of congregation while Aaron was conducting his sacrifices outside, Moses and Aaron would have found the sons' bodies when they entered the tent, so how could they have then come out of the tent and blessed the people without mentioning what they had seen?

4. As the *Biur* points out, a "strange incense" would have been one that was offered on the altar, or one that was composed of unauthorized ingredients.

5. In the Lutzki 672 manuscript, an additional comment is inserted here, adopting Wessely's opinion that the term *esh zarah* does not literally mean "strange fire"; rather, *esh* is the equivalent of *isheh* ("burnt sacrifice"), since it is a sacrifice that can be said to be "presented," not the fire.

**10:3. And Moses said to Aaron, "This is precisely what the Lord has declared [that is, this death is in accordance with the admonition previously given to us by the Lord], saying, 'In those who are permitted to come close to Me, I will show Myself holy [in other words, superhuman, omnipotent, punishing them miraculously when they fall short of their obligations], and thus I will command respect of all the people.'" And Aaron kept silent [he resigned himself].**

*This is precisely what the Lord has declared (hu asher dibber YHVH).* There is no need to search out where He made such a declaration, for this is analogous to [Laban and Bethuel's statement to Abraham's servant], "Let her [Rebecca] become the wife of your master's son, as the Lord has decreed" [Gen. 24:51].[6] The meaning is, "Know that so He has decreed in His wisdom, to show Himself holy, that is, to demonstrate His holiness and greatness, by punishing His chosen ones who are close to Him, in order that all the people should hear and be afraid, and that they should reason [that such a demonstration could be made] *a fortiori* with respect to themselves" (see Rashi).[7] I hereby revoke what I wrote on this verse in *Bikkurei ha-Ittim* 5588 [1827], p. 145.[8]

**10:4. Then Moses called Mishael and Elzaphan, sons of Uzziel, uncle of Aaron, and he said to them, "Come near, transport your brothers [that is, your relatives] far from the Sanctuary, outside of the camp."**

6. Although there is no record of such an actual decree, Shadal's comment on Gen. 24:51 explains that God had effectively revealed His will by means of the incident of Rebecca at the well (as recounted by the servant to Laban and Bethuel in Gen. 24:42-48).
7. Rashi's comment on this verse says that when God judges the righteous, He incurs the people's fear, exaltation, and praise, and if this is the case, then it is all the more so when He judges the wicked.
8. There, Shadal expressed the view that the phrase *hu asher dibber YHVH* was to be taken as a rhetorical question: "Is this what the Lord has declared?" In other words, "Is this act that your sons committed a fulfillment of God's declaration that He would show Himself holy by means of those who would come close to him?" Shadal goes on to identify where God had made such a declaration: "And Aaron and his sons I will sanctify to be priests to Me... And they [the people] will know that I, the Lord, am their God, Who brought them out of the land of Egypt, to reside among them" (Exod. 29:44, 46).

# Shadal on Leviticus

**10:5.** They drew near, and they transported them in their tunics outside of the camp, as Moses ordered.

**10:6.** And Moses said to Aaron, and to Eleazar and Ithamar his sons, "Do not let your heads have unkempt hair, and do not rend your garments, otherwise you will die, and the entire assembly will incur the anger (of the Lord). But your brothers, (that is) all the house of Israel, may weep (the death of) those whom the Lord has burned.

**10:7.** "And from the entrance of the tent of congregation do not go forth, otherwise you will die, for you have upon you the oil of anointing of the Lord." And they followed the order of Moses.

**10:8.** And the Lord spoke to Aaron, saying:

**10:9.** "Wine, or (other) intoxicating liquor, do not drink, neither you nor your sons, when you enter into the tent of congregation, otherwise you will die: a perpetual statute for all the ages to come.

*Wine, or (other) intoxicating liquor, do not drink.* Not that Nadab and Abihu sinned on account of drunkenness, for it is unlikely that they would have drunk wine on the morning of that awesome day; rather, because they died for having added something that God had not commanded them, God wanted to alert Aaron and his sons to be particular as to the matters of the service, not to change even a minor thing. It is as if He said, "I know that from this day forward, you would not dare to do anything on your own initiative, but I hereby command you to guard yourselves even from error. Therefore, do not drink wine or other intoxicating liquor when you enter into the tent of congregation, so that you do not come to forget anything. Not only must you take such care when performing the service, but also when you give instruction to others as to what is sacred or profane, or pure or impure, or as to any other laws of God, you must take care not to drink, so that you do not err in instruction and sin to God."

**10:10.** "Likewise when you must distinguish [decide] between that which is sacred and that which is not, and between the impure and the pure—

**10:11.** "Or teach the children of Israel any of the statutes that the Lord has commanded them through Moses."

*when you enter... when you must distinguish... or teach.* Drinking is forbidden to the priests during all the activities that are unique to them, and these are of three categories. The first is the conduct of the service in the Sanctuary, and this is what is referred to by "when you enter into the tent of congregation." The second is instruction as to the sacred and profane or pure and impure in matters pertaining to the service and the Temple—that is, pronouncing judgment whenever a doubt arises among the priests themselves. The third is instruction of all the laws to the children of Israel, to inform them what they must do, what is forbidden, and what is permitted. Perhaps instruction in matters of leprosy [*tsara'at*] is included in the second category, for it involves distinguishing between the pure and the impure.

**10:12.** And Moses said to Aaron, and to Eleazar and Ithamar, his remaining sons, "Take the flour offering remaining after the part of it that was burned in sacrifice to the Lord, and eat it in unleavened loaves by the altar, for it is a most holy thing.

**10:13.** "You will eat it in a holy place, for it is your right and the right of your sons (to be received) from the sacrifices to be burned to the Lord, for so I was commanded.

**10:14.** "And the breast of waving and the leg of tribute you will eat in a pure place [that is, one that is also outside the Tabernacle], you and with you your sons and your daughters, for they have been constituted as your right and that of your children (to be received) from the sacrifices of contentment of the children of Israel.

**10:15.** "They will bring of them the leg of tribute and the breast of waving, together with the tallows to be burned in sacrifice, so that a waving may be made of them before the Lord, and they will belong to you, and to your children with you, in perpetual right, as the Lord has commanded."

**10:16.** Moses then sought account of the goat of the sacrifice of aspersion and found that it had been burned; and he became indignant with Eleazar and Ithamar, remaining sons of Aaron, saying:

*the goat of the sacrifice of aspersion.* From this it can be inferred that there was only one goat (the one mentioned above, Lev. 9:3), and if so, [the day that Nadab and Abihu died] was not the first of the month [of Nisan], and the "eighth day" [of the installation, mentioned in Lev. 9:1] was the eighth day of the month, for the Tabernacle was erected on the first of the month, and prior to the eighth day they [Aaron and his sons] sat at the entrance of the tent of congregation for seven days [as they had been commanded in Lev. 8:33]; thus it follows that the Tabernacle was then already in place. At this time there was not yet any "goat of the prince" [i.e., the princes of the tribes had not yet brought their inaugural offerings, as described in Numbers ch. 7], and thus it follows that the princes began to bring their offerings only after the eighth day. [Although it says in Num. 7:1 that the princes' offerings began] *be-yom kelot Mosheh lehakim et ha-mishkan* (lit. "on the day that Moses finished erecting the Tabernacle"), it was not precisely on that same day, but after the installation. Similarly, although it is written there [Num. 7:10 and 7:84] that the [princes began the] inauguration of the altar *be-yom himmashah oto* (lit. "on the day it was anointed"), it says afterwards [Num. 7:88] that this was *aharei himmashah oto* ("after it was anointed").

However, the Sages (as cited by Rashi) said [in *Sifra* and *Zevahim* 101a] that there were three goats,[9] but that they had eaten two of them

---

9. That is, on the day that Nadab and Abihu died, three goats had been offered: the kid of the installation sacrifice (Lev. 9:3), the goat of the first prince's inaugural offering, and the goat that was brought on the first day of every month.

because those two had a status of holiness for that occasion alone, and they had burned only the goat of the sacrifice of the first day of the month, as that offering had a status of holiness for all generations to come. Yet it seems that according to the plain meaning, the text should have specified which goat it was that Moses sought account of, and since it mentions only "the goat of the sacrifice of aspersion," it can be inferred that there was only one goat. As for Rashi's comment on the end of the next verse, that the aspersion sacrifice of the eighth day was not brought for the purpose of propitiation, this is not so, for above in Lev. 9:7 it is written, "…and make the people's sacrifice and propitiate for them," and the "people's sacrifice" consisted of a kid, a calf, and a ram (above, Lev. 9:3).

**10:17. "How is it that you have not eaten the sacrifice of aspersion in the holy place? For it is a most holy thing, and it is a thing that was assigned to you, because (eating it) you were to assume the sins of the assembly, and to propitiate for them before the Lord.**

*How is it that you have not eaten.* "Even though you are *onenim* [i.e., in the first stage of mourning], you should have eaten the aspersion sacrifice, for I already told you, 'Do not let your heads have unkempt hair… And from the entrance of the tent of congregation do not go forth' [above, vv. 6, 7]; in other words, you are not to express any feeling for what happened to you."

**10:18. "Its blood has not yet been brought into the Sanctuary [in which case the sacrifice of aspersion would have had to be burned; see Lev. 6:23]; you should therefore have eaten it in a holy place, as I have prescribed."**

**10:19. And Aaron said to Moses, "Behold today they (my sons) presented before the Lord their sacrifice of aspersion and their burnt offering, and then such things [that is, the death of the two sons] happened to me; if on this very day I had eaten a sacrifice of aspersion, could that have pleased the Lord?" [In other words, "Having just now been stricken by the heavenly wrath, how could I**

**have considered myself acceptable to God and worthy to propitiate on behalf of others? And if I had so presumed, could such arrogance on my part not have irritated the Divinity all the more?"]**

*Behold today they (my sons) presented.* "I, together with my four sons, brought our sacrifice of aspersion and our burnt offering to propitiate for ourselves, but nevertheless such things happened to me—my two sons died. If so, we are not acceptable before the Omnipresent, and thus if the eating of the aspersion sacrifice is, as you have said, for the purpose of propitiating for the assembly, could it be that we would have propitiated for the assembly while we ourselves were reproached by God? And if we had nevertheless eaten it and had boasted of ourselves that we were still acceptable before Him and worthy of propitiating for the nation, would this have been pleasing in God's sight? Indeed, He would have been all the angrier with us for our insolence."

According to the Korem (and Rashbam's comment is similar), the meaning is, "Although I suppressed my pain and did not weep, in order to justify Heaven's judgment in public, would it have been pleasing in God's sight to eat the meat of the aspersion sacrifice in a [feigned] state of happiness and serenity while my heart was full of sadness and woe, given that the meat of the holy things is properly eaten in joy and not like the bread of sorrow?" However, according to this interpretation, it would be hard to understand the relevance of the phrase "Behold today they presented," etc. A. H. Mainster responds that "behold today" refers to the first day that they brought offerings: "It would have been fitting for this day to be one of great joy for us, but on the contrary, such things happened to me..." Yet there remains a difficulty as to [the need for] the phrase "their sacrifice of aspersion and their burnt offering," and therefore I maintain my interpretation.

**10:20. Moses heard, and it pleased him.**

# Shemini

**11:1. And the Lord spoke to Moses and to Aaron, saying to them:**

The purpose of the dietary prohibitions is to separate [Israel] from the nations and to elevate the soul, for the eating of loathsome things results in spiritual diminution. The reason is not the preservation of health, for indeed camel flesh is good for one's health and is much favored by the people of the East.

**11:2. "Speak to the children of Israel, saying: These are the animals that you may eat, among all the beast [quadrupeds] existing on the earth.**

**11:3. "Whichever among the quadrupeds is furnished with hooves and has a splitting of the hooves [that is, which has them cloven in two] and is a ruminant, that you may eat.**

*furnished with hooves (mafreset parsah).* The hoof is a single nail resembling a shoe, unlike the nails on each toe like those of the cony and the hare (Rashbam).

*and has a splitting of the hooves (ve-shosa'at shesa).* With the hoof divided in two, not one whole hoof like that of the horse or donkey. The principal meaning of the noun *parsah* ("hoof") is "cleft," and it was originally applied to animals with split hooves; later it was transferred to the horse's hoof, which is not split. For this reason, after the verse said *mafreset parsah* ("furnished with hooves"), it had to add *ve-shosa'at shesa* to exclude the horse and the donkey. Nevertheless, v. 4 below says *u-mi-mafrisei ha-parsah,* meaning "and among the cloven-hoofed," in accordance with the principal meaning of the word.

**11:4. "These, however, you shall not eat among the ruminants and the cloven-hoofed: the camel, for it is a ruminant but does not have a cloven hoof; impure it is for you.**

**11:5. "And the cony [?], for it ruminates but does not have a cloven hoof; impure it is for you.**

*the cony (ha-shafan).* This is the *coniglio,*[10] which dwells among the rocks (Ps. 104:18, Prov. 30:26). In Latin, the word *cuniculus,* which means *shafan,* also denotes "burrows" in the earth. Perhaps, too, the Hebrew *shafan* is related to *tsafan* ("to hide"), since the *shafan* hides within the clefts of the rocks. Note that Scheuzer, in his book *Physique Sacrée,* and also Valmont de Bomare, in *Dictionnaire d'Histoire Naturelle,* say that the *coniglio* is a ruminant.[11]

**11:6. "And the hare, for it ruminates but does not have a cloven hoof; it is impure for you.**

*the hare (ha-arnevet).* The hare (Ital. *lepre*) is a ruminant, and so wrote Linnaeus and others, even though it does not have a double stomach like other ruminants.[12]

---

10. This Italian word may be translated as "rabbit" or "cony," the latter term appearing in some traditional English Bible versions as a synonym for "hyrax." The "true" cony, however, is the pika, which—unlike the hyrax—is a relative of the rabbit and hare (*Encyclopaedia Britannica,* s.v. "Hyrax"). Shadal's Italian text translation renders *shafan* as *coniglio,* but with a question mark indicating doubt; it is unclear whether Shadal was aware of the distinction between the rabbit and the various kinds of "conies." In any case, *shafan* should be understood here as the hyrax, since rabbits are not native to the land of Israel (see Natan Slifkin, *The Torah Encyclopedia of the Animal Kingdom,* vol. 1, s.v. "Hyrax"). Modern Hebrew, however, uses the word *shafan* for "rabbit," while *shefan ha-sela'im* ("rock rabbit") is used for "hyrax."
11. Modern science disagrees; however, Slifkin (*Torah Encyclopedia,* s.v. "Hyrax") explains that although the hyrax does not technically chew its cud, it is possible that the hyrax regurgitates and rechews undigested food; otherwise, its classification as a "ruminant" [*ma'aleh gerah*] may have been based on its complex gut or manner of chewing, in keeping with the concept that "the Torah speaks in the language of men."
12. Again, modern science disagrees, but Slifkin (*The Camel, the Hare and the Hyrax,* pp. 133-136) suggests that the term *ma'aleh gerah* here is an idiom that refers to ruminant-style chewing or else cecotrophy, which is the consumption of food pellets that have been digested, retained in the caecum (a pouch connected to the large intestine), and then excreted.

**11:7.** "And the swine, for it is furnished with hooves and has a splitting of hooves, but is not a ruminant; impure it is for you.

**11:8.** "Of their flesh you shall not eat, and their carcass you shall not touch [when you wish to eat a holy thing or enter into the Temple]; impure they are for you.

*and their carcass you shall not touch.* Cf. below, v. 11, "and their carcass you shall abhor"; when you wish to be pure in order to eat holy things or to enter the Sanctuary, do not touch their carcass.[13]

**11:9.** "These (animals) you may eat among all those that are in the water: all those that have fins and scales, (living) in the water, in the seas (that is), or in the streams; those you may eat.

**11:10.** "And all those that do not have fins and scales, (living) in the seas or in the streams, of any species swarming [exclusively] in the water, and of every species of living things that are in the water [including the amphibians], abhorrent things are for you.

*of any species swarming in the water.* Those that live only in the water.

*and of every species of living things that are in the water.* Amphibians that live [on land and] also in the water (Mendelssohn).

**11:11.** "And abhorrent they must be to you: of their flesh do not eat, and their carcass you shall abhor.

*and their carcass you shall abhor.* As far as practical law [*halakhah*] is concerned, this has no application, but according to the plain meaning

---

13. This comment accords with Rashi (following *Sifra*), who notes that Israelites who are not priests are not otherwise forbidden to touch the carcass of an impure animal. See also Maimonides, who says that "whoever desires to remain in his state of impurity and not enter the camp of the Divine Presence is permitted to do so" (*Sefer ha-Mitsvot*, Pos. 109).

[*peshat*], impure [i.e., forbidden] species of fish cause [ritual] impurity when they die.

**11:12. "Every aquatic animal that does not have fins and scales, abhorrent is to you.**

**11:13. "These, then, you shall abhor among the flying creatures; they shall not be eaten, abhorrent things they are: the eagle, the sea eagle, and the black eagle.**

*the sea eagle (ha-peres).* The Hebrew is from *paras*, meaning "breaking, cleaving."[14]

*the black eagle (ha-ozniyyah).* The Hebrew is from *oz* ("strength"), with the addition of the letter *nun* instead of a doubled letter [*zayin*], on the model of *ma'uzneha* ("its strongholds") [Isa. 23:11].

**11:14. "The kite, and the merlin, with its various species.**

*the merlin (ha-ayah).* A species of falcon that emits the cry *yaya*.

**11:15. "Every crow, with its various species.**

**11:16. "And the ostrich, and the falcon, and the seagull, and the hawk with its various species.**

*the hawk (ha-nets,* Ital. *sparviere).* The Hebrew is from *nitsots* ("spark," "gleam"): "The hawks [*i sparvieri*], whose eyes shine in the dark" (Virey, [*Storia dei costumi e dell'instinto degli animali,*] vol. II, p. 300).

**11:17. "And the pelican, and the cormorant, and the owl.**

---

14. According to Slifkin, the *peres* is the bearded vulture, which is "famed for making pieces. It eats bones, which it does via picking them up, flying high over rocks, and then dropping them and smashing them to pieces." (http://www.rationalistjudaism.com/, Sept. 28, 2016.) Some English versions, including the King James, translate *peres* as "ossifrage," from the Latin for "bone breaker."

**the pelican** *(ha-kos).* Which has beneath its mouth a kind of sack or cup (Heb. *kos*) that it fills with water and fish.

**11:18. "And the swan, and the cuckoo, and the vulture.**

**the cuckoo** *(ha-ka'at).* Which emits the cry *ku-ku*.

**11:19. "And the stork, the parrot with its various species, and the hoopoe, and the bat.**

**the bat.** It is not a bird, but it resembles a bird, and for this reason it is mentioned last (Wessely's comment is similar).

**11:20. "Any swarming winged thing, walking on four (feet), an abhorrent thing is [must be] for you.**

**11:21. "These only may you eat among all the swarming winged things walking on four (feet): those that have legs above their feet, with which to leap over the earth [that is, those that have four legs and two additional hind legs that are longer and serve for leaping].**

**11:22. "Of these you may eat: the locust, with its various species; the *sol'am*, with its various species; the *ḥargol*, with its various species, and the cricket, with its various species.**

**11:23. "And every (other) swarming flying creature, having four feet, an abhorrent thing is for you.**

**11:24. "And from the following you will contract impurity, whoever touches its carcass will be impure until the night.**

**11:25. "And whoever lifts up (even without contact) of its carcass will wash his clothes and will be impure until the night.**

**11:26. "All the animals furnished with hooves, which do not have splitting (in them) and are not ruminants, are impure for you; whoever touches them (when they are dead) will be impure.**

# Shadal on Leviticus

***All the animals furnished with hooves,*** *etc.* These are the horse, the donkey, and the zebra (Wessely).

***All the animals*** *(le-khol ha-behemah).* This verse specifies what is meant by the phrase "And from the following you will contract impurity *(u-le-elleh tittamma'u)*" [above, v. 24]. Mendelssohn's answer offers nothing,[15] for the phrase "are impure for you" is [not the predicate of the sentence, but rather] a general statement following particulars, as if it were written, "From all the animals furnished with hooves... you will contract impurity, for they are impure for you" (similar to vv. 27 and 28 below). This is how the grammar of the verse's language appears to me, even though I have not translated it accordingly.[16]

**11:27. "And those among the quadruped animals that walk on their hands [that is, whose soles are divided into digits] are impure for you; whoever touches their carcass will be impure until the night.**

***But those... that walk on their hands.*** All those that do not have hooves (a nail resembling a shoe), but whose feet are divided into digits, such as dogs and other beasts (Wessely).

**11:28. "And whoever lifts up their carcass will wash his clothes and will be impure until the night; (those animals) are impure for you.**

---

15. Mendelssohn's comment answers an implied question as to whether the letter *lamed* in *le-khol ha-behemah* serves the same function as the *lamed* in *u-le-elleh tittamma'u*, a question that Shadal would answer in the affirmative. Mendelssohn, however, maintains that the two *lameds* serve different functions; the phrase "are impure for you" is the predicate of the sentence in v. 26, and thus the subject phrase *le-khol ha-behemah* cannot mean "from all the animals," and the *lamed* in *le-khol* simply means "in general."

16. If Shadal had translated this verse in accordance with his comment, the translation might have read, "From all the animals furnished with hooves, which do not have splitting (in them) and are not ruminants. They are impure for you; whoever touches them (when they are dead) will be impure."

**11:29.** "These are impure for you among the swarming things [small quadrupeds] that swarm upon the earth: the weasel, and the mouse, and the toad, with its various species.

**11:30.** "And the mournful-sounding toad,[17] and the mole, and the lizard, and the turtle, and the chameleon.

*and the mole (ve-ha-koaḥ).* In the Syriac translation, this is *ḥulda*, which is "mole" in Syriac; in [Hebrew] poetic language it is called *ḥafarperet* ("the burrowing one"). However, the *ḥoled* [the first animal named in the previous verse], which is *ḥuldah* in Rabbinic Hebrew, is the weasel.

*and the turtle (ve-ha-ḥomet).* The *ḥomet* is said to be the snail, but that is not a "swarming thing" *(sherets)* because it has no legs. I say that it is the *testudo* [Latin for "tortoise"], from the Syriac *ḥumtena*, which is a "bulwark" or "fortification."

**11:31.** "These are the ones that are impure for you among all the swarming things [small quadrupeds]; whoever touches them after they die will be impure until night.

**11:32.** "Likewise every object on which any of them comes to fall, after they die, will be impure; any utensil, whether of wood, or of cloth, or of leather, or of sack (cloth), any utensil of which some use is made, will be immersed in water and will remain impure until night; then it will be pure.

**11:33.** "And if any of them falls into an earthenware vessel, everything inside it will be impure, and it [the vessel] you shall break.

**11:34.** "Every edible thing that has touched water will become impure [if it is found inside an earthenware vessel in which one of

---

17. The Hebrew is *anakah*, a word that also means "groan, cry, moan." Luzzatto's Italian translation is *la botta dal suono lugubre*. The "toad" of the previous verse (Heb. *tsav*) is *rospo* in the Italian; both *rospo* and *botta* mean "toad."

those animals has fallen]; likewise any potable liquid in any vessel will become impure [if an impure animal falls into it].

11:35. "And everything on which falls (some piece) of their carcass will become impure; whether it is an oven or a stove, it will be broken in pieces. They are impure, and impure they will be for you.

*Whether it is an oven or a stove.* Even if fixed to the ground, it is susceptible of impurity, even though such fixed objects do not generally contract impurity (see Wessely).

11:36. "But a spring or a cistern, (any) receptacle of water [that is not movable], will be pure; and (even so) one who touches their carcass [even in water] will become impure.

*one who touches their carcass.* If one is in the water (in a spring or cistern) and there he touches a carcass, even if the carcass is in the water, it cannot be said that the water receptacle (*mikveh*) prevents him from contracting impurity (the opinion of Hillel in *Torat Kohanim*; see Wessely).

11:37. "If something of their carcass falls upon the product of any vegetation that has been sown, (that product attached to the soil) is pure [it does not contract impurity].

*any vegetation that has been sown.* [This statement serves] to declare pure that which is attached to the ground (Rashbam and Wessely).

11:38. "But when a vegetable product has touched water, and then (some piece) of their carcass falls upon it, it becomes impure for you.

11:39. "If one of those animals that is permitted to you for eating dies (of itself), one who touches its carcass will be impure until the night.

**11:40.** "And one who eats of its carcass will wash his clothes, and he will be impure until the night; and one who lifts up its carcass will wash his clothes, and he will be impure until the night.

**11:41.** "And every swarming thing that swarms on the earth is an abhorrent thing; it must not be eaten.

**11:42.** "Whether they walk on their bosom or go on four (feet), or they have many feet, in sum, any swarming thing that swarms on the earth, do not eat them, for they are objects to be abhorred.

**11:43.** "Do not render yourselves abhorrent by [that is, eating] any of the swarming animals, and do not render yourselves impure by means of them, which would cause you to be brutalized.

*which would cause you to be brutalized (ve-nitmetem)*. The Hebrew is from [the same root as], "[We are] reputed dull [*ve-nitminu*] in your sight" (Job 18:3) (as per the alternative view cited by Ibn Ezra).[18] It is as I said above [at Lev. 11:1], that the eating of loathsome things results in spiritual diminution, as if the soul were brought down from a human elevation to an animal level, as it is written [in Job 18:3], "Wherefore are we counted as beasts, and reputed dull in your sight?"

**11:44.** "For I, the Lord, am your God; therefore sanctify yourselves and be holy, for holy am I; and do not render yourselves impure through any swarming thing that creeps upon the earth.

**11:45.** "For it is I, the Lord, Who brought you out of the land of Egypt, to be your God; be holy, then, for holy am I.

---

18. In his comment on Lev. 11:43, Ibn Ezra first expresses the view that *nitmetem* (נטמתם) is the equivalent of נטמאתם ("you will be rendered impure"), but he notes that some say the word is from a different root (i.e., טמה, "to be stupid"), and he cites the example *ve-nitminu* in Job 18:3.

**11:46.** "This is the law concerning the quadrupeds and the flying creatures, and every living thing that creeps in the water, and every animal swarming on the earth.

**11:47.** "In order (that one may know) to distinguish between the impure and the pure, and between the animal that may be eaten and the animal that must not be eaten.

# *Tazria*

*When a woman gives birth • Purity and impurity •*
*"Leprosy" (tsara'at) • Symptoms in skin or clothing*

**12:1. And the Lord spoke to Moses, saying:**

**12:2. "Speak to the children of Israel as follows: When a woman proliferates and gives birth to a male, she will be impure for seven days. She will be impure, as she is in the days of her menstruation [that is, not only with respect to holy things, but also for her husband].**

***When a woman proliferates*** *(tazria).* The Hebrew is derived from *zera* (lit. "seed"), in its secondary meaning, which denotes "fruit."

***as she is in the days of her menstruation.*** She will have the same degree of impurity as in the days of her menstruation.

***as… in the days of*** *(ki-y'mei,* lit. "as the days of"). The Hebrew is the equivalent of *ke-vi-y'mei.* The meaning is not that the number of the days of her impurity will be seven, like the days of menstruation, for below [v. 5], in the case of a woman who gives birth to a female and is impure for fourteen days, it likewise says that "she will be impure for two weeks, as during her menstruation." Rather, the meaning is that she will be forbidden to her husband as well, which is not the case during the days of her *dam tohar* ("blood of purity").[1]

**she will be impure for seven days.** Here I think it appropriate to express my view briefly on all matters of impurity [*tum'ah*] and purity [*tohorah*]. I say that impurities are divided into two categories: those whose purification involves the bringing of a sacrifice and those whose purification does not involve the bringing of a sacrifice. Let us begin with the impurity of *tsara'at* ("leprosy"),[2] which is the most severe impurity in the first category. Many have thought that the reason for keeping the *metsora* ("leper") at a distance is because this disease is contagious through touch, but it seems to me that if the Torah had been concerned about contagion, how many other diseases are contagious— and yet the Torah did not prescribe any regulation for them. How is it that the Torah did not command a thing concerning pestilence?[3]

In my opinion, a change in the appearance of the skin was thought by the ancients to be a sign of God's reproach, and they considered the leper to be stricken with a plague of God as a punishment for some serious sin; for this reason they would keep apart from the leper as they would from one who was excommunicated by the Omnipresent. Similarly, a change in the appearance of a garment or a house was considered a sign of God's reproach, as if the stricken garment or house were despised by the Omnipresent by reason of some great sin that had been committed within them. Because all of this supported a faith in Divine Providence and in God's reward and punishment, the Torah upheld this belief and commanded that the leper be kept distant, the stricken garment burned, and the stricken house demolished, and that the [cured] house be ritually

---

1. After the initial stage of seven days following the birth of a male or fourteen days following the birth of a female, there is a second stage of 33 or 66 days during which the mother may not enter the Sanctuary (below, vv. 4, 5). However, any blood that she sees during this stage does not give her the status of a *niddah* (menstruant) as it normally would; such blood is called *dam tohar*.
2. For a discussion of this translation, see footnote 7 at Lev. 13:2.
3. In Hebrew, *eikh lo tzivetah davar al devar ha-dever*—an example of Shadal's fondness for plays on words.

sprinkled. It also commanded that one who was healed of leprosy would bring a sacrifice, so that immediately after the removal of God's reproach and excommunication, which had prevented the leper from being seen before Him, the leper would come to the house of God and submit before Him, thanking Him for bringing him close once more and asking Him not to rebuke him again or keep him distant.

This is the meaning of the phrase, "And thus the priest will propitiate before the Lord for the one who is purified" (Lev. 14:31): by means of the sacrifice, God will become reconciled with him and will extend His mercy toward him. Indeed, the significance of [the purification ceremony involving] the two birds, the cedar wood, the hyssop, the scarlet wool, and the sprinklings (Lev. 14:4-7) seems entirely to symbolize and allude to atonement for sin, in order to let it be known that the leper is no longer excommunicated by the Omnipresent. The scarlet wool alludes to sin, for sins were described in terms of redness—as it is written, "Though your sins be as scarlet" (Isa. 1:18)—in reference to the shedding of blood, for there is no greater sin. The cedar and the hyssop symbolize the great and the small—as in, "And he [Solomon] spoke of trees, from the cedar that is in Lebanon to the hyssop that springs out of the wall" (I Kings 5:13)—and thus the cedar wood, hyssop, and scarlet wool symbolize sins both great and small.

The blood of the slaughtered bird (Lev. 14:6) symbolizes a great cleansing, that is, the cleansing of a great sin, "For it is the blood that can propitiate for the life (of a man)" (Lev. 17:11), while the living water (Lev. 14:5, 6) symbolizes a small cleansing, that is, the cleansing of a minor sin. The two birds are the leper's atonement and symbolic substitute; one of them is slaughtered and its blood propitiates for life, while the other remains alive, is bound together with the "sins" (that is, the cedar wood, hyssop, and scarlet wool) and is dipped in blood and water, and the leper is sprinkled with it. This symbolizes that his sins have been atoned for and he has returned to a state of purity. Afterwards the living bird is allowed to go free through the field, symbolizing that the leper is no longer enclosed outside the camp but comes out of his enclosure and enters into any place that he wishes.

Similar to the case of the leper is that of the menstruant, the man or woman who has a discharge, and the woman who gives birth, for all of these are as if excommunicated by the Omnipresent, since the (involuntary) issuance of blood or seed is [as it were] the beginning of death, suggesting that this man or woman is under a death sentence. For this reason we are commanded to keep separate from them and to avoid their touch, and therefore when they become pure, they bring a sacrifice and the priest atones for them as he does for a leper. The menstruant, however, is not obligated to bring a sacrifice, for the Torah has consideration for the women of Israel and does not burden them with traveling from their homes to the house of God every month. It should not be said that the reason she has no obligation to bring a sacrifice is that it is unlikely that she would ask God that she should never be a menstruant again,[4] for indeed she might ask that the next time she becomes a menstruant, her period of impurity should not last unduly long and thereby render her as one who has a discharge. In a similar vein, the woman who gives birth is in need of atonement [and must bring a sacrifice], not in order to ask that she never give birth again, but to ask that she not die in childbirth, for the blood emitted by a woman giving birth is a symbol of death, and every such woman is in a dangerous situation.

On the other hand, the forms of impurity whose purification does not involve the bringing of a sacrifice are the impurities from contact with a dead [human] body, the carcass of an animal that has died of itself, and [human] seed that is not the result of a disease. These have nothing to do with propitiation, because they are not things that descend from Heaven. Rather, they are matters that depend on human will; if one wants, one becomes impure from them, and if one does not want, one does not become impure from them (we are not concerned with rare cases, and thus there is no particular command for one in whose proximity a person dies suddenly, or the like). Therefore it would not likely be thought of such impure persons that they were truly excommunicated by the Omnipresent. Nevertheless, the dead human body and the animal carcass do cause impurity, for there is no greater Divine reproach than death, and if the leper and the person with a discharge cause impurity

---

4. In contrast, as Shadal notes earlier in this comment, the healed leper brings a sacrifice because he is asking God "not to rebuke him again or keep him distant."

to one who touches them because they are excommunicated by the Omnipresent, then all the more so should the dead body or the carcass. Due to the severity of the dead body's or carcass's impurity, even the one who touches it is excommunicated for seven days and requires sprinkling with the water of aspersion.

A slaughtered animal, however, is not impure, for its death was not by the hand of Heaven or by way of reproach, but rather by a human hand and for human good. In contrast, a human murder victim, even though he was killed by a human hand, is impure, for a human being is subject to Providence and Divine reward and punishment—unlike an animal—and therefore it is appropriate to think of a dead human being, even if his death was by a human hand, as having died as a result of God's decree and reproach. Such a thought is inappropriate with respect to an animal that was slaughtered or otherwise killed.

The impurity occasioned by contact with human seed is for the honor of the Temple, so that one should not enter the house of God or eat sacred meats on the same day that one engaged in physical pleasure (not of a necessary nature, like eating or drinking). This is analogous to the command [to the men] before the giving of the Torah (Exod. 19:15), "Be prepared for the third day; do not approach a woman." This prohibition would serve to exalt the honor and glory of the Sanctuary and its holy things in the mind of the entire community, as it would exalt the magnificence of the Divine service in the minds of the priests who performed it, and all of this would be of great benefit in increasing the fear of God in the hearts of the priests and the people.

The sprinkling of the water of aspersion is an allusion to atonement for sin. The red heifer (Num. ch. 19), with its redness, symbolizes sin. Similarly, the cedar wood, hyssop, and scarlet wool symbolize great and small sins, and by burning them together [with the heifer, Num. 19:6], it is as if the sin is nullified, and their ashes are a sign of such nullification. Therefore the sprinkling of these ashes purifies the impurity caused by contact with a dead body, which is a severe form of impurity. And yet, even though the sin is burned, it is not entirely nullified, for the ashes that remain of it still retain something of the sin, and thus they impart a slight degree of impurity to one who touches them. This slight impurity is removed through immersion.

# Shadal on Leviticus

One need not wonder how it is that the red heifer purifies the impure but imparts impurity to the pure,[5] for the heifer removes a severe form of impurity but imparts [merely] a slight impurity. To what is this analogous? To the case of a copper vessel that is first scoured with sand; such scouring removes that which cannot be removed by washing with water, but afterwards it is necessary to rinse the vessel with water to remove the sand that adheres to it. Thus it is written (Lev. 6:21), "a copper vessel… will have to be cleansed and rinsed." The person who does the scouring will also have to rinse off his hands because of the dirt that adheres to them. Similarly, the heifer's ashes perform a powerful cleansing and remove the severe impurity, but after such cleansing an immersion is also needed, both for those who handle the "water of sprinkling" [*mei niddah*, in which the ashes are mixed, Num. 19:9] and for the person whom they sprinkled.

**12:3. "Then on the eighth day will be circumcised the flesh of his [the newborn's] foreskin.**

***Then on the eighth day will be circumcised.*** This verse, which at first glance seems to have no connection to what precedes or follows it, teaches us why the commandment of circumcision is precisely on the eighth day, not the seventh or tenth, which are numbers commonly associated with the Torah's commandments. Circumcision is fixed on the eighth day because during the first seven days, the mother is in a state of severe impurity, like that of menstruation, and the blessed Giver of the Torah did not want the child to be circumcised until his mother became pure. This is for one of three reasons: first, as per R. Simeon bar Yohai (*Niddah* 31b), so that it should not occur that everyone is rejoicing but the father and mother are sad, for on the eighth day the woman who has

---

5. Classical sources regard this aspect of the red heifer ritual as a mysterious paradox. Solomon himself, the wisest of men, was said to be baffled by it (*Eccles. Rabbah* 7:23, no. 4). See also *Num. Rabbah* 19.1, which states the paradox and offers the response, "Said the Holy One, blessed is He, 'I have framed a law [*ḥukkah*, i.e., a statute for which no rational explanation can be given], I have decreed a decree; you are not permitted to transgress my decree.'"

given birth becomes pure for her husband. Second, as per R. Ovadiah Sforno, because the fetus is nourished in the mother's womb by means of menstrual blood, and during the first seven days this blood is digested, so that on the eighth day the child attains the purity to enter into the holy covenant [of circumcision]. To these I would add a third reason, which is that the foreskin was considered by the Israelites as a kind of impurity, as it is written (Isa. 22:1), "For henceforth there shall no more come into you [Jerusalem] the uncircumcised and the impure." Thus the Torah commanded that on the day that the woman who has given birth is cleansed of her impurity, the child also becomes pure by means of circumcision.

**12:4. "Afterwards she will remain for thirty-three days in (a state of) cleansing of purification: any holy thing she shall not touch, and into the Temple she shall not enter, until the days of her purification are completed.**

**12:5. "And if she gives birth to a female, she will be impure for two weeks, as during her menstruation, and sixty-six days she will remain in cleansing of purification.**

**12:6. "And the days of her purification for a son or for a daughter having been completed, she will bring a lamb born within the year, for a burnt offering, and a young dove or a turtledove, for a sacrifice of aspersion, to the entrance of the tent of congregation, to the priest.**

**12:7. "He will present it before the Lord, and he will propitiate for her; and she will become pure of her flow of blood. This is the law of the one who gives birth, whether for (the birth of) a male or for a female.**

*He will present it (ve-hikrivo).* The pronominal suffix [*-o,* indicating a masculine direct object] refers back to [the missing but understood masculine noun] *korban* ("sacrifice," "offering"), which comes on the strength of the verb *hikriv*; the sense of the verse is, "He will present the aforementioned sacrifice, which is a burnt offering and a sacrifice of aspersion" (see my comment on "Do not give false testimony against your neighbor" (Exod. 20:13)).[6]

The term *korban* may include many animals and everything that a person presents to God on a single occasion, as we find [e.g., Num. 7:13, 15], "And his offering [*korbano*] was: one silver plate... One young bull, one ram...."

**12:8. "And if her resources are not sufficient for (to be able to bring) a lamb, she will take two turtledoves, or two young doves, the one for a burnt offering, and the other for a sacrifice of aspersion; and the priest will propitiate for her, and she will become pure."**

**13:1. The Lord spoke to Moses and Aaron, saying:**

**13:2. "When one has in the skin of his body a prominence, a scab, or a spot, and this becomes in the skin of his body the disease of leprosy,[7]**

6  There, Shadal explains that in this phrase (Hebrew *lo ta'aneh be-re'akha ed shaker*, lit. "Do not testify against your neighbor false witness"), the verb *ta'aneh* carries with it the missing but understood noun *aniyyat*, "the testifying of," so that the correct interpretation is, "Do not testify against your neighbor the testifying of a false witness."

7. Luzzatto translates the Hebrew *tsara'at* as *lebbra* (Italian for "leprosy") without comment, and likewise translates *tsarua* and *metsora* as *lebbroso* ("leprous one," "leper"). In his time and place, *lebbra* or "leprosy" was the conventional term used for *tsara'at,* and there were attempts to identify it with various ailments (see, for example, Benedetto Frizzi, *Dissertazione sulla lebbra degli Ebrei* (Trieste, 1795)). Shadal himself made no such attempts. He was familiar with Frizzi's work, which he called a "most learned dissertation," and he noted that the author (a Jewish physician) had sought to demonstrate that "the Mosaic and rabbinic dispositions concerning *lebbra* were all in harmony with medical doctrines" with respect to the prevention of contagion, but Shadal expressed doubt that *tsara'at* was a contagious disease ("Breve Prospetto della Legislazione Mosaica," *L'Educatore Israelita*, 1st year, 2nd ed. (1853), p. 295). He cited evidence that Geonic authorities regarded the Torah's *tsara'at* regulations as no longer binding after the Temple's destruction, and he questioned whether they would have abolished those regulations if the disease were contagious. He

**the matter will be brought to Aaron the priest, or to one of his sons
the priests.**

---

further noted that the *Tur* and R. Joseph Caro, whose legal codes are
concerned only with the laws that remain in force in the Exile, make
no mention of the *tsara'at* regulations (ibid., n. 3). See also Shadal's
discussion of *tsara'at* in his commentary to Lev. 12:2.

Although the identification of *tsara'at* with "leprosy" is in keeping with many Bible translations, modern authorities distinguish it
from the illness that is now called "leprosy" or "Hansen's disease,"
which was found to be a bacterial infection by Gerhard Henrik Ar-
mauer Hansen in 1873. "Identification of the two ailments derives
from the fact that in the Septuagint, *tzara'at* is translated as *lepra*.
The church fathers, relying on this Greek translation, assumed that the
degenerative disease that they were familiar with, which was known
as *lepra*, was indeed the biblical *tzara'at*" (Ephraim Shoham-Steiner,
trans. Haim Watzman, *On the Margins of a Minority: Leprosy, Madness, and Disability Among the Jews of Medieval Europe* (Detroit:
Wayne State U. Press, 2014, p. 26, notes omitted)).

The *lepra*, or *aphe lepras*, of the Septuagint was a condition
characterized by scaling of the skin, but there is little evidence that
"leprosy" (i.e., Hansen's disease) existed in the ancient Middle East;
moreover, because mold or mildew can cause scaling and depigment-
ed lesions in humans and can also infest houses, *tsara'at* might be
understood as "mold" (Heller, Heller, and Sasson, "Mold: 'Tsara'at,'
Leviticus, and the History of a Confusion," *Perspectives in Biology
and Medicine* 46(4):588-591 (Autumn 2003)). Others have suggested
that the diagnosis may include such diseases as psoriasis, seborrheic
dermatitis, syphilis, impetigo, scarlet fever, and lupus erythematosus
(Grzybowski and Nita, "Leprosy in the Bible," *Clinics in Dermatology* 34(1):3-7 (Jan.-Feb. 2016)). Melanoma has also been suggested (Chaim Trachtman, "Tzaraat as Cancer" TheTorah.com (2016),
https://thetorah.com/article/tzaraat-as-cancer).

On the other hand, some traditional authorities (e.g. Maimonides, *Tum'at Tsara'at* 16:13) express the view that *tsara'at* cannot
be identified with any naturally occurring disease and that it was a
miraculous Divine punishment. Luzzatto himself maintained that the
laws of *tsara'at* were religious and not medical in nature, and he cited
the opinion of Josephus (*Antiquities* 3:13) that this disease could be
cured only through prayer (*L'Educatore Israelita*, p. 295).

*the matter will be brought to Aaron (ve-huva el Aharon*, lit. "will be brought to Aaron" [with the subject of the phrase unstated; "the matter" is supplied in translation]). So also below (Lev. 14:2), "the matter will be brought to the priest," for it is [actually] the priest who goes to him, but the meaning is that the matter will be told to the priest. Compare:

- "When they have any suit, it is brought to me [*ba elai*]" (Exod. 18:16, where the unstated subject of the verb *ba* is to be understood as "the suit," not "the litigant");
- "The dispute of the two will be brought [*yavo*] to the tribunal" (Exod. 22:8);
- "Neither does the cause of the widow come [*yavo*] to them" (Isa. 1:23) (Joseph Shabbetai Basevi).

**13:3. "The priest will see the disease in the skin of the body, and finding in the infected part that the hair has turned white, and that the part appears deeper than (the rest of) the skin of his [that individual's] body, it is the disease of leprosy, and the priest, having seen it, will declare him impure.**

*The priest will see the disease in the skin of the body.* According to A. H. Mainster, the text here is speaking of an infection that is not white, but rather greenish or reddish or of some other appearance, and it is for this reason that the infected part appears deeper than the rest of his skin. So indicates the following verse: "If, however, it is a white spot… and it does not appear deeper than (the rest of) the skin." Thus Rashi [who apparently assumed that the infection in v. 3 is white] was confused as to this matter and wrote [in his comment on v. 4], "I do not know how to explain this."

There is proof [for Mainster's view] below (Lev. 14:37): "That the alteration of the walls of the house consists of greenish or reddish stains, and that these appear lower (than the surface) of the wall"; for according to Mainster, white [areas] appear to be raised and others appear to be lower. This is indeed true of a stain per se that is not described as having the appearance of some sort of body, but if the stain is described as resembling some body, then it will always appear to us as if it is

116

raised, for the mind hastens to think that this body is imposed upon that background. Therefore a sunlit area appears deeper than a shaded area, as the shadow takes the form of some body, and the mind immediately concludes that this body is raised from the ground or the wall. Similarly, letters appear to us as shapes that stand out from the paper. For a different opinion, see *Netivot ha-Shalom* and Reggio.[8]

**13:4. "If, however, it is a white spot in the skin of his body, and it does not appear deeper than (the rest of) the skin, nor has its hair turned white, the priest will order that the disease remain enclosed [that is, that the individual stay in a room apart] for seven days.**

*the priest will order that the disease remain enclosed* (*ve-hisgir ha-kohen et ha-nega,* lit. "and the priest will enclose the disease"). He will order the person who has the disease to stay in his house and not to touch anyone else until it is ascertained whether he is pure or impure. According to the Rosh [R. Asher ben Yehiel], the meaning is that the priest was to make a mark around the diseased spot as an indication, in order to see afterwards whether or not it had spread. In that case, however, the words "for seven days" would not fit in well (Shalom Simeon Modena).

**13:5. "The priest will see him on the seventh day, and finding that the disease has remained in its state, the disease (that is) not having spread in the skin, the priest will again make him stay enclosed for seven days.**

---

8. The commentary on this verse in *Netivot ha-Shalom* says that the infected area appears deeper than the rest of the skin just as a sunlit area appears deeper than a shaded area. This comment presupposes that the infected area in v. 3 is white, *contra* Shadal and Mainster. Reggio comments on v. 4 that there is a distinction between bright whiteness (such as that of snow) and dull whiteness (such as that of wool), and that the infected area mentioned in v. 3 is bright white and thus appears deeper than the rest of the skin, while the spot mentioned in v. 4 is dull white and does not appear deeper; therefore, in the latter case, the person must be enclosed for seven days so that the priest can observe whether the spot turns bright white or remains the same.

# Shadal on Leviticus

*in its state (be-einav,* lit. "in its eyes"). See v. 37 below.

**13:6. "The priest will see him again on the seventh day, and finding that the part has faded, and the disease has not spread in the skin, the priest will declare him pure; it is a *mispaḥat*[9]; and the individual will wash his clothes, and he will be pure.**

*has faded (kehah).* The Heb. indicates "weakness" or "loss of strength" (Wessely).

**13:7. "If, however, the *mispaḥat* will spread in the skin, after having been seen by the priest when it was declared pure, it will be seen again by the priest.**

**13:8. "And the priest, seeing that the *mispaḥat* has spread in the skin, will declare the disease impure; it is leprosy.**

**13:9. "When someone has the disease of leprosy, the thing will be brought to the priest.**

**13:10. "The priest will see, and finding in the skin a white prominence, and this having turned the hair white, but there being in that prominence some healthy part with flesh of a natural color—**

*turned (hafekhah).* The Hebrew is an intransitive verb, [and the phrase should be understood] as the equivalent of "in the infected part... the hair has turned [*hafakh*] white" [above, v. 3], "when he has completely turned [*hafakh*] white" [below, v. 13]. This means that the prominence has "turned," i.e., its hair has turned or become white, an expression similar to *ke-elah novelet aleha* ("like a terebinth whose leaf fades") [more literally, "like a terebinth that fades [with] its leaf," Isa. 1:30].

*some healthy part with flesh of a natural color (u-miḥyat basar ḥai,* lit. "a rawness of raw flesh"). The color of [naturally] ruddy flesh;

---

9. Left untranslated by Shadal, *mispaḥat* has been rendered by others as "scab" or "rash."

the Hebrew does not mean "the healthiness of healthy flesh," for it is actually diseased flesh and long-established leprosy.[10]  Accordingly, Rosenmueller attested that with leprosy, sometimes the skin is white and underneath it there grows flesh that is red and spongy.

**13:11. "That is long-established leprosy in the skin of his body, and the priest will declare him impure; he will not make him stay enclosed, for he is impure.**

**13:12. "If, however, the leprosy goes sprouting in the skin, and the leprosy covers all the skin of the infected individual from the head to the feet, wherever the sight of the priest reaches—**

*the skin of the infected individual (or ha-nega,* lit. "the skin of the disease"). The body in which the disease is (Wessely); perhaps the diseased person himself is referred to as *nega.*

**13:13. "The priest, perceiving the leprosy covering all of his body, will declare pure the infected individual; when he has entirely become white, he is pure.**

*the leprosy covering all of his body.* At the end stage of the disease, the leprosy goes forth and spreads throughout the body, and within ten or twelve days it is healed (Rosenmueller).[11]  Similarly, the *Ba'al ha-*

10. Here Luzzatto's commentary appears to differ at least in part from his text translation.
11. This reference is to Rosenmueller's comment on Lev. 13:12 (*Scholia in Leviticum,* p. 82), where he specifies that he is speaking of the type of leprosy that is called "*the Yaws*" in English. However, modern medical science clearly distinguishes between what is now known as "leprosy" (i.e., Hansen's disease) and yaws. Although both diseases are bacterial infections that can lead to skin lesions and disfigurement, they are caused by different types of bacteria (see *Oxford Textbook of Medicine,* vol. 1, pp. 575, 604). More importantly, Rosenmueller's description of the supposed end stage of yaws does not seem to be in keeping with modern knowledge, which means that this disease, like Hansen's, most likely cannot be identified as *tsara'at.*

*Turim* wrote that when the disease spreads, then it no longer penetrates the depth of the flesh, and this is a sign that it is close to being healed, but when it does not spread throughout the body, then it consumes and descends into the flesh underneath.

**13:14. "But as soon as there appears in him flesh of a natural color, he will be impure.**

**13:15. "The priest, seeing the flesh of a natural color, will declare him impure; the flesh of a natural color is impure; it is leprosy.**

**13:16. "If, however, the flesh of a natural color once again changes to white, the matter will be brought to the priest.**

**13:17. "The priest will see it, and finding the infected part to have become white, the priest will declare pure the infected individual; pure he is.**

**13:18. "When a person has in his skin an ulcer, and he is healed of it—**

**13:19. "And then in the site of the ulcer there arises a white prominence, or a white-reddish spot, it will be shown to the priest.**

**13:20. "The priest will see, and finding its appearance lower than the skin, and its skin having turned white, the priest will declare it impure; it is the disease of leprosy that sprouted in the ulcer.**

**13:21. "If, instead, the priest will see that there is no white hair in it, nor is it lower than the skin, and it has faded, the priest will cause the individual to be enclosed for seven days.**

**13:22. "And if it spreads in the skin, the priest will declare him impure; it is the disease (of leprosy).**

**13:23. "If, however, the spot remains in its place, without spreading, it is the scar of the ulcer, and the priest will declare it pure.**

**13:24.** "When a person has in his skin a burn, and then the site of the healed burn presents a white-reddish or white spot—

**13:25.** "And the priest, having seen it, finds in the spot that the hair has changed (and turned) white, and it appears deeper than the skin, it is leprosy sprouted in the burn, and the priest will declare the individual impure; it is the disease of leprosy.

**13:26.** "But if the priest, having seen it, finds that the spot does not have white hair, nor is it lower than the skin, and it has faded, the priest will hold the individual enclosed for seven days.

**13:27.** "Then the priest will see him on the seventh day, and if it has spread in the skin, the priest will declare the individual impure; it is the disease of leprosy.

**13:28.** "If, however, the spot remains in its place, without spreading in the skin, and has faded, it is a prominence produced by the burn, and the priest will declare the individual pure, for that is the scar of the burn.

**13:29.** "When a man or a woman has an (external) disease in the head or in the beard—

**13:30.** "And the priest, seeing the infected part, finds it to appear deeper than (the rest of) the skin, and there being in it thin yellow hair, the priest will declare the individual impure; that is a *netek*,[12] it is leprosy of the head or of the beard.

**13:31.** "If, however, the priest, seeing the site of the *netek*, finds it not to appear deeper than the skin, nor to have black hair in it, the priest will hold enclosed for seven days the disease of the *netek*.

---

12. Left untranslated by Shadal, *netek* has been understood by others as a "scall" or "scaly patch."

**13:32.** "Then the priest will see the disease on the seventh day, and finding that the *netek* has not spread, nor that yellow hair has formed in it, and that the *netek* does not appear deeper than (the rest of) the skin—

*the* netek *has not spread.* It does not say "in the skin" [as in 13:22 and 13:27 above]; this is a spreading plain and simple. Afterwards the individual shaves [next v.], and then they are to see whether or not the *netek* spreads "in the skin" [v. 34] (A. H. Mainster). Support for this view is found in v. 36: before the shaving, if the *netek* has not spread and there is no yellow hair in it, the priest will enclose the individual, but after the shaving, if it has spread "in the skin," the individual is [definitely] impure. In that case, the priest does not inspect the *netek* for yellow hair, nor does he enclose the individual to see if yellow hair will grow in it, since the spreading is "in the skin" [and this one symptom is sufficient] (Mainster).

**13:33.** "The individual will shave himself and leave the *netek* unshaven, and the priest will hold the *netek* enclosed again for seven days.

**13:34.** "Then the priest will see the *netek* on the seventh day, and finding that the *netek* has not spread in the skin, nor that it appears deeper than the skin, the priest will declare the individual pure, and the latter will wash his clothes and be pure.

**13:35.** "If, however, the *netek* spreads in the skin, after (the individual) was declared pure—

**13:36.** "And the priest, seeing it, finds the *netek* to have spread in the skin, the priest is not to inspect for yellow hair; (the individual) is impure.

**13:37.** "If, however, the *netek* remains in its state, and black hair grows in it, the *netek* is healed, the individual is pure, and the priest will declare him pure.

*If, however, the* netek *remains in its state (be-einav).* From here there is proof that the expression *be-einav* [lit. "in its eyes"; cf. Lev. 13:5] refers to its size, not its appearance.

*in its state.* That is, the spreading has not gone away; [nevertheless,] if black hair grows in it, the *netek* has healed and the individual is pure (Wessely).

**13:38. "When a man or a woman has in the skin of the body many white spots—**

*many white spots (beharot beharot levanot).* It seems to me (against the accents) that this is a usage analogous to *ḥomarim ḥomarim* ["heaps and heaps," Exod. 8:10] and *be'erot be'erot ḥemar* ["many pools of bitumen," Gen. 14:10].[13]

**13:39. "And the priest sees that there are in the skin of the body faded white spots, that is a *bohak*[14] sprouted in the skin; the individual is pure.**

**13:40. "When one's head remains hairless, he is bald; he is pure.**

*When one's head, etc.* The words "white hair," which Wessely (on v. 42 below) deleted from Rashi's comment on this verse, do not appear in the 5278 edition or in the *ḥumash* with three Targumim, Venice 5351 (1591).[15]

---

13. Here, the first word *beharot* is accented with a disjunctive *etnaḥta*, which would indicate that the Masoretes understood the phrase to mean "spots, white spots."
14. Left untranslated by Shadal, *bohak* has been understood by others as "freckled spot" or "rash."
15. Rashi's comment on v. 40 states that the bald person is not subject to the laws of the *netek* in the head or beard, but rather to those of an infection on the skin of other parts of the body, for which the symptoms of impurity are the presence of some flesh of a natural color (*miḥyah*) or the spreading of the infection. In some editions, the words "white hair" precede *miḥyah*, but Wessely expresses the view that "some erring student" added these words, since the Rabbis

**13:41.** "And if on the front part his head remains hairless, he is bald in front; he is pure.

**13:42.** "If, however, in the baldness in entirety or only in front there is an infected white-reddish site, it is leprosy sprouted in his baldness in entirety or in front.

**13:43.** "The priest will see him, and finding the prominence of the infected site white-reddish in his baldness in entirety or in front, resembling the leprosy of the skin (of the other parts) of the body—

**13:44.** "He is a leprous individual, impure he is; the priest will declare him impure; he has the disease (of leprosy) on the head.

**13:45.** "The leprous one, then, in whom the disease (of leprosy) is (recognized), will have his clothes torn and his head disheveled, and he will go veiled to his upper lip; and (when going out) he will cry, 'Impure, impure.'

***The leprous one, then, in whom the disease (of leprosy) is (recognized)*** *(ve-ha-tsarua asher bo ha-nega).* Even if he has only one diseased site (*nega*); this is the distinction between the terms *tsarua* ("leprous one") and *metsora* ("leper").

***he will cry, 'Impure, impure.'*** But was he not to dwell outside the camp? Rabbi Abraham Grego, of blessed memory, said that the meaning is [that he would make this cry only] when he went from his house to the outside of the camp. This is correct; it is for this reason that his clothes were to be torn like those of a mourner, for he was to be put at a distance from

---

deduced from the phrase *tsara'at porahat* ("leprosy sprouted") in v. 42 that only *mihyah* and spreading, and not white hair, are symptoms of impurity in a bald person. Chavel's edition of Rashi does not contain the words "white hair." Rosenbaum and Silbermann's edition has these words in parentheses but notes that they "must have got into the text by error," since the Mishnah, in *Nega'im* 10:10, restricts the relevant symptoms to *mihyah* and spreading (Leviticus volume, p. 165).

the society of his friends, and he was going out to dwell alone in a place of imprisonment.

**13:46. "For as long as the disease lasts in him, he will be (regarded as) impure; impure he is; he will dwell apart, outside of the camp will be his habitation.**

**13:47. "And when a cloth has a leprous change, whether this occurs in a woolen cloth or a linen cloth**[16]—

**13:48. "Whether in the warp or in the weft of the linen or the wool, or in leather, or in any leatherwork—**

*in the warp (vi-sh'ti).* The word *sheti* indicates "establishment, foundation" (*shetot*), for the warp is the foundation in the weaving, into which the weft is intermingled.

**13:49. "And the changed part is greenish or reddish, in the cloth or in the leather, whether in the warp or in the weft, or in any leather implement, it is a leprous change, and it will be shown to the priest.**[17]

---

16. The Lutzki 672 manuscript adds a brief note here, "Frizzi lebbra pag. 66." This is a reference to Benedetto Frizzi, *Dissertazione sulla lebbra degli Ebrei* (Trieste, 1795), in which the author discusses "leprosy" of clothing (pp. 62-68) and cites evidence that bubonic plague fluids could leave indelible greenish or yellowish stains on clothing, and that such stains, if not washed with strong alkalines, could cause further contagion. Frizzi says that this evidence offers a notable parallel to the "Mosaic system" (p. 66). Perhaps Shadal later deleted this note in light of his doubt as to whether *tsara'at* was a contagious disease (see his article, "Breve Prospetto della Legislazione Mosaica," *L'Educatore Israelita*, 1st year, 2nd ed. (1853), p. 295).

17. Although Shadal's text translation of the word *yerakrak* in this verse is *verdiccia* ("greenish"), the Lutzki 672 manuscript contains a comment saying that *yerakrak* means "yellow," and that there is proof for this from the phrase, "The wings of the dove are covered with silver, and her pinions with the shimmer of gold [*bi-y'rakrak*]" (Ps. 68:14).

**13:50.** "And the priest, having seen the change, will cause the changed object to be enclosed for seven days.

**13:51.** "Then he will see the changed part on the seventh day, (and finding) that the change has spread in the cloth, whether in the warp or in the weft, or in the leather, in whatever work that has been made of leather, that change is an acute leprosy; it is impure.

**13:52.** "And he will burn the cloth, whether the warp or the weft, of wool or of linen, or whatever leather implement, in which there is the change, for it is acute leprosy; it must be burned.

**13:53.** "If, however, the priest sees that the change has not spread in the cloth, whether in the warp or in the weft, or in whatever leather implement—

**13:54.** "The priest will command, and the object in which there is the change will be washed; then he will again cause it to be enclosed seven days.

**13:55.** "And the priest will see after the changed object has been washed, and finding that the change has not changed color and has not spread, it is impure; you must burn it; that is a profound change in its reverse side and in its top side.

*after the changed object has been washed (hukkabes).* See what I wrote at Isa. 34:6.[18]

*has not changed color (eino,* lit. "its eye"). Has not changed its appearance; the word *eino* does not mean the same as *einav* ("its state," "its size," lit. "its eyes") [see Lev. 13:5, 13:37].

18. There, commenting on the phrase *huddashenah me-ḥelev* ("it is made fat with fatness"), Shadal says that *huddashenah* is in the *hotpa'el* conjugation, like *hukkabes* in the present verse. He explains that this conjugation is equivalent in meaning to the *pu'al* (passive intensive) conjugation, as *hukkabes* has the same meaning as *kubbas* in the phrase *ve-khubbas shenit* ("will be washed again," Lev. 13:58).

# Tazria

*in its reverse side and in its top side (be-karaḥto o ve-gabaḥto,* lit. "in its back baldness or in its front baldness"). See Saadiah Gaon and Ibn Ezra.[19]

**13:56.** "But if the priest sees that the change has faded, after the object was washed, he will tear out that piece of the cloth, or of the leather, or of the warp, or of the weft.

**13:57.** "If, however, (the change) reappears in the cloth, whether in the warp or in the weft, or in whatever implement of leather, it is springing (leprosy); you must burn it [that object] in which there is the change.

**13:58.** "However, the cloth, or the warp, or the weft, or whatever implement of leather, from which the change has disappeared after washing, will be washed again; then it will be pure.

*from which the change has disappeared (ve-sar mehem ha-naga). Sar* means "to cease or discontinue," as in:

- "The scepter shall not be lacking [*yasur*] from Judah" (Gen. 49:10);
- "My strength would leave me [*ve-sar mimmenni*]" (Judges 16:17);
- "His folly will not leave him [*tasur me-alav*]" (Prov. 27:22).

**13:59.** "This is the law concerning the leprous change of a cloth of wool or of linen, whether of the warp or of the weft, or of whatever implement of leather, where (the object) must be declared pure or impure."

---

19. Ibn Ezra's comment on this phrase cites and endorses Saadiah Gaon's interpretation, which is followed in Shadal's translation. However, the *Sifra*, Onkelos, and Rashi interpret *be-karaḥto o ve-gabaḥto* to mean "in its old, worn-out state or in its new state."

# *Metsora*

*"Leprosy" (tsara'at), continued • Purification*
*procedure • Infection of a house • Bodily discharges*

**14:1. And the Lord spoke to Moses, saying:**

**14:2. "This will be the law of the leper, on the day of his purification. The matter will be brought to the priest.**

***The matter will be brought to the priest*** *(ve-huva el ha-kohen,* lit. "will be brought to the priest" [with the subject of the phrase unstated; "the matter" is supplied in translation]). See above at Lev. 13:2. Wessely's comment is far-fetched; similarly, at v. 3 below, his comment on the word *ve-hinneh* is incorrect.[1]

---

1. Wessely's comment on the phrase "will be brought to Aaron" in Lev. 13:2 understands the unstated subject of the phrase as "the leper," and he says, "Even if the leper is wise and qualified to instruct, and he knows that he is definitely impure, he is compelled to come to the priest, for the impurity and purity of skin diseases must be determined by a priest." Wessely's comment on the word *ve-hinneh* in v. 3 says that "it becomes clear to him [the priest] that it is, in fact, as the leper who was brought out to him has said, that the disease has healed."

128

**14:3.** "And the priest will go forth out of the camp, and finding that the disease of leprosy is healed [has disappeared] from the leper—

**14:4.** "The priest will command, and there will be provided for the one who is to be purified two live birds, pure [permissible to eat], and some cedar wood, and some scarlet wool, and some hyssop.

**14:5.** "And the priest will command, and one of the birds will be slaughtered into an earthenware vessel, upon living water [that is, the bird will be slaughtered so that its blood goes into a vessel containing water from a spring or river].

*upon living water.* The dipping [described in the next verse] was to be in blood and also in water, for the blood was mixed with water; cf. v. 51 below, "And he will dip them in the blood of the slaughtered bird *and* in the living water."

**14:6.** "He will take the live bird, and the cedar wood, and the scarlet wool, and the hyssop, and he will dip [the last three, bound together] and the live bird in the blood of the slaughtered bird (that is) together with the living water.

**14:7.** "And he will sprinkle seven times upon the one who is to be purified of leprosy, and he will declare him pure; then he will let the live bird go free through the countryside.

**14:8.** "And the one who is to be purified will wash his clothes, and he will shave all of his hair, and he will bathe in water, and (thus) he will be pure, and then he will enter into the camp; but he will remain for seven days outside his tent.

**14:9.** "And on the seventh day he will shave all of his hair, his head, his beard, and his eyebrows; all hair in sum he will shave; and he will wash his clothes, and he will bathe in water, and he will be pure.

# Shadal on Leviticus

**14:10. "And on the eighth day he will take two immaculate lambs, and one ewe-lamb born within the year, immaculate, and three tenths (of an *ephah*) of fine flour, (to make of it) a flour offering with oil, and a *log* of oil.**

*and one ewe-lamb.* Rashi interpreted this as an aspersion sacrifice (*ḥattat*); see above, Lev. 4:32.

**14:11. "And the purifying priest will present the individual who is to be purified, and those [the lambs, etc.], before the Lord, at the entrance of the tent of congregation.**

**14:12. "The priest will take one of those lambs, to make of it a sacrifice of repentance, as well as the *log* of oil, and he will make of them a waving before the Lord.**

*and he will make of them a waving (ve-henif otam tenufah).* The sacrifice required a live waving; cf. below, v. 24, and also Lev. 23:20. Similarly, there was the "waving" (*tenufah*) of the Levites (Num. 8:11, 21). The Sages understood this literally, expressing the view that the priest was to lift them with his hands.[2] However, some say that he was to lead them around the altar; it is said that Saadiah Gaon, in his Arabic translation, translated this in the sense of "leading" or "leading around" (see Gesenius, [*Hebrew and Chaldee Lexicon*] on the root *nuf*).

**14:13. "And he will slaughter the lamb in the place where the sacrifices of aspersion and the burnt offerings are slaughtered, in a holy place; for the sacrifice of repentance belongs to the priest as does the sacrifice of aspersion; it is a most holy thing.**

**14:14. "And the priest will take some of the blood of the sacrifice of repentance, and he will place it on the top of the right ear of the one**

2. See *Lamentations Rabbah*, proem 23: "'And the strong men shall bow themselves' (Eccl. 12:3): these are the priests; Rabbi Abba bar Kahana said, 'Aaron waved twenty-two thousand Levites on one day.'"

who is to be purified, and on the thumb of his right hand, and on the big toe of his right foot.

14:15. "And the priest will take some of the *log* of oil, and he will drip it on the palm of the left hand of the priest (himself).

14:16. "And the priest will wet the finger of his right hand with the oil that is in the palm of his left hand, and he will sprinkle some of that oil with his finger seven times before the Lord.

14:17. "And some of the rest of the oil that is in his palm the priest will place on the top of the right ear of the one who is to be purified, and on the thumb of his right hand, and on the big toe of his right foot, over the (previously applied) blood of the sacrifice of repentance.

14:18. "And the remainder of the oil that is on the priest's palm he will place upon the head of the one who is to be purified; thus the priest will propitiate for him before the Lord.

14:19. "Then the priest will make the sacrifice of aspersion [consisting of the above-mentioned ewe-lamb], and he will propitiate for the one who is to be purified of his impurity; then he will slaughter the burnt offering [that is, the other lamb].

14:20. "The priest will cause the burnt offering and the flour offering to burn on the altar; and the priest thus propitiating for him, he will be pure.

14:21. "And if he is poor, and his resources do not reach (so far), he will take a lamb for a sacrifice of repentance, of which the waving will be made, to propitiate for him, and a tenth (of an *ephah*) of fine flour infused with oil, for a flour offering, and a *log* of oil.

14:22. "And two turtledoves, or two young doves, as his resources will permit, of one of which will be made a sacrifice of aspersion, and of the other a burnt offering.

# Shadal on Leviticus

**14:23.** **"On the eighth day after his purification, he will bring them to the priest, at the entrance of the tent of congregation before the Lord.**

***On the eighth day after his purification, he will bring them*** *(ve-hevi otam ba-yom ha-shemini le-tohorato,* וְהֵבִיא אֹתָם בַּיּוֹם הַשְּׁמִינִי לְטָהֳרָתוֹ) [which may alternatively be translated as "he will bring them, on the eighth day, for his purification"]. Rashi connected the words *ha-shemini* and *le-tohorato* [understanding the phrase to mean "on the eighth day after his purification"], but this was not the opinion of the accentuator [who marked the word *ha-shemini* with a disjunctive *tevir*]; if it were as Rashi explained, then the words *ve-hevi otam* would have had to be set off with a *munaḥ revia.*[3] In any case, however, the meaning is the same, for the sprinklings with the bird's blood and so forth [as described above, vv. 5-8] were for the purpose of purifying the leper, while the sacrifices [on the eighth day] were the completion of his purification (9 Marḥeshvan 5625 [1865]).

**14:24.** **"And the priest will take the lamb destined for a sacrifice of repentance, and the *log* of oil; and the priest will make of them a waving before the Lord.**

**14:25.** **"The lamb of the sacrifice of repentance will be slaughtered, and the priest will take some of the blood of the sacrifice of repentance, and he will place it on the top of the right ear of the one who is to be purified, and on the thumb of his right hand, and on the big toe of his right foot.**

---

3. That is, in order to connect the words *ha-shemini* and *le-tohorato* as per Rashi (and Shadal's own translation), the disjunctive quality of the *tevir* marking *ha-shemini* would have had to be effectively reduced by accenting the preceding word *otam* with the stronger disjunctive *revia.* However, the words *ve-hevi otam* are in fact accented with a *kadma ve-azla,* and the *azla* is a weaker disjunctive than the *tevir.* Hence it follows that the Masoretes meant to separate the words *ha-shemini* and *le-tohorato,* thus favoring the translation "he will bring them, on the eighth day, for his purification."

14:26. "And some of the oil the priest will drip on the palm of the left hand of the priest (himself).

14:27. "And the priest will sprinkle with the finger of his right hand some of the oil that is on his left palm, seven times before the Lord.

14:28. "Then the priest will place some of the oil that is on his palm on the top of the right ear of the one who is to be purified, and on the thumb of his right hand, and on the big toe of his right foot, (that is) on the same places where the blood of the sacrifice of repentance was applied.

14:29. "And the remainder of the oil that is on the priest's palm he will place upon the head of the one who is to be purified, to propitiate for him before the Lord.

14:30. "Then he will make one of the turtledoves, or one of the young doves, that he will have been able to provide—

14:31. "Of those (I say) which his resources will have reached, (he will make) one into a sacrifice of aspersion, and the other into a burnt offering, besides the flour offering; and thus the priest will propitiate before the Lord for the one who is to be purified.

14:32. "This is the law of one who has the disease of leprosy, and who is of limited means in (the time of) his purification."

14:33. And the Lord spoke to Moses and to Aaron, saying:

14:34. "When you have entered into the land of Canaan, which I am about to give you in possession, and it happens that I order a leprous change in some house of the country of your possession—

14:35. "The owner of the house will go to announce to the priest, saying, 'A kind of leprous change has shown itself to me in the house.'

**14:36.** "And the priest will command that the house be cleared out, before the priest goes to see the change, (and that is) so that [in case the house is declared impure] all that is in the house does not become impure; and afterward the priest will go to see the house.

**14:37.** "He will observe the change, and finding that the change in the walls of the house consists of greenish or reddish stains, and that these appear deeper than (the surface of) the wall—

*stains (sheka'arurot).* Onkelos translated this as *paḥatan,* meaning "pits"; the Hebrew is from the root *ka'ar* ["to be concave"]. Leprous changes affecting houses were so called because they were a sort of concavity; the latter part of the verse specifically states that they appeared "deeper than (the surface of) the wall."

**14:38.** "The priest will come out of the house to the entrance thereof, and he will order that the house remain closed seven days.

**14:39.** "The priest will return on the seventh day, and seeing that the change has spread in the walls of the house—

**14:40.** "The priest will command, and the stones in which there is the change will be removed (from the wall) and thrown outside the city, into an impure place.

**14:41.** "And the house will be scraped on the inside, around (these stones); and the soil that is scraped from it will be spilled outside the city into an impure place.

*that is scraped (hiktsu).* This word and *hiktsot* ["has been scraped," in v. 43] are from the root *katsah* (קצה, "to cut"), which here is the equivalent of the root *katsa* (קצע, "to scrape"). However, Rashi derived [the words *hikstu* and *hiktsot*] from *katsah* [in the sense of "end" or "edge," interpreting the phrase to mean] "the soil that is scraped off at the edges of (*bi-k'tsot,* בקצות) the change round about." This reading of Rashi's comment is found in a manuscript in my possession and in [the supercommentary of] Mizrahi, but in some early printed editions [the word בקצות] was written [in the abbreviated form] 'בקצו, and [some] later versions misunderstood this and wrote it as בקצוע [which would render Rashi's interpretation as "the soil that is scraped off *in the scraping of the change round about*"].

**14:42. "Other stones will be taken, and they will be put in the place of the first ones, and other soil will be taken, and the house will be plastered.**

**14:43. "If, however, the change returns to spring forth in the house, after the stones have been removed, and after the house has been scraped, and after it has been plastered—**

***removed (ḥillets)... scraped (ḥiktsot).*** These verbs are vocalized with a *ḥirek* instead of a *pataḥ* [i.e., the expected forms would have been *ḥallets and ḥaktsot*, in the *pi'el* infinitive]; compare:

- *ad hishmidkha otam* [instead of *hashmidkha*, Deut. 7:24];
- *teḥillat dibber YHVW be-Hoshea* [instead of *dabber*, Hos. 1:2];
- *kol yemei hisgir oto* [instead of *hasgir*, Lev. 14:46].

If the word *ḥiktsot* were in the passive *nif'al* conjugation (as was Rashi's opinion), its proper form would have been *ḥikkatsot*; rather, it seems that it is an active verb [irregularly vocalized] with a *ḥirek,* like *hishmidkha,* and similarly *ḥillets* instead of *ḥallets.* However, the verb *ḥittoaḥ* ("it has been plastered") is undoubtedly passive.[4]

**14:44. "The priest will come, and seeing that the change has spread in the house, it is an acute leprosy in that house; (the house) is impure.**

---

4. In keeping with Shadal's understanding of the series of verbs in this verse, the proper translation might have been "after one has removed the stones, and after one has scraped the house, and after it has been plastered." In his translation, however, Shadal chose to render all three of the verbs in the passive voice.

*the change has spread* *(pasah)*. The correct explanation is that of Wessely, that the return of the change and its sprouting in the new stones after the previous stones have been removed is called *pisyon* ("spreading").[5]

**14:45.** "And he will have the house thrown down, its stones, its timbers, and all the soil of the house; and he will send (the entirety) outside the city, to an impure place.

**14:46.** "Anyone, then, who has entered that house in the course of the days in which the house was ordered to remain closed will be impure until night.

**14:47.** "And one who has slept in that house will have to wash his clothes [besides his body]; and likewise one who has eaten in that house will have to wash his clothes.

**14:48.** "But if the priest, having come, sees the change not spread in the house, after the house has been plastered, the priest will declare the house pure, for the change has been healed.

**14:49.** "And he will take, in order to make aspersions upon the house, two birds and some cedar wood, and some scarlet wool, and some hyssop.

**14:50.** "And he will slaughter one of the birds into an earthenware vessel, upon living water.

---

5. Wessely notes that even if the change that appears in the new stones is smaller in measurement than the change that appeared in the previous stones, the new change can properly be said to have "spread" in relation to the previous change, which has been removed altogether. This is *contra* Nachmanides, who interprets the word *pasah* in this verse as "recurred" rather than "spread." In so interpreting, Nachmanides was seeking to avoid a halakhic difficulty, since the Rabbis had ruled that a recurring change renders a house impure even if it has not "spread." Wessely's interpretation, too, would avoid this difficulty.

**14:51.** "And he will take the cedar wood and the hyssop and the scarlet wool and the living bird, and he will dip them in the blood of the slaughtered bird and in the living water, and he will sprinkle upon the house seven times.

**14:52.** "He will sprinkle (that is) the house with the blood of the bird and with the living water, doing so with the living bird, and with the cedar wood, and with the hyssop, and with the scarlet wool.

**14:53.** "Then he will let the living bird go free, outside the city, through the countryside; and thus propitiating for the house, it will be pure.

**14:54.** "This is the law for any disease of leprosy, and for the *netek*—

**14:55.** "And for leprosy of clothes and of houses—

**14:56.** "And for prominences, and for scabs, and for spots—

**14:57.** "According to which judgment will have to be given, when one [individual or object] is impure, and when one is pure. This is the law of leprosy."

**15:1.** And the Lord spoke to Moses and to Aaron, saying:

**15:2.** "When someone has a discharge [blennorrhea][6] from his member, such a flow of his is impure.

**15:3.** "And this will be his impurity [that is, such will be the diseased conditions that will render him impure], in his flow: whether his

6. Italian *blennorrea*. This disease is defined as an inordinate secretion and discharge of mucus, but the word is also an old term for "gonorrhea." Scientific opinion has been said to be "nearly unanimous" that the disease referred to in Lev. 15:2-15 is gonorrhea (Milgrom, *Leviticus: A Book of Ritual and Ethics*, p. 159, citing Preuss, *Biblisch-talmudische Medizin*, trans. Rosner).

member issues (liquid) so that his flow dribbles, or whether his member seems to be blocked by the (density of) his flow, (either of these things) is [produces] his impurity.

15:4. "Whatever bed on which the person with blennorrhea lies will be impure, and whatever implement on which he sits will be impure.

15:5. "And whoever touches his bed will wash his clothes and will bathe himself in water, and he will be impure until night.

15:6. "And one who sits upon an implement on which the person with blennorrhea has sat will wash his clothes and will bath himself in water, and he will be impure until night.

15:7. "And one who touches the body of the person with blennorrhea will wash his clothes and will bath himself in water, and he will be impure until night.

15:8. "And when the person with blennorrhea has spit upon a pure individual, the latter will wash his clothes and will bath himself in water, and he will be impure until night.

15:9. "And any riding implement on which the person with blennorrhea rides will be impure.

15:10. "And whoever touches any object that has been underneath him will be impure until night, and one who lifts these things will wash his clothes and will bath himself in water, and he will be impure until night.

15:11. "And anyone who has been touched by the person with blennorrhea without having his hands rinsed will wash his clothes and will bath himself in water, and he will be impure until night.

15:12. "An earthenware vessel that is touched by the person with blennorrhea will be broken; and if it is a wooden vessel, it will be rinsed.

**15:13.** "When the person with blennorrhea is clean [healed] of his flow, he will count [that is, let run] seven days (from the moment) of his impurity, then he will wash his clothes and bathe his body in living water, and he will be pure.

**15:14.** "And on the eighth day he will take two turtledoves, or two young doves, and he will come before the Lord, at the entrance of the tent of congregation, and he will give them to the priest.

**15:15.** "And the priest will make of the one a sacrifice of aspersion, and of the other a burnt offering; and thus the priest will propitiate for him before the Lord for his flow.

**15:16.** "A man from whom issues a flow of seed will bathe his entire body in water, and he will be impure until night.

*a flow of seed (shikhvat zera).* After [any form of] the verb *hayah* ("to be") (as in the next verse) or the verb *yatsa* ("to come forth"), [the word *shikhvah*] denotes a spreading out, as in *shikhvat ha-tal*, "the expanse of dew" (Exod. 16:13). After the verb *shakhav* ("to lie"), the word denotes a lying [with someone].

**15:17.** "And any garment, and whatever hide, on which there is a flow of seed will be washed in water, and it will be impure until night.

**15:18.** "And when a man lies carnally with a woman, they will bathe themselves in water, and they will be impure until night.

**15:19.** "A woman, when she has a discharge—her flow will consist of blood in her sexual organ—for seven days she will be in her menstruation [she will be considered in a state of menstruation], and whoever touches her will be impure until night.

**15:20.** "And any object on which she lies during her menstruation will be impure, and likewise anything on which she sits will be impure.

**15:21.** "And anyone who touches her bed will wash his clothes and bathe himself in water, and he will be impure until night.

**15:22.** "And anyone who touches any implement on which she has sat will wash his clothes and bathe himself in water, and he will be impure until night.

**15:23.** "And if, touching the bed, he is upon it, or (he sits) on the implement on which she is seated, he will be (equally) impure (only) until night.

*And if, touching the bed, he is upon it, etc.* The verses above referred to one who touches her bed or seat even if he does not lie or sit on it, and even if she is not there at the time, while here it adds that even if he lies on the bed or sits on the implement and she herself is sitting on it at the time, he is impure only until night (Wessely and Reggio). The words *be-nog'o vo* [lit. "when he is touching it," which phrase appears in the Hebrew after "on which she is seated"] refer back to the beginning of the verse: "And if, when he is touching it"—that is, if the aforementioned person who is doing the touching is on the bed, etc.; this was the opinion of the accentuator (A. H. Mainster).[7]

**15:24.** "But if someone lies with her, he will incur (the same impurity of) her menstruation, and he will be impure seven days; and any bed on which he lies will be impure.

**15:25.** "If a woman has her discharge of blood for several days, outside the time of her menstruation, or she has the discharge beyond (the customary duration of) her menstruation, for the entire time of her impure discharge she will be (considered) as in the days of her menstruation; impure she is.

---

7. Literally translated, the verse says, "And if he is on the bed or on the implement on which she is seated, when he touches it…" The word *alav*, the last word of the phrase "on which she is seated," is marked with a disjunctive *tipḥa*, indicating that everything in the verse up to that point is to be taken as a single unit, and that the subsequent phrase "when he touches it" modifies that entire unit.

15:26. "Every bed on which she lies on any of the days of her discharge will be for her as the bed of her menstruation; and every implement on which she sits will be impure, as it would be impure for her menstruation.

15:27. "And anyone who touches them will be impure; and he will wash his clothes and bathe himself in water, and he will be impure until night.

15:28. "If she then remains clean [healed] of her discharge, she will count [let run] seven days, and then she will be pure.

15:29. "And on the eighth day she will take two turtledoves, or two young doves, and she will bring them to the priest at the entrance of the tent of congregation.

15:30. And the priest will make of the one a sacrifice of aspersion, and of the other a burnt offering. Thus the priest will propitiate for her before the Lord, for her impure discharge.

15:31. "Make the children of Israel hold themselves far from their impurity; otherwise they would die for their impurity, contaminating My seat that is amidst them [that is, entering the Temple in a state of impurity].

15:32. "This is the law regarding the person with blennorrhea, and one from whom issues a flow of seed, for which he becomes impure—

15:33. "And the menstruating woman, with regard to her (regular) menstruation, and one who has a flow, whether male or female, and one who lies with an impure woman.

# *Aḥarei Mot*

*One goat for the Lord, another for Azazel* • *"Of all your errors you will become pure"* • *"The life of the animal is in the blood"* • *"Do not do any of all these abominations"*

**16:1. The Lord spoke to Moses, after the death of the two sons of Aaron, who, having presented themselves [arbitrarily] before the Lord, died.**

*after the death.* Even though they had not entered the Holy of Holies [and thus the mention of their death may not seem strictly relevant to the admonition in the next verse], their death resulted from their making light of the honor and fear that was owed to God's Sanctuary and its service. In a manuscript of Rashi's commentary in my possession, there is an addition [to the comment on this verse]: "Any place that produces a heavy mist and induces sweat, such as an underground chamber surrounded with an enclosure of stones, is called a *taḥav* [תחב]" (although earlier [in the same comment] the word is written טחב, with a *tet*).[1]

---

1. This addition serves to explain Rashi's comment, taken from the *Sifra*, that the reason why the command in the next verse (that Aaron should generally avoid entering the Holy of Holies) is said to have been given "after the death of the two sons of Aaron" is that this statement is like a physician's warning to a patient, "Do not eat cold

# Aḥarei Mot

**16:2. The Lord, that is, said to Moses, "Speak to Aaron your brother, so that he does not enter at any time into the Sanctuary, beyond the door-curtain (which is) before the cover that is upon the Ark; otherwise he would die, for within a cloud I will appear above the cover.**

***so that he does not enter at any time*** *(be-khol et*, lit. "at every time")*.* At no time [is he to enter].

***for within a cloud I will appear above the cover.*** For even when I reveal Myself above the cover, this will be only within the cloud, for the glory of God is a hidden thing; and therefore even the high priest must take care not to enter therein.

***so that he does not enter at any time into the Sanctuary, beyond the*** ***door-curtain*** (וְאַל־יָבֹא בְכָל־עֵת אֶל־הַקֹּדֶשׁ מִבֵּית לַפָּרֹכֶת). The accents of this verse are quite strange, because the *etnaḥ* [major disjunctive] should properly have been placed [not at the end of the phrase *mi-beit la-parokhet*, "beyond the door-curtain," but rather] at the end of the phrase *ve-lo yamut*, "otherwise he would die" [as in the following re-accentuation]:

וְאַל־יָבֹא בְכָל־עֵת אֶל־הַקֹּדֶשׁ מִבֵּית לַפָּרֹכֶת אֶל־פְּנֵי הַכַּפֹּרֶת אֲשֶׁר עַל־הָאָרֹן וְלֹא יָמוּת

Perhaps the accentuators agreed with Rabbi Judah (*Menaḥot* 27b), that if one goes "beyond the door-curtain," one merely transgresses a warning ["so that he does not enter"], but that if one comes "before the cover," the death penalty is incurred ["otherwise he would die"]. Possibly it might further be said that in the time of the Second Temple, someone might have thought, "Now that there is no Ark and no cover, it should be

things or sleep in a damp place [*taḥav*], so that you do not die as so-and-so did." The proper spelling of *taḥav* is טחב, with a *tet*. Chavel notes that a similar addition is found in the first printed edition of Rashi (Reggio di Calabria, 1475): "A place that produces a heavy mist and induces sweat, such as an underground chamber surrounded with an enclosure." This abbreviated version of the statement does not contain the misspelling תחב.

permissible to enter the Holy of Holies," and for this reason, the Rabbis saw fit to split the verse as if it contained two statements: "So that he does not enter at any time into the Sanctuary, beyond the door-curtain" (even if there is no Ark or cover there, it is forbidden to enter therein, but) "before the cover that is upon the Ark" (let him not enter at any time) "otherwise he will die"; i.e., when there is an Ark, there is a death penalty, and when there is no Ark, there is no death penalty, but there is still a warning. Then the [Masoretic] accentuators (who lived after the closing of the Talmud) marked the accents in accordance with the reading that had been received orally from the Rabbis of the Second Temple era.[2]

**16:3. "(Only) after having done these things will Aaron enter into the Sanctuary, after having made (that is) a young bull into a sacrifice of aspersion, and a ram into a burnt offering.**

**16:4. "He will don a sacred tunic, of linen, and trousers of linen he will have on his flesh, and with a belt of linen he will be girt, and with a mitre of linen he will bind (his head); they are sacred vestments, and he will bathe his body in water before donning them.**

**16:5. "And from the congregation of the children of Israel he will receive two goats for a sacrifice of aspersion, and a ram for a burnt offering.**

**16:6. "Aaron will bring forth the bull of the sacrifice of aspersion, belonging to him, and he will propitiate for himself and for his house.**

**16:7. "And he will take the two goats, and he will present them before the Lord, at the entrance of the tent of congregation.**

---

2. It should be pointed out that in *Menaḥot* 27b, a majority of the Rabbis opposed Rabbi Judah's view and split the verse differently: one who enters the Sanctuary transgresses the warning "so that he does not enter," but one who goes beyond the door-curtain and comes before the cover incurs the death penalty.

**16:8. "Aaron will draw lots with respect to the two goats: (on) one lot will be (written) 'For the Lord,' and (on) the other, 'For Azazel.'**

*lots (goralot)*. *Garalon* in Arabic means "stone."

*Azazel.* It seems that this was, in ancient times, the name of the evil god, the Satan, *El Az* ("mighty god"), and that the word Azazel is derived from the phrase *az az el* ("Mighty, mighty is God"). Among the monotheists, who did not believe in the existence of a god of evil, this word remained and conveyed the meaning of "total evil, perdition," just as even today one says "Satan" to indicate any great evil or doom. The goat was let loose to its doom in the desert, so that it would die of hunger. At a time when the land of Israel had ample room for the Israelites, who were the smallest of nations, it was possible to find within their territory a broad, uninhabited area in which the goat could wander and die, but with the passage of time, when the nation increased and the land was more fully settled, so that there was no longer any uninhabited area, they were constrained to make a new rule that the goat should be pushed off a cliff [see, e.g., *Yoma* 67a], for otherwise it would enter into an inhabited city.

The purpose of sending the goat to Azazel seems to be in keeping with the expression, "And You will cast all their sins into the depths of the sea" (Micah 7:19), for the priest, by means of his statement [below, v. 21], would place all of the sins of the people upon the goat, and then he would send it away, along with all the sins, to an uninhabited area, and the people would be left clean of all their sins.

**16:9. "And Aaron will present the goat upon which has fallen the lot for the Lord, and he will make of it a sacrifice of aspersion.**

**16:10. "And that goat upon which has fallen the lot for Azazel will be kept alive before the Lord, to propitiate upon it, to then send it to Azazel, to the wilderness.**

**16:11. "Aaron will present the bull of the sacrifice of aspersion belonging to him. and he will propitiate for himself and for his house [that is, he will implore Divine pardon for his own sins and for**

those of his family]; then he will slaughter the bull of the sacrifice of aspersion belonging to him.

16:12. "And he will take the paddle full of lit coals from upon the altar, before the Lord, and his fists full of aromatic powdered incense, and he will bring it beyond the door-curtain.

16:13. "And he will place the incense on the fire, before the Lord; and the cloud of the incense will conceal the cover that is upon (the Ark of) the law, and thus he will not die.

16:14. "And he will take of the blood of the bull, and he will sprinkle of it with his finger toward the cover, to the east; and before the cover (on the floor) he will sprinkle of that blood seven times with his finger.

16:15. "Then he will slaughter the goat of the sacrifice of aspersion belonging to the people, and he will bring its blood beyond the door-curtain, and he will do with that blood as he did with the blood of the bull, and he will sprinkle it toward the cover and before the cover.

16:16. "Thus he will propitiate for the Sanctuary [purifying it with these aspersions] from the impurities of the children of Israel, from their faults, and from all their errors, and he will do the same for the tent of congregation, which dwells with them in the midst of their impurities.

*Thus he will propitiate for the Sanctuary from the impurities of the children of Israel, from their faults.* The aspersions purify the Sanctuary from the impurities that the Israelites might have done to it, whether intentionally or unintentionally, but the propitiation is not effective for the person who rendered the impurity, for he is to bear his sin. The purpose of this propitiation is that in the event that one of the people comes to the Sanctuary in a state of impurity, the people should not think that the Sanctuary has been rendered impure, and that all of the services performed in it have been disfavored; rather, they should think that it has been restored to its purity and holiness by means of the high priest's aspersions.

**16:17. "No person may be found in the tent of congregation when he enters to propitiate in the Sanctuary, until he has come forth (from it). He will thus propitiate for himself, and for his house, and for all the assembly of Israel.**

**16:18. "Then he will go forth to the altar that is before the Lord, and he will propitiate for it; that is, he will take of the blood of the bull and of the blood of the goat, and he will place it on the prominences of the altar round about.**

***Then he will go forth to the altar that is before the Lord.*** The golden altar; see Exod. 30:10 ["And Aaron will make expiation upon its prominences once a year. Of the blood of the sacrifice of aspersion (of the day of) expiation, once a year, he will expiate upon it..."]. The words of Ibn Ezra [in his comment here] are erroneous; see Wessely, and see the *Me'ammer*, who seeks to defend Ibn Ezra.[3]

---

3. Ibn Ezra asserts that the "altar" referred to here is the altar of the sacrifices [*mizbaḥ ha-olah*], which was outside the Sanctuary. To the contrary, Wessely (in the *Biur* to Mendelssohn's *Netivot ha-Shalom*) cites *Yoma* 58b in support of the view that the altar in question is the golden altar of the incense, which was within the Sanctuary. Wessely says that if Ibn Ezra's view was based on the phrase "Then he will go forth [*ve-yatsa*] to the altar," which might be construed as implying that the priest was to exit the Sanctuary, such a reading would have been based on a misunderstanding of the verb *yatsa*, which (when not followed by the preposition *min*, "from") may simply mean to move from one point to another within a given space without leaving that space. However, the *Me'ammer* (commentary by R. Wolf Meir, which is included in the 1862 Prague edition of *Netivot ha-Shalom*) counters that Wessely, "in his haste to pursue Ibn Ezra," disregarded the fact that at v. 16, on the phrase "and he will do the same for the tent of congregation," Ibn Ezra commented, "He was to sprinkle seven times before the cover *and on the altar of the incense.*" Thus, according to the *Me'ammer*, Ibn Ezra's comment on v. 18 does not mean that in this instance there was no sprinkling on the golden altar as well.

**16:19.** "And he will sprinkle upon it of that blood with his finger seven times, and thus he will purify it and sanctify it from the impurities of the children of Israel.

**16:20.** "Having finished propitiating for the Sanctuary, for the tent of congregation, and for the altar, he will cause to be brought forth the live goat.

**16:21.** "Aaron will place both of this hands on the head of the live goat, and he will confess over it all the sins of the children of Israel, all their faults and all their errors, and he will place them [symbolically, with the act of his hands and with his words] on the head of the goat, which by means of an appropriate person, he will send into the wilderness.

*appropriate (itti).* [The Hebrew is an adjective] derived from *et* ("time") [that is, "appropriate for this time or occasion"], just as *mezumman* ("ready, prepared") is derived from *zeman* ("time"). Perhaps this is the derivation of the word *atid* ("future"), similar to *ittit* [the feminine form of *itti*], from *et*.[4]

**16:22.** "The goat will carry upon itself all of their sins into an uninhabited land, and he will let the goat go in the wilderness.

**16:23.** "Aaron, having re-entered the tent of congregation, will take off the linen vestments that he donned before entering the Sanctuary, and he will leave them there.

**16:24.** "He will bathe his body in water in a holy place, and he will don his (usual) garments; and having come forth from there, he will make the burnt offering belonging to him and the burnt offering given by the people, and he will propitiate for himself and for the people.

---

4. Perhaps Shadal's thinking might have been influenced by the fact that the word *ittit* would have been pronounced by Italian Jews as *ittid*.

**16:25. "And he will burn on the altar the tallow of the sacrifice of aspersion.**

*And he will burn, etc.* In a manuscript Rashi in my possession it is written, "The Targum translates this as *ve-yat tarbei ḥatvata* ("and the tallows of the sacrifices")—the *emurim* (sacrificial portions) of the bull and the goat he will burn on the altar." The meaning is that two sacrifices of aspersion are included here, that of the bull and that of the goat.[5]

**16:26. "And the one who will have led the goat to Azazel will wash his garments, and he will bathe his body in water, and afterwards he will be able to re-enter the camp.**

**16:27. "But the bull of the sacrifice of aspersion, and the goat of the sacrifice of aspersion, the blood of which will have been brought into the Sanctuary in order to make the propitiations, will be transported outside the camp and burnt, with their skin, their flesh, and their waste.**

**16:28. "And the one who burns them will wash his garments, and he will bathe his body in water, and afterwards he will be able to re-enter the camp.**

**16:29. "This will be for you an everlasting statute: in the seventh month, on the tenth of the month, you shall afflict your persons [by fasting], and you shall do no work, neither the native nor the foreigner who dwells among you."**

*you will afflict your persons (te'annu et nafshoteikhem).* Cf. *ve-nefesh na'anah tasbi'a* ("[And if you draw out your soul to the hungry,] and satisfy the afflicted soul," Isa. 58:10); *va-y'annekha va-yar'ivekha* ("He made you suffer privations and hunger," Deut. 8:3) [i.e., the root *anah*, "to suffer," can imply hunger or fasting].

---

5. In standard printed editions of Rashi, the comment consists only of the phrase, "The *emurim* of the bull and the goat." Also, in standard printed editions of Targum Onkelos and the Jerusalem Targum, the phrase in question reads *ve-yat tarba de-ḥatata* ("and the tallow of the sacrifice," in the singular).

**16:30.** **"For on this day (the high priest) will propitiate for you, to purify you; of all your errors you will become pure before the Lord [in other words, of the sins unknown to the one who committed them].**

*will propitiate for you.* [The unstated subject of this phrase is] the priest, by means of the services that he will perform (Wessely).

*of all your errors you will become pure before the Lord.* This refers to the sins that have been forgotten by or hidden from the person who committed them.

**16:31.** **"A day of great rest it is for you, and you will afflict your persons—an everlasting statute.**

**16:32.** **"The priest who will be anointed (high priest), and installed to officiate in place of his father, will make the propitiations, and will don the garments of linen, sacred vestments.**

*and will don (ve-lavash).* This verb is connected to *ve-khipper* ("will make the propitiations"); i.e., the one serving as a priest in place of his father will make the propitiations on this day, and he will perform the services in white garments; so translated Mendelssohn.

**16:33.** **"He will make the propitiations for the most holy place, for the tent of congregation, and for the altar, and for the priests, and for all the people of the assembly.**

**16:34.** **"The thing will be for you an everlasting law, so that there may be propitiation for the children of Israel, (to purify them) of all their errors, once a year." And he carried out all that the Lord commanded Moses.**

**17:1.** **The Lord spoke to Moses, saying:**

# Aḥarei Mot

*The Lord spoke, etc.* After the Tabernacle had been erected, He began to command them concerning matters of holiness, that they should be holy since the God Who dwelled among them was holy. Thus He admonished them as to forbidden foods, impure things, and illicit relations, as well as matters of conduct between man and his fellow, for He loves justice and compassion among human beings. Afterwards He admonished them concerning the holiness of the priests (in the *parashah* of *Emor* [Lev. ch. 21-22]).

Although the prohibition of the consumption of tallow and blood [below, vv. 6, 10-14] applies to ordinary meat [*hullin*] as well [as consecrated meat], it is promulgated only by way of honor to the One Above, for tallow and blood were considered to be Divine foodstuffs. Indeed, blood was selected to be brought upon the altar because the soul resides within it, and therefore it propitiates for the soul. Perhaps tallow was so selected even before the giving of the Torah, because it melts and goes up in the fire and produces more smoke than the flesh, and thus it has a function similar to that of incense. The prohibition of blood has another reason besides the one stated here, for drinking it is an act of cruelty and fosters an evil trait in the soul. Therefore blood is prohibited even with respect to a wild beast [*hayyah*] that is not sacrificed upon the altar, unlike the case with tallow.

**17:2.** **"Speak to Aaron and to his sons, and to all the children of Israel, and say to them: This is what the Lord has commanded.**

**17:3.** **"If anyone of the house of Israel slaughters a bovine, ovine, or caprine animal in the camp, or slaughters it outside the camp—**

*If anyone... slaughters, etc.* Scripture [in vv. 3-7] is speaking of ordinary meat [*hullin*], for in the wilderness the people were forbidden to consume meat privately [without sharing it with others as part of a "sacrifice of contentment"]; this is in accordance with R. Ishmael's opinion [in *Hullin* 16b], and this is closest to the plain meaning of the verses (Wessely).[6]

---

6. Wessely (in the *Biur* to Mendelssohn's *Netivot ha-Shalom*) explains that according to R. Akiva (*Hullin* 17a), this entire section (vv. 3 through 9) is speaking of consecrated sacrificial meat and requires such sacrifices to be slaughtered and offered at the tent of congregation,

# Shadal on Leviticus

Subsequently, in vv. 8 and 9, Scripture speaks of consecrated sacrificial meat [*mukdashin*]. That is, first there is a prohibition on slaughter away from the tent of congregation in general, so that the people should not come to slaughter to satyrs [v. 7], and then [the Torah] says, "If a person might say, 'I will make a burnt offering or other sacrifice to God in my home.' know that anyone who makes a burnt offering or other sacrifice and does not bring it to the entrance of the tent of congregation, [that person will become extinct]."

**17:4. "—and does not bring it to the entrance of the tent of congregation, to make [of the blood and the tallow] a sacrifice to the Lord, before the tabernacle of the Lord, that will be considered to that man as homicide; he has shed [human] blood, and that man will become extinct from the midst of his people.**

**17:5. "So that those animals that the children of Israel wish to slaughter in the open field, they bring (instead) to the Lord, to the entrance of the tent of congregation, to the priest, and they make of them sacrifices of contentment to the Lord.**

**17:6. "And the priest will scatter its blood on the altar of the Lord at the entrance of the tent of congregation, and he will burn its tallow, in a propitiatory scent, to the Lord.**

**17:7. "Let them no longer make their sacrifices to the satyrs, after which they are wont to fornicate [in other words, to which they are wont to render worship]. This will be for them an everlasting statute, for all the ages to come [that is, to distance themselves from that cult, and from the immoral practices that accompany it; however, eating**

---

and that under this view, there was never a prohibition on the slaughter and consumption of meat for private purposes only [*besar ta'avah*]. Wessely goes on to explain that according to the view of R. Ishmael, that *besar ta'avah* was forbidden until the people entered the land of Israel, vv. 3-7 require all slaughtering, for any purpose, to take place at the tent of congregation, while vv. 8 and 9 specifically penalize one who slaughters an animal for consecrated purposes at the tent of congregation but then offers it as a sacrifice at another location.

**meat without bringing the animal to the Temple was permitted once they entered the promised land; see Deut. ch. 12]."**

*an everlasting statute.* The prohibition against sacrificing to satyrs.

**17:8. And to those same ones He said, "Anyone of the house of Israel, or of the foreigners who will dwell among them, who may make a burnt offering or (other) sacrifice—**

**17:9. — "and does not bring it to the entrance of the tent of congregation to render it to the Lord, that individual will go extinct from his people.**

*to render it to the Lord (or, "to make it the Lord's," la-asot oto la-YHVH).* It does not say "to bring a sacrifice to the Lord," as in v. 4 above, because here [in v. 8] it has already said "who may make a burnt offering or (other) sacrifice."

**17:10. "And anyone of the house of Israel, and of the foreigners dwelling among them, who eats any kind of blood... I will turn Myself against the person eating the blood, and I will cause him to go extinct from the midst of his people.**

**17:11. "For the life of the animal is in the blood, and I have conceded it to you [that is, I have conceded it to be burned] on the altar, to propitiate for your persons, for the blood—that can propitiate for the life (of man).**

*for the blood—that can propitiate for the life (ki ha-dam hu ba-nefesh yekhapper,* lit. "for the blood, in the life it propitiates"). It propitiates for the life; see Rashi.[7]

---

7. Rashi's comment on this verse states that since the life of every creature is dependent on blood, God has given over blood to propitiate for the life of man; "let life come and propitiate for the life."

# Shadal on Leviticus

**17:12.** "Therefore I said to the children of Israel, 'Let no person among you eat blood, and likewise let no foreigner dwelling among you eat blood.'

**17:13.** "And any one of the children of Israel, or of the foreigners dwelling among them, who takes in hunting any wild beast or flying creature that is permitted to eat, will pour out its blood and cover it with earth.

***and cover it with earth.*** [Some say that this is] so as not to leave it on the ground for the souls of the dead to come and drink it, in accordance with the belief of ancient peoples, as seen in Homer.[8] Rosenmueller said that this was by way of according honor to the blood, so that the wild beasts should not drink it. To me it seems that this was so that the blood should not remain and cause one who saw it to think that it was human blood, and that the blood of an innocent person had been shed in the land of Israel, which was holy (Shalom Simeon Modena).

**17:14.** "For the life of every animal is the blood that it has in its body; therefore I have said to the children of Israel, 'Do not eat the blood of any animal, for the life of every animal is its blood; whoever eats it will go extinct.'

***For the life of every animal is the blood that it has in its body*** *(ki nefesh kol basar damo be-nafsho hu)*. In the phrase *damo be-nafsho* (lit. "its blood in its soul") *nafsho* is the equivalent of *gufo* ("its body") (Arnheim).[9]

---

8. In Homer's *Odyssey* 11:35-39, Odysseus (Ulysses) offers sacrifices to the dead at the entrance of Hades, and all the souls rush to the sacrificial pit to drink blood. The ancient Greeks believed that the dead lost their memory, but that after drinking blood they regained it and became omniscient (see Lada Stevanović, *Laughing at the Funeral: Gender and Anthropology in the Greek Funerary Rites*, p. 63). See also below, Lev. 19:26.
9. In Heymann Arnheim's *Die fünf Bücher Moses nebst den Haftaroth* (Prague, 1855), the phrase *ki nefesh kol basar damo be-nafsho hu* is translated in German as *Denn das Leben alles Fleisches ist das Blut*

154

**17:15.** "And any person, whether native or foreign, who eats of an animal that died of itself or is torn apart [by some wild beast] will wash his clothes, and will bathe himself in water, and will be impure until night; then he will be pure.

**17:16.** "And if he does not wash [his clothes], and does not bathe his body, he will incur sin [entering the Temple, or eating a holy thing]."

*he will incur sin.* If he eats something holy or enters the sanctuary, or if he does not warn those who touch him. According to A. H. Mainster, it is one who delays purifying himself who incurs sin.

**18:1.** And the Lord spoke to Moses, saying:

**18:2.** "Speak to the children of Israel, and say to them: I, the Lord, am your God.

**18:3.** "You must not imitate the practices of the land of Egypt, where you dwelled; nor may you imitate the practices of the land of Canaan, where I am about to cause you to enter; nor may you follow their statutes.

*nor may you follow their statutes.* Of all the abominations recorded here, we do not find any that were a matter of statute except the passing of children through [the fire of] Molech. Apparently, just as the practice of levirate marriage is a statute among us, so some of the illicit relations were a matter of statute among those nations under particular circumstances.

---

*in seinem Leibe,* "For the life of all flesh is the blood in its body." In a footnote, Arnheim says, "There is a play on words here with *nefesh,* 'life' and 'body.'" In other words, two forms of the word *nefesh* appear in v. 14, the first denoting "life" and the second denoting "body." It should be observed that in Arnheim's rhythmic German translation of the phrase, the words *Leben* and *Leibe* themselves form an alliterative play on words.

# Shadal on Leviticus

**18:4.** **"My laws you will fulfill, and My statutes you will observe and follow. I, the Lord, am your God.**

**18:5.** **"Observe My statutes and My laws, in fulfilling which man acquires life [wellbeing]. I am the Lord [Who imposes them upon you].**

*acquires life (va-ḥai bahem,* lit. "and lives in them"). Society will survive in peace, for if one were to associate [incestuously] with one's close relatives, every family would become a society unto itself, separated from the others. "But this assertion, in my opinion, is worthless, for if incestuous relations were permitted, there would be no families whatsoever in the world, and the reason is that if one were to engage in such relations, there would be no love or reverence or peace in the world, as in the era of the Flood" (Shalom Simeon Modena).[10] Perhaps (as per A. H. Mainster) it was the law in Egypt that the people of one family or tribe were forbidden to intermarry with those of another family or tribe (for the nation was divided into castes), and thus they were sometimes compelled to enter into consanguineous marriages.[11]

---

10. The first view presented in this comment is certainly Shadal's own, because it recurs at the end of his comment on the phrase "None of you must approach any flesh of his own body" (v. 6, below). The second, differing view, although presented in first person ("in my opinion"), thus cannot be Shadal's own. Because he attributes it to his student Modena, I have set if off with quotation marks to make it appear as if Modena himself is speaking, although this is not the usual format of Shadal's commentary.

11. Ancient sources such as Herodotus described Egyptian society as subject to a caste system, though modern scholarship has found evidence of a certain degree of social mobility (see, for example, Célestin Bouglé, *Essays on the Caste System,* pp. 14-16). As for incestuous relations, one modern source asserts that "during the Pharaonic period consanguineous marriages were possible," though rarer than once thought, and that "[w]ithin the royal family the practice may have been more common than it was among the commoners.... When practiced it was almost always a marriage between a half-brother and a half-sister." (Paul John Frandsen, *Incestuous and Close-Kin Marriage in Ancient Egypt and Persia,* p. 39.)

# Aḥarei Mot

**18:6.** **"None of you may approach any flesh of his own body [that is, any close, consanguineous relative] to uncover her shameful parts [that is, you must not consort with any close relative of yours, nor with one who is the wife of a close relative of yours, for the wife is regarded as if forming part of the husband]. I am the Lord.**

*flesh of his own body (she'er besaro).* From the expression *akh atsmi u-v'sari attah* ("you are entirely my bone and my flesh," Gen. 29:14). The word *she'er*, too, denotes "flesh," as in *va-yamter aleihem ke-afar she'er* ("He caused flesh also to rain upon them as the dust," Ps. 78:27).

*None of you may approach any flesh of his own body.* The purpose of the sexual prohibitions was not, as Maimonides maintained (*Guide for the Perplexed* 3:49), to limit intercourse, for the Torah did not forbid the taking of many wives (except in the case of a king), nor was their purpose to increase intercourse with one wife; rather, they were all for the benefit of society. The prohibition of relations with another's wife has an obvious purpose, which is to avoid the violence, rivalry, and murder that result from adultery. Even if a man were to consent to this and to offer his wife to a rich man, this practice would be forbidden because of the corruption that the resulting destruction of virtue would cause to the nation as a whole. Sodomy and bestiality are prohibited because of their unnatural character, and because if they were permitted, the taking of women [by men] would decrease.

The purpose of the incest prohibitions is to further the wellbeing of the home, the perfection of virtuous traits, and the wellbeing of the state. The taking of one's mother, the wife of one's father, the father's sister, or the wife of the father's brother are acts against the honor of the father and mother, and the depreciation of parental honor would cause destruction of virtue and undermine the family regime. Similarly, a son's wife is the equivalent of a daughter to her father-in-law and mother-in-law, and if her father-in-law were to take her, this would result in the depreciation of the honor of the father-in-law, the mother-in-law, the father, and the mother. So also, taking a woman and her daughter would confer equal status upon them both and would thus cause depreciation of the mother's honor.

# Shadal on Leviticus

The reason for the prohibition of taking a woman and her sister is clearly expressed by the word *litsror* ("causing her anguish," v. 18 below), and that is so as not to create jealousy between two sisters and to make them into rivals who hate each other, in contrast to their rightful nature of loving one another. It is well known that hatred between relatives is harsher than hatred between strangers, for the force of their previous love is commensurate with the power of their subsequent hatred, and this causes destruction of virtue and great damage to the wellbeing of the home. Likewise, taking the wife of one's brother would cause jealousy and hatred between the brothers. Even in the case of a brother who dies and leaves children, if the surviving brother takes his sister-in-law, this would cause hatred between him and his brother's children, and also between his own children and his brother's children, resulting in destruction of virtue and damage to the wellbeing of the home. This would not occur, however, in the case of a brother who dies and leaves no children [in which case the law of levirate marriage applies; see Deuteronomy ch. 25].

The prohibition of taking one's sister seems to be based on the wellbeing of the state, for if taking a sister were permitted, most men would marry their sisters, each family would thus become a people unto itself, the families would not intermarry or mix with each other, and the nation would not become one people, but would turn into many peoples that would be distant from each other and not love one another.[12]

***to uncover her shameful parts*** *(le-gallot ervah)*. The "exposure of shameful parts" [*gillui ervah*] is a euphemistic term for intercourse. It

---

12. Shadal's view corresponds to the position later taken by, among others, Sigmund Freud, who claimed that "psychoanalytic investigations have shown beyond the possibility of doubt that an incestuous love choice is in fact the first and regular one" (Freud, *A General Introduction to Psychoanalysis* (trans. Riviere), pp. 220-21). However, this view has been contested by others, including researchers who found that there was a complete absence of love affairs or marriages between males and females who were raised from childhood in the same communal children's facilities on Israeli kibbutzim, and that such avoidance was entirely voluntary (see, for example, Arthur P. Wolf, *Incest Avoidance and the Incest Taboos*, pp. 45-47).

does not necessarily refer to a permanent taking, but may also refer to a casual instance of intercourse, as in, "Nor may you approach a woman, to uncover her shameful parts, during the impurity of her menstruation" (below, v. 19). When the term *gillui ervah* is used in connection with a man, as in "the shameful parts [*ervat*] of your father" or "the shameful parts [*ervat*] of your brother" [below, vv. 7, 16], the reference is to the shameful parts of his wife, for a man and his wife are considered as one flesh [cf. Gen. 2:24]. In v. 10, a man and his offspring are also considered as one flesh.

Note that Scripture always assigns the admonition to the male, for he is the initiating party, and if the sexual union in question is forbidden to the male, it would not likely be permitted to the female (and thus the prohibition is not spelled out with respect to the female, except in the case of a woman who engages in bestiality [below, v. 23], for in that case she is the initiating party, bringing the animal toward herself). However, it is not to be inferred from here that everything forbidden to a male is correspondingly forbidden to a female. Rather, that which is openly prohibited is prohibited [*heikha de-gelei gelei*], and that which is not is not. For example, the father's sister is prohibited to a male [i.e., the nephew], while the father's brother is permitted to take the niece.

If you were to ask, "If so, given that 'the shameful parts of your daughter-in-law' are mentioned [below, v. 15], why is there no mention of a prohibition with respect to a son-in-law and a mother-in-law?"—this is already included in the prohibition of taking a woman and her daughter [below, v. 17]. And if you were to ask, "Given that 'the shameful parts... of your daughter's daughter' are mentioned [below, v. 10], why is there no mention of a prohibition with respect to a grandson and his grandmother, whether his father's mother or his mother's mother?"—it seems to me that Scripture speaks of the typical case, for it may be likely for a grandfather to desire his granddaughter, but it would be quite unlikely for a young man to desire his father's mother or his mother's mother, who is so much older than he.[13]

---

13. A man's grandmother is, in fact, classified as one of the "secondary" kin who are forbidden under Rabbinic law; see note to v. 14 below.

# Shadal on Leviticus

**18:7.** "The shameful parts of your father and the shameful parts of your mother (together) you must not uncover [that is, do not commit incest with your mother, for since she forms part of your father, the outrage done to her is at the same time done to him]: she is your mother; you must not uncover her shameful parts.

*The shameful parts of your father and the shameful parts of your mother (together) you must not uncover.* That which constitutes the father's shameful parts and also the mother's shameful parts—that is, the mother, who is a close relation in two respects [i.e., your mother as well as your father's wife] (Nachmanides). Under Rashi's interpretation, the phrase "she is your mother" presents a difficulty.[14]

**18:8.** "The shameful parts of your father's wife [that is, of your stepmother] you must not uncover: she is the shameful parts of your father [that is, she forms part of him].

**18:9.** "The shameful parts of your sister, daughter [also] of your father or daughter [only] of your mother, born (that is) at home (with you) or born outside—you must not uncover her shameful parts.

*born (that is) at home (with you), etc.* It would seem to me that this phrase comes to explain what comes before: "your sister, daughter of your father" is the one "born at home," since she was born with you in the same home, while "your sister... daughter of your mother" is the one "born outside," since she was born of another man and apparently in a different house. According to this, however, would there not be a difficulty [i.e., a redundancy] with what is added subsequently (in v.

---

14. Rashi interprets the phrase "the shameful parts of your father" in this verse as referring to the father's wife, implying that this includes either the mother or a stepmother. However, the subsequent phrase "she is your mother" seems to contradict this interpretation. Note that according to the plain meaning of the phrase "the wife of your father" in v. 8 below, this is the first mention of a stepmother prohibition, but according to Rashi (following *Sanhedrin* 54a), this phrase repeats the mother/stepmother prohibition of v. 7 but impliedly extends it to conduct that occurs after the father's death.

11), "The shameful parts of the daughter of your father's wife, begotten by your father—she is your sister"? But my student Rabbi Abraham Hai Mainster says that a sister who is not from the same mother is not mentioned at all in v. 9; rather, this is the correct interpretation: "The shameful parts of your sister (the daughter of your mother, for the terms 'brother' and 'sister,' without more, are those from the same mother; cf. 'When a brother of yours, son of your mother... seduces you secretly [to idolatry]' (Deut. 13:7); 'If only you were like my brother, who nursed from my mother's breasts' (Songs 8:1)), whether she is *also* your father's daughter or *only* your mother's daughter, that is, whether she is born at home or born outside," as I have explained [this last phrase].

**18:10. "The shameful parts of your son's daughter, or of your daughter's daughter—you must not uncover her shameful parts, for they are your shameful parts [they are as if the flesh of your own body].**

*The shameful parts of your son's daughter, etc.* The prohibition of one's own daughter is not mentioned, for she has already been included in the prohibition of one's mother (that a son must not commit incest with his mother, and similarly a daughter with her father), and also in the prohibition of taking a mother and her daughter [below, v. 17].

*they are your shameful parts.* They are your own bone and flesh, and so this is as if you are uncovering your own shameful parts.

**18:11. "The shameful parts of the daughter of your father's wife, begotten by your father [but from another mother]—she is your sister; you must not uncover her shameful parts.**

**18:12. "The shameful parts of your father's sister you must not uncover; she is your father's flesh.**

**18:13. "The shameful parts of your mother's sister you must not uncover, for she is your mother's flesh.**

# Shadal on Leviticus

**18:14.** "The shameful parts of your father's brother you must not uncover; (that is) you must not approach his wife; she is your aunt.

*The shameful parts of your father's brother.* "The shameful parts of your mother's brother" are not mentioned, and in fact the wife of the mother's brother is not included in the [Torah's] class of forbidden relations, but is only in the secondary class forbidden under Rabbinic law.[15] The reason for this distinction is that the father's brother is from the same family as ours, unlike the mother's brother, who is from a different family, and the taking of his wife (once she is widowed or divorced) is not an "abomination." If you were to say that the mother's sister, too, is from a different family [and yet is a forbidden relation (v. 13)], this is not a valid claim, for the mother's sister is the mother's "flesh," unlike the wife of the mother's brother, who has no natural kinship with us.

**18:15.** "The shameful parts of your daughter-in-law you must not uncover; she is your son's wife; you must not uncover her shameful parts.

**18:16.** "The shameful parts of your brother's wife you must not uncover; she is the shameful parts of your brother.

**18:17.** "The shameful parts of a woman and of her daughter you must not uncover; not even her son's daughter or her daughter's daughter may you take, to uncover her shameful parts; they are one same flesh; it would be turpitude.

*it would be turpitude (zimmah).* The verb root *zamam* refers to a thought that one conceals; the word is derived from *zemam*, which is the Aramaic word for the "bit" or "muzzle" that stops up an animal's mouth. The thoughts that one conceals are mostly evil ones, but they may also

---

15 Twenty categories of women are classified as *sheniyyot*, or "secondary" kin who are forbidden to a man under Rabbinic law; these include his maternal or paternal grandmother, his great-granddaughter, and the wife of his mother's brother (see Maimonides, *Mishneh Torah, Ishut* 1:6).

be good ones. With respect to forbidden relations, the only one called *zimmah* is the taking of a woman and her daughter (in the present verse and in Lev. 20:14, below), because this is such an abominable act that one who does it is compelled to conceal it. In Ezek. 22:11 it is written, "And each has lewdly [*ve-zimmah*] defiled his daughter-in-law," for this act is similar to the taking of a woman and her daughter. Likewise, "And a man and his father go to the same maid" (Amos 2:7); this is mentioned as a thoroughly contemptible indecency. Later, the word *zimmah* was used for any indecent, abominable act, while *mezimmah* was used for any thought that a person would conceal in his heart, as in, "No purpose [*mezimmah*] of Yours can be thwarted" (Job 42:2). *Mezimmah* was also used as a synonym for "wisdom" or "cleverness," in other words, a person's ability to think thoughts and conceal them in his heart until the time comes to put them into effect, as in, "Discretion [*mezimmah*] shall watch over you, discernment shall guard you" (Prov. 2:11) (8 Tevet 5617 [1857]).

**18:18. "Nor may you take a woman while already having a sister of hers, causing her anguish, uncovering her [the second one's] shameful parts together with her, (that is) in her lifetime.**

*nor may you take, etc.* In vv. 18, 19, and 20, the list of forbidden relations [between men and women] concludes with those whose prohibition is not permanent but only temporary. The [taking of a wife's] sister is permitted after her sister's death, the menstruant is permitted at the end of her impurity, and a married woman is permitted after she is widowed or divorced (8 Tevet 5617).

**18:19. "Nor may you approach a woman, to uncover her shameful parts, during the impurity of her menstruation.**

**18:20. "And with the wife of your neighbor you must not lie carnally, contaminating yourself with her.**

**18:21. "And of your offspring you must not give to make of it a sacrifice to the Molech; doing so, you would dishonor the name of**

your God [that is, the idolatrous peoples would say that the Israelites know the inferiority of their own God, and thus they sacrifice animals to Him, but to other deities their own children]. **I am the Lord.**

**18:22.** "And with a male you must not have the intercourse of (a man with) a woman; it is an abominable thing.

**18:23.** "Nor may you have intercourse with any beast, contaminating yourself with it; and a woman must not place herself before a beast to cover herself with it; it is a (depraved) mixing.

**18:24.** "You must not contaminate yourselves with any of these things, for with all of these things were contaminated the peoples that I am about to chase away from your presence.

**18:25.** "And the country became impure from it, and I demanded account of them for their misdeeds, and the country vomited out its inhabitants.

*And the country became impure, etc.* According to R. Joseph Shabbetai Basevi, "the country" [*ha-arets*] means "the inhabitants of the country," as in, "And the people of all the countries [*ve-khol ha-arets*, lit. "and all the land"] went to Egypt" (Gen. 41:57), and the phrase [translated here as] "and I demanded account of them" [*va-efkod... aleha*, lit. "and I demanded account of it"] means "of its inhabitants." Then "the country vomited out its inhabitants," i.e., the country itself. However, according to R. Eliezer Elijah Igel, the phrase "and the country became impure" is itself to be taken literally, and the phrase *va-efkod avonah aleha* [lit. "and I demanded account of it for its misdeeds"] does not refer to the vomiting out of the country's inhabitants. Rather, the reference is to other punishments and plagues with which God struck the country, such as famine and pestilence; ultimately the country could no longer bear its inhabitants, who had brought such plagues upon it, and it vomited them out.[16]

---

16. Note that Shadal's own translation of this verse does not conform entirely to either Basevi's or Igel's interpretation, but incorporates elements of both.

18:26. "Observe you, therefore, My statutes and My laws, and do not do any of all these abominations, neither the native nor the foreigner dwelling among you.

18:27. "For those who inhabited that land before you practiced all these abominations, and the land became impure from it.

18:28. "Do not, then, make that land vomit you out, having contaminated it, as it vomited out [that is, as it is about to vomit out] the people who were before you.

18:29. "For whoever commits any of these abominations—the persons who have done so will go extinct from the midst of their people.

18:30. "Maintain, therefore, obedience to Me, so as not to practice any of the abominable statutes that were practiced before you, so that you do not become impure. I am the Lord your God [who requires this of you]."

# *Kedoshim*

*"Holy you must be" • Acts of charity and kindness*
*• "Judge your neighbor with justice"*
*• Sins against God and one's fellow • Illicit relations*

**19:1.** And the Lord spoke to Moses, saying:

**19:2.** "Speak to all the congregation of the children of Israel, and say to them: holy you must be, for holy am I, the Lord your God.

**19:3.** "You shall respect each one his father and his mother, and you shall observe My Sabbaths. I am the Lord your God.

**19:4.** "Do not turn to the idols, and gods of cast metal do not make for yourselves. I am the Lord your God.

**19:5.** "And when you make a sacrifice of contentment to the Lord, you shall make it so that it is accepted of you.

**19:6.** "On the day on which you make your sacrifice, it may be eaten, and also on the day after; but that which is left over of it until the third day must be burned.

**19:7.** "And if it is eaten on the third day, it becomes an abhorrent thing; it will not be accepted.[1]

**19:8.** "And one who ate of it [on the third day] incurs a sin, for he has profaned a holy thing to the Lord; and that individual will go extinct from the midst of his people [one who made an edible sacrifice was required to consume it within a short time, so that he would have to share it with his friends and with the poor].

**19:9.** "And when you reap the harvest of your land, you must not finish reaping the extremities of your field, nor gather (from the ground) the ears fallen in the harvest.

*you must not finish reaping the extremities of your field.* [The Torah] here mentions the prohibition on eating a sacrifice later than the day after [it was offered] and immediately follows it with [the law of *pe'ah*,] "the extremities of the field," because the reason it was commanded that the sacrifice be eaten within one or two days was that the offeror would be compelled to invite others to his sacrifice, so that they would eat it with him. If he were permitted to salt the meat of the sacrifice and preserve it for days or months, he alone would eat it with his household, but since the eating was forbidden later than the day after, he would be compelled to offer some of it to others, and this would bring about an act of charity and kindness—similar to leaving the extremities of the field [for the poor].

We do in fact find, in connection with sacrifices, that people were invited to eat of them; for example:

- "For the Lord has prepared a sacrifice, He has consecrated His guests" (Zeph. 1:7);
- "Invite Jesse to the sacrifice" (1 Sam. 16:3);
- "Sacrifices of peace-offerings were due from me; this day have I paid my vows. Therefore came I forth to meet you..." (Prov. 7:14-15).

---

1. See Shadal's discussion of this law in his comment at Lev. 7:18.

**19:10.** "Nor shall you gather the clusters of grapes that remain on your vine, nor shall you gather (from the ground) the fallen grains; (but) you shall leave them for the poor and for the foreigner. I am the Lord your God.

**19:11.** "Do not steal, and do not deny and do not lie to one to the harm of another.

**19:12.** "And do not swear in My name for falsehood; in doing so, you would profane the name of your God. I am the Lord.

**19:13.** "Do not defraud your neighbor, and do not rob (what is his); do not let the reward of the day laborer remain with you until the next day.

***Do not defraud*** *(lo ta'ashok).* One who defrauds [*oshek*] does not take from another's hand, but keeps to himself what he owes the other (Wessely). With regard to the origin of the word, it seems to me that the verb root *ashak* is derived from the root *akash* ("to pervert, to be crooked").

**19:14.** "Do not curse a deaf person, and before a blind person do not place a stumbling block; but you shall fear your God. I am the Lord.

***Do not curse a deaf person,*** *etc.* An admonition to one who causes harm in secret and says, "No one will see me."

**19:15.** "Do not do injustice in judgment; do not give deference to the poor person, and do not convey esteem to the great [powerful] person; judge your neighbor with justice.

**19:16.** "Do not be a talebearer [a sower of discord] among your people; nor may you remain a [passive] onlooker upon danger to the life of your neighbor. I am the Lord.

# Kedoshim

**19:17. "Do not hate your brother in your heart; (rather) reprove your neighbor, and (thus) you will not incur sin on his account.**

*and (thus) you will not incur sin on his account (ve-lo tissa alav ḥet).* If you hate him without reproving him, you will incur sin on his account, but if you reprove him and he does not accept the reproof, it seems that no sin is upon you if you hate him. Wessely's comment regarding hatred in one's heart makes no sense,[2] nor did he understand the wise opinion of the Rabbis in *Torat Kohanim* [*Sifra, Kedoshim* 4:8]. He thought that they interpreted the expression *lo tissa* in the sense of "raising one's voice" [*nesi'at kol*].[3] However, this was not their intended meaning; they said only that if you cause another's face to blanch in public, you incur a sin. If their meaning had been in accordance with Wessely's opinion, they ought to have said, "One might have thought that you were permitted to reprove him in a loud voice, but we learn otherwise from the phrase *lo tissa.*" However, from the Rabbis' actual statement—"One might have thought that you were permitted to reprove him and cause his face to change appearance, but we learn otherwise from the phrase *lo tissa alav ḥet*"—it is clear that their intended meaning was that your reproof should not be without compassion or mercy, for otherwise you would incur a sin.

**19:18. "Do not take revenge, and do not nourish hatred against the children of your people; but love for your neighbor that which you love for yourself. I am the Lord.**

*and do not nourish hatred (ve-lo tittor*, from the root *natar).* According to the plain meaning, *netirah* is revenge taken after the passage of time,

---

2.  In his comment in *Netivot ha-Shalom* on the phrase "Do not hate your brother in your heart," Wessely distinguished between "hatred in one's soul," which he said was not subject to rational choice or human control, and "hatred in one's heart," which he said was a matter of voluntary choice.
3.  In his comment on the phrase *ve-lo tissa alav ḥet*, Wessely interpreted these words to mean, "Do not raise your voice to announce his sin in public."

as in, "And He reserves wrath [*ve-noter*] for His enemies" (Nahum 1:2) (Wessely).[4]

***but love for your neighbor that which you love for yourself*** *(ve-ahavta le-re'akha kamokha).*[5] All sins that one commits against one's fellow are abhorrent per se, except for the taking of revenge, which appears to be proper justice. Therefore [the Torah] says with regard to it, "Love for your neighbor that which you love for yourself—just as you would not wish for others to take revenge on you, so you should not take revenge on your neighbor, even if your revenge would have been justified. And likewise in all matters, you should love for your neighbor that which you love for yourself."

Mendelssohn interpreted this phrase as meaning, "Love your neighbor with all the kinds of love with which you love yourself," the equality being in the quality of the love and not the quantity, where there is no conflict between the two objects of love [i.e., you and your neighbor].[6] This, however, comes close to the character trait of Sodom ("What is mine is mine, and what is yours is yours"—*Avot* 5:10), for how can I do good for my friend without my incurring a loss or burden, whether light or heavy? Of necessity there must always be a conflict between my benefit and the benefit of another, and it is impossible for me to give my friend even a small coin [*perutah*] without losing that coin from my own pocket.

---

4.  As Wessely goes on to point out in his comment to this verse, the Rabbis construed *netirah* to include bearing a grudge without any intention of taking revenge, and they also limited the prohibition of *netirah* to monetary matters, as stated in *Torat Kohanim* (*Sifra, Kedoshim* 4:11): "How far does the power of *netirah* extend? If one said to another, 'Lend me your spade,' and he did not lend him, and the next day the other said to him, 'Lend me your sickle,' and he answered, 'Here it is; I am not like you, who did not lend me your spade'—therefore the Torah says *lo tittor*."
5.  This phrase has more commonly been translated, "Love your neighbor as yourself."
6.  In his comment, Mendelssohn further explains that the Torah does not command one to benefit another where this would result in an undue burden on oneself, and that in such a case one's self-love takes precedence.

# Kedoshim

**19:19. "My statutes you shall observe; your animal you shall not mate with different species; your field you shall not sow with mixed species; nor shall you wear a garment woven of different materials (that is)** *shaatnez* **[of linen and wool].**

*shaatnez.* According to Jablonski and Forster, the word *shaatnez* is Egyptian and its original form is *shontnes*, meaning a wool and linen garment of many colors. All kinds of mixtures were prescribed by idolatrous statutes among the ancients.

**19:20. "If a man lies carnally with a woman who is the slave of a man, and held by him as if she were a wife, but who has not been redeemed, nor has she obtained her freedom, she will be (considered as if) unbound (in matrimony), (and thus) they will not be put to death, for she was not freed [in other words, a woman must not be at the same time a wife and a slave, and as long as the master does not free her, he does not have the right to have her and her lover punished as adulterers].**

*she will be (considered as if) unbound* (bikkoret tihyeh). [The word *bikkoret* is to be understood] as Nachmanides interprets it, [as the equivalent of] *hefker* ("unclaimed"); that is, she is not legally considered as a married woman, since she has not been freed, but she is to be considered as *hefker* so that they are not put to death as adulterers. In my opinion and Ibn Ezra's, she is an Israelite and not a Canaanite, but according to the Rabbis, even a Canaanite slave woman, once freed, may be validly married like any Israelite woman.[7]

The reason for this commandment is so that the master should not think to use the woman as a servant and also for sexual purposes; rather, either he should free her and take her as a wife, according to the right of daughters of Israel, or else she should remain unclaimed by him and anyone else alike.

---

7.  Ibn Ezra expresses the view that the woman in question is an Israelite who has been sold into servitude by her father as provided in Exod. 21:7. According to the Rabbis, however, the woman is a Canaanite slave (*Keritot* 11a).

# Shadal on Leviticus

The culpability [*asham*] in this case is unintentional—resulting from ignorance of the law—as in the cases enumerated in Lev. ch. 5, since the man who lies with her thinks that she is actually *hefker* and thus permitted to any man, though in fact this is not so. Rather, she is considered *bikkoret* ("unbound") only after the fact, so that they should not be put to death, but she is not *bikkoret* in the sense that anyone who likes may have sexual relations with her in the first place.

**19:21.** **"He will bring his sacrifice of repentance to the Lord, at the entrance of the tent of congregation, a ram (that is) in a sacrifice of repentance.**

**19:22.** **"And the priest will propitiate for him before the Lord, with the ram of the sacrifice of repentance, for the sin that he committed, and the sin committed by him will be pardoned for him.**

**19:23.** **"When you have entered into the [promised] land, and you will have planted any fruit-bearing tree, you must prohibit for yourselves its first produce; for three years it will be for you (as if) precluded; it must not be eaten.**

*it will be for you (as if) precluded (yihyeh lakhem arelim)*. The word *yihyeh* ("it will be") refers back to *piryo* ("its produce"). The word *peri* ("produce, fruit") is a collective noun that takes a plural adjective, on the model of, "And My people [*ammi*, singular] are in suspense [*telu'im*, plural]" (Hosea 11:7). Here, too, the phrase is to be construed as if it said, "Its fruit [*piryo*, singular] will be for you precluded fruits [*perot arelim*, plural]." See Maimonides, *Guide for the Perplexed* 3:37).[8]

---

8. There, Maimonides explains that the prohibition against eating the fruit of a tree for the first three years was intended to prevent the application of a method of witchcraft, as described in the ancient source "The Nabatean Agriculture," by which a "rotten substance" would be scattered around or under a newly planted tree to accelerate its productiveness. Maimonides notes that after three years, most fruit trees in the land of Israel bore fruit in the ordinary course of nature, without the application of such witchcraft.

# Kedoshim

**19:24.** "And in the fourth year all of your produce will be holy, in homage to the Lord. [The fruits themselves, or other foods of equal value, were to be eaten in the holy city.]

**19:25.** "In the fifth year, then, you will eat its produce [without any restriction], and doing that, you will have an abundant harvest. I am the Lord your God.

*I am the Lord your God (ani YHVH Eloheikhem).* Wherever it is written כִּי אֲנִי הֹ׳ אֱלֹהֵיכֶם [*ki ani YHVH Eloheikhem*, with a conjunctive-disjunctive *merkha-tipḥa* marking the words *ani YHVH*], God's name is linked with the word *ani* [and the phrase means "for I, the Lord, am your God"]. However, where the [introductory] word *ki* does not appear [and the accents do not link the words *ani YHVH*], God's name is linked with the word *Eloheikhem* [and the phrase means "I am the Lord your God"]. See my comment on the phrase *anokhi YHVH Elohekha* (Exod. 20:2).[9]

**19:26.** "You must not eat with the blood [that is, the meat of an animal that has not been well drained of blood. According to others, "around the blood," an expression alluding to the superstitious practice of slaughtering some animals over a pit, thinking to attract there the shades of the dead; see *Odyssey*, Book 11]; nor follow (superstitious) omens and auguries.

*You must not eat with the blood (al ha-dam*, lit. "upon the blood"). They would pour the blood into a pit and eat there the sacrifices they had made to demons and the souls of the dead, believing that they would come there to drink the blood, and that as a reward, the demons and souls would come to them in a dream and tell them the future (Nachmanides).[10]

**19:27.** "Do not cut in a circle the extremities (of the hair) of your head, and do not destroy the extremities of your beard.

---

9. There, Shadal notes that the accentuators, who set off the word *anokhi* with a disjunctive *tipḥa*, indicated that the phrase should be understood as "I am the Lord your God," and not "I, the Lord, am your God."
10. See also above, Lev. 17:13, and the footnote to that verse.

*and do not destroy the extremities of your beard (ve-lo tashḥit et pe'at zekanekha).* This "destruction of the extremities" [*hashḥatat pe'ah*] is mentioned in conjunction with the "incision for a dead person" [next v.]. Similarly, with respect to the priests (below, Lev. 21:5), it says, "Nor shall they shave [*lo yegalleḥu*] the extremities of their beard, nor shall they make any incision on their body"; see Ibn Ezra's comment there.[11]

According to the plain meaning [*peshat*], all Israelites are forbidden to "destroy" their beards for purposes of mourning the dead, while the priests are forbidden even to shave, also for the dead.[12]

**19:28. "And do not make any cutting in your bodies for a dead person, nor shall you make in yourselves incised writing. I am the Lord.**

*incised (ka'aka).* The Hebrew is related to the roots *taka* ("to thrust, insert") and *shaka* ("to sink, immerse").

**19:29. "Do not profane your daughter by prostituting her; in so doing, the country would be given over to fornication, and it would be filled with turpitude.**

*Do not profane (al teḥallel) your daughter by prostituting her.* After warning against incised writing, which is a symbol of subjugation to idolatry, [the Torah] forbids dedicating one's daughter to idolatry by

---

11. Commenting on Lev. 21:5, Ibn Ezra says that the prohibitions in that verse refer to mourning practices, and that the meaning of Lev. 19:27 is thus "clarified" [*hitbarer*]. In turn, Ibn Ezra's comment on Lev. 19:27 notes that "some say" this verse is juxtaposed with the prohibition of making an incision for a dead person because there were those who cut the extremities of their hair or "destroyed" the extremities of their beard for mourning purposes.

12. However, the normative halakhic view is that the prohibitions of this verse are of general application; authoritative sources such as *Makkot* 20a and *Shulḥan Arukh, Yoreh De'ah* 181 make no mention of the mourning context. These sources define "destruction" of the beard as its removal by razor, as opposed to scissors. *Makkot* 21a equates the kind of "shaving" [*gilluaḥ*] forbidden to priests (Lev. 21:5) with "destruction" with a razor.

prostituting her for the honor of idolatry. Because such women were called *kedeshot* ("sacred prostitutes"), a term related to *kedushah* ("holiness"), the text employs the terminology of *ḥillul* ("profanation") and says *al teḥallel*, in order to make it known that such an act is not sanctification but profanation.

Who will not laugh at Ibn Ezra, who interprets this verse to mean that after forbidding the cutting of one's body, [the Torah] forbids a young woman to make incisions in her flesh, for that will lead her to expose her flesh, and since a woman's voice is considered to be enticing [*ervah*], all the more so is making such incisions.

**19:30. "You shall observe My Sabbaths, and you shall respect My temple. I am the Lord.**

**19:31. "Do not turn to the *ovot* [demons, or shades of the dead, which ventriloquists used to cause people to believe that they made to speak] and to the *yidde'onim* [?][13]; do not seek to contaminate yourselves with them. I am the Lord your God.**

**19:32. "Before the hoary head you shall rise, and you shall respect the face of the old person, and you shall fear your God. I am the Lord.**

**19:33. "And when a foreigner dwells with you in your country, you must not oppress him.**

**19:34. "The foreigner dwelling with you must be equal for you to a native of yours, and you shall love for him that which you love for yourself, for you (too) have been foreigners in the country of Egypt. I am the Lord your God.**

*and you shall love for him that which you love for yourself (ve-ahavta lo kamokha)*. The ancient peoples loved only their fellow nationals, and

___

13. Left untranslated by Shadal due to uncertainty, this word has been understood by others as "familiar spirits," "wizards," or "necromancers."

the oppression of foreigners was not abhorrent in their eyes. Therefore it says here, "You shall love for him that which you love for yourself," i.e., treat him as you would want others to treat you if you were a foreigner. This is similar to what I wrote above (v. 18) on the phrase "Love for your neighbor that which you love for yourself."

**19:35. "Do not do iniquity in matters of justice, in the measure of length, in weight, and in the measure of volume.**

*in the measure of length... and in the measure of volume (ba-middah... u-va-mesurah). Middah* means the measurement of length, while *mesurah* refers to a containing vessel, such as the *ephah* or the *se'ah* (Wessely). The root *madad* ("to measure") originally denoted the spreading of one thing over another, as in, "And he [Elijah] stretched himself [*va-yitmoded*] upon the child" (1 Kings 17:21), and thence this term came to be used for the measurement of length, which involved the passing of a rope or a measuring rod over the object to be measured. Subsequently the term *medidah* was transferred to refer also to measurement with a container, as in, "They measured [*va-yamoddu*] [the manna] with the omer" (Exod. 16:18); "Who has measured [*madad*] the waters in the hollow of his hand?" (Isa. 40:12).

Wessely attacked Rashi [for limiting the term *mesurah* to a liquid measure], but he did not know that Rashi, too, mentioned both liquid and dry measures; so it appears in manuscript and in the printed versions of Venice and Amsterdam.[14] Although Rashi, in commenting on *Bava Metsi'a* 61b, did write that *mesurah* is a liquid measure, there he was expressing that view in interpreting the *baraita*,[15] but here he correctly explained the meaning of the word as used in this verse.

---

14. Although some editions give Rashi's comment on the word *u-va-mesurah* in this verse as, "This is a liquid measure," both the Chavel and the Rosenbaum-Silbermann editions have it as, "This is a liquid and dry measure."
15. The *baraita* in question, in discussing the law of honest measurements in Lev. 19:35, says that one should not fill up a *mesurah* in such a way as to make foam.

**19:36.** "You shall have just balances, just weights, a just *ephah*, and a just *hin*. I am the Lord your God, Who brought you out of Egypt.

**19:37.** "You shall thus observe all My statutes and all My laws, and carry them out. It is I, the Lord [Who requires this of you]."

**20:1.** And the Lord spoke to Moses, saying:

**20:2.** "To the children of Israel themselves you shall say: Whoever of the children of Israel, or of the foreigners dwelling in Israel, gives of his own offspring to the Molech must be put to death; the people of the country must stone him.

**20:3.** "And I will turn Myself against that individual, and I will make him go extinct from among his people [see Gen. 17:14]; for of his offspring he has given to the Molech, so as to render My temple impure [in the opinion of others], and to profane My holy name [see above, Lev. 18:21].

*And I will turn Myself against that individual.* After he is stoned, to cause him "to go extinct from among his people," that is, to bring it about that no descendants will remain from him and that his name will be erased, for this is what is meant by *karet* ("excision").[16]

*so as to render My temple impure.* For in God's Temple they would sacrifice oxen, sheep, or goats, while on the altar of Molech they would sacrifice human beings. Thus, it would seem as if the table of the Lord was contemptible [cf. Malachi 1:7], because they would offer upon it [merely] the tallow and blood of animals, while the altar of Molech was pure and honorable, for their they would offer human sacrifice (Abravanel).

---

16. The reference to Gen. 17:14 in Shadal's translation is to his comment on the phrase, "That person will be cut off [taken away] from among his people (*ve-nikhretah ha-nefesh ha-hi*)," where he explains that *karet* is to be understood as a "punishment by the hand of Heaven," i.e., that the person would go childless and die before his time, contra Clericus, who maintained that *karet* meant "banishment."

**20:4. "But if the people of the land close their eyes when that man gives of his offspring to the Molech, so as not to put him to death—**

*the people of the land.* These are the members of his family, as it says subsequently [next. v.], "against his kin."

**20:5. "I will turn Myself against that man and against his kin, and I will cause him and all (his accomplices), who stray after him to go fornicating after the Molech, to become extinct from among their people.**

**20:6. "And if a person turns himself to the *ovot* or the *yidde'onim*, fornicating after them, I will turn Myself against that individual, and I will cause him to go extinct from among his people.**

**20:7. "Sanctify yourselves and be holy, for I, the Lord, am your God.**

**20:8. "Observe My statutes and carry them out; I, the Lord, have declared you holy [I chose you, so that you should be so].**

**20:9. "So anyone who curses his father or his mother will be put to death; his father or his mother he has cursed; the guilt of his death is in him.**

*the guilt of his death is in him (damav bo, lit. "his blood is in him").* That which is found in Rashi's comment [in some editions], "Compare *damo be-nafsho* (lit. "its blood in its soul") [see above, Lev. 17:14], is an error; it should read, "Compare *damo be-rosho* ("His blood shall be upon his own head," Josh. 2:19). After some years I found a small Bible [with Rashi] printed in Amsterdam in the year 5460 (1700) in which it was written, in parentheses, ס״א בראשו ("in other books, *be-rosho*").[17]

**20:10. "And when one commits adultery with a married woman—commits adultery with the wife of his neighbor!—the adulterer and the adulteress will be put to death.**

---

17. The reading *be-rosho* is generally found in current editions of Rashi.

*commits adultery with the wife of his neighbor!* [This extra phrase is] like "his father or his mother he has cursed" [in the preceding verse] (Ibn Ezra), that is, "a man who does such an evil thing."[18]

20:11. **"And when one lies with the wife of his father, he has uncovered the shameful parts of his father; both of them will be put to death; the guilt of their death is in them.**

20:12. **"And when one lies with his daughter-in-law, they will both be put to death; they have committed a [depraved] mixing; the guilt of their death is in them.**

20:13. **"And when one has with a male the intercourse of (a man with) a woman, they have both committed an abomination; they will be put to death; the guilt of their death is in them.**

20:14. **"And when one takes a woman and her mother, it is turpitude; they will be burned, he and they, so that there may not be turpitude among you.**

*and they.* The two women, if the first one knows that the man has taken the second, and she nevertheless remains with him and subjects herself to intercourse with him (Samuel Solomon Olper).

20:15. **"And when one has his intercourse with a beast, he will be put to death, and (also) the beast you shall kill.**

20:16. **"And when a woman places herself before any beast to cover herself with it, you shall kill the woman and the beast; they must be put to death; the guilt of their death is in them.**

---

18. Compare Shadal's comment on Gen. 9:5, where the verse reads, "And of your blood, which is of your life, I demand account. From every animal I demand account of it; and from man, from man his brother, will I demand account of the life of man." Shadal points out that the phrase "from man his brother" is a kind of elliptical phrase that serves only to add force to the command, and for comparison he cross-refers to the extra phrase here.

# Shadal on Leviticus

*the guilt of their death is in them.* This is said of the animal as well here, but not in the verse above, for here the animal is the active agent (Isaac Pardo). Therefore in the verse above, the participants are mentioned separately, and it says, "He will be put to death, and (also) the beast you shall kill," while here they are mentioned together: "You shall kill the woman and the beast." It is true that the animal has no knowledge of good or evil, and thus it would not be strictly correct to say of it that "the guilt of its death is in it," but the Torah spoke in this way in order to impress more greatly on people's hearts that any perpetrator of an abominable act will receive punishment.

**20:17. "And when one takes his sister, the daughter of his father or the daughter of his mother, and sees her shameful parts, and she sees his shameful parts [while they should have held such a union in horror, and sibling intimacy should not have exceeded its proper limits], it is an ignominious thing, and they will go extinct in the sight of their compatriots [that is, the extinction of their name will not be long in coming]; he uncovered the shameful parts of his sister! He will bear the punishment for it.**

*and sees her shameful parts, etc.* For even such sight is indecent between a brother and sister, because they grow up together and their hearts are [normally] hardened against each other[19]; therefore it is appropriate to be strict with them even with regard to such sight, and because they thought to act in secret, they are punished by going extinct in the sight of their compatriots.

*it is an ignominious thing (ḥesed).* Cf. "Lest he that hears it revile you [yeḥassedkha]" (Prov. 25:10). A similar word occurs in Aramaic; see Rashi [who notes that the Aramaic equivalent of the Hebrew ḥerpah ("shame, disgrace") is ḥissuda].

---

19. Here, Shadal appears to be taking a position that differs from the view that he expresses in his comment on Lev. 18:6, that "if taking a sister were permitted, most men would marry their sisters."

# Kedoshim

**20:18. "And when one lies with a menstruating woman and uncovers her shameful parts—he has denuded her font, and she has uncovered her own font of blood!—they will both go extinct from among their people.**

**20:19. "And the shameful parts of your mother's sister, or of your father's sister, you must not uncover, for [one who did this] would uncover his own flesh, and [the man and the woman] would bear its punishment.**

*And the shameful parts of your mother's sister, etc.* Much further study is needed as to why in this section, which deals with punishments, this verse alone appears in the form of an admonition ("you must not uncover") rather than providing a punishment ([which would have been introduced with the formula] "and when one lies with..."). Among all the commentators, only Rashi makes note of this.[20] Another matter for further study is the reversal of the order in which the illicit relations are listed in the *parashah* of *Aharei Mot* [Lev. ch. 18] and in this *parashah*. Also, the prohibition of taking two sisters is omitted here, perhaps because it is permitted to take one after the other dies. As for Ibn Ezra's intimation that this omission is for the sake of Jacob's honor, this is "tasteless food without salt" [cf. Job 6:6], and Abravanel has refuted him.[21]

As to the punishment for the one who takes his father's sister or his mother's sister, concerning which the verse states that the parties to this offense "would bear its punishment," without specifying what

---

20. Rashi comments on this verse that the Torah here repeats the admonition given above, in Lev. 18:12-13, to make it known that the prohibitions regarding one's parents' sisters extend to sisters on their father's side as well as sisters on their mother's side.

21. Ibn Ezra's comment says that "the enlightened one will understand" why the punishment for taking two sisters is omitted here. Abravanel, noting that Ibn Ezra was making a veiled reference to the fact that Jacob had married two sisters, says that Ibn Ezra's opinion makes no sense, given that the prohibition was not yet in force in Jacob's time, but came into effect only after the Torah was given. Abravanel goes on to say that the reason why the punishment for taking two sisters is omitted here is simply that this punishment is the same as the one for all the other incest offenses, namely *karet*.

their penalty would be, perhaps it is the same as in the subsequent verse, which states that they [a man and his aunt] "will bear the punishment of their sin; they will die without offspring," i.e., the punishment for both of these [pairs of offenders] is to die childless.

Yet another matter for study is why the verse mentions the mother's sister before the father's sister. Joseph Shabbetai Basevi says that since a son is more affectionate toward his mother than toward his father, it is likely that he will desire his mother's sister rather than his father's sister.

It seems to me that vv. 19, 20, and 21 deal with matters that are distinct and different from those at issue in other illicit relationships, for when the prohibition of lying with a menstruating woman is mentioned in v. 18, this completes the discussion of illicit relationships in which one engages out of desire, and henceforward [God] admonishes a man who has no children and takes a woman to obtain offspring from her. For this reason He begins with admonitory language and says, "You must not uncover..." In other words, "Do not think that what I admonished you about in the previous section concerned only one who acts out of desire, and not one who acts for the sake of obtaining offspring and perpetuating his name," for levirate marriage [*yibbum*] for the purpose of perpetuating a [deceased and childless] brother's name was commonly practiced among them, and perhaps even with respect to other illicit relationships [besides a sister-in-law], they would sometimes take a permissive position if the purpose was for the sake of Heaven. Thus, relations with the mother's sister, the father's sister, the uncle's wife, and [in most circumstances] the brother's wife are forbidden, and in each of these cases the punishment is to die without children, as opposed to what the man taking these women would have intended, which was to obtain offspring.

A man taking a woman for the purpose of having children would undoubtedly choose a woman who had already given birth, and therefore there was no need to mention here the permitted case of *yibbum*, for this practice was observed when there was no offspring, and if the brother died childless, it would follow that the dead man's wife had never given birth (it is possible that she might have borne another man's child before marrying the brother in question, but Scripture speaks of the common case, in which she would have married the brother as a virgin and not a widow). If the living brother was seeking a wife to obtain progeny [for himself], he would not [normally] choose the widow of his brother who died childless. Thus, as I have said, in all of these cases [in vv. 19-21] the punishment is to die without children; this is stated explicitly in the two verses that follow the present one (v. 19), but in this verse the penalty for the offense is not spelled out; rather, it says that the offenders "would bear its punishment." It may be assumed that the intended meaning is as it is specified in the two subsequent verses, in which it is written, "They will bear the punishment of their sin; they will die without offspring" (v. 20), and "They will be deprived of offspring" (v. 21). Everything I have written concerning this verse and the two that follow is merely conjecture.

**20:20. "And when one lies with his aunt, he uncovers the shameful parts of his uncle; they will bear the punishment of their sin; they will die without offspring.**

**20:21. "And when one takes the wife of his brother, it is a disgraceful action; he has uncovered the shameful parts of his brother; they will be deprived of offspring.**

***it is a disgraceful action*** *(niddah hi).* [This phrase refers to] the cohabitation (Rashi), not the woman [although the Hebrew might have been understood to mean "she is a woman who should be kept apart"], for otherwise it would have said *niddah hi lo* ("she is, *to him,* a woman who should be kept apart"). Rather, *niddah* [as used here] is a noun that signifies "distancing," as in *niddat devotah* ("her menstruation," lit. "the distancing of her menstruation," Lev. 12:2).

**20:22. "You shall observe, then, all of My statutes and all of My laws, and you shall carry them out; otherwise the country to which I am about to lead you to dwell in will vomit you out.**

**20:23. "And do not follow the statutes of the nations that I am about to drive out from your presence, for they have done all these things and they became intolerable to Me.**

# Shadal on Leviticus

**20:24.** "And so I said to you, 'You will possess their land, and I will give it to you to possess, (it being) a land that flows with milk and honey.' It is I, the Lord, your God, Who have distinguished you from the other peoples.

**20:25.** "And you shall distinguish the pure beasts from the impure, and the pure flying creatures from the impure, and you shall not render yourselves abhorrent through [that is, eating] those beasts and those flying creatures, or any animal crawling on the ground that I have marked out to you to be held as impure.

**20:26.** "And you shall be holy to Me, for holy am I , the Lord; and I have selected you from the other peoples, so that you be Mine.

**20:27.** "And a man or a woman, those who have to themselves [that is, purport to have] *ov* or *yidde'oni*, will be put to death; they will be stoned; the guilt of their death is in them."

# *Emor*

*Priestly restrictions • Animals acceptable for sacrifice •*
*"You shall not slaughter on one same day the mother and*
*its offspring" • "These are My solemn occasions" • The*
*blasphemer's punishment*

**21:1. The Lord said to Moses, "Say as follows to the priests, sons of Aaron: No one of his class may render himself impure through any dead person [that is, no one who is from the lineage of Aaron may touch a dead body, nor be in a house where a dead body is].**

*No one of his class (be-ammav,* lit. "in his people") *may render himself impure through any dead person.* No man among the clan [*am*] of priests may become impure through a dead person; cf. "he shall take to wife a virgin of his class [*me-ammav*]" (v. 14 below) (Rashbam), for according to the plain meaning, she [i.e., the wife of the high priest] must be a member of the priestly clan.[1]

---

1. Philo (*Special Laws* 22:110) maintained that the high priest's wife had to be the daughter of a priest. However, this does not appear to be the normative halakhic view. The Jerusalem Talmud (*Yevamot* 8:2), interpreting Lev. 21:14, states that the requirement of *me-ammav* excludes a convert, the implication being that the high priest may marry a virgin from any tribe of Israel. This view is specifically

# Shadal on Leviticus

**21:2.** **"Except for one who is his flesh [his close relative, and typically lives] near him: for his mother (that is), and for his father, and for his son, and for his daughter, and for his brother.**

**21:3.** **"As well as for his virgin sister, close to him [living in the paternal house], who has not had a husband; for her, he will render himself impure.**

*who has not had a husband.* For if she had been married, presumably she would have had children who would have taken care of her burial. The Torah spoke only of the typical case, for most married women have children; [even] if she did not have children, perhaps her husband would have rendered himself impure for her as if she were a *met mitsvah* [i.e., a dead person with no one else to bury her], or else he would have hired buriers.

**21:4.** **"The chief of his class [see v. 10] (however) must not (ever) render himself impure, for it would profane him.**

*The chief of his class (ba'al be-ammav).* The high priest (Onkelos and Wessely).[2]

**21:5.** **"They [the priests] shall not make a baldness in their head [they must not tear their hair for the death of anyone], nor shall they shave the extremities of their beard, nor shall they make any incision in their body.**

---

adopted by Rabbi S. R Hirsch and the Netsiv in their comments on Lev. 21:14.

2.  At one point, Shadal took the alternate view (found in the Lutzki 672 manuscript) that *ba'al be-ammav* means "any husband of the priestly clan," and that the plain meaning of the verse is that no priest may render himself impure by burying his wife, as there will generally be other family members (such as her children or her parents) who would be obligated to assume this responsibility. Shadal notes that the halakhic view is less strict and allows a priest to bury his wife as long as she was from a class of women that he was permitted to marry.

**21:6. "Holy they must be to their God, so as not to dishonor the
name of their God; for they present the sacrifices to be burned to the
Lord, the bread of their God, and so they must be holy.**

**21:7. "They shall not take a woman (who has been) a harlot, or
debased, and likewise a woman divorced from her husband they
shall not take; for he is holy to his God.**

*or debased (va-ḥalalah).* According to Ibn Ezra, this is a woman who
is less "flagrant" [*mefursemet*] than a harlot [*zonah*], and according to
A. H. Mainster, this even includes a victim of rape.[3]

*a woman divorced from her husband (ve-ishah gerushah me-ishah).*[4]
Know that the example [of a supposedly parallel usage] given by

---

3.  Milgrom asserts that "it is altogether plausible that in the biblical
    period rape disqualified a woman from marrying a priest" (*Leviticus:
    A Book of Ritual and Ethics*, p. 264). Arnold Ehrlich, in his comment
    on the word *va-ḥalalah* in Lev. 21:7, says that the term includes a
    rape victim. However, R. David Zvi Hoffmann, in his comment
    ad loc., says (with respect to the *peshat*, or plain meaning), "It is
    impossible to agree with the later exegetes who say that *ḥalalah*
    means a woman who has been raped, for if so, the prohibition of
    the *zonah* ('harlot') would be entirely superfluous." The halakhic
    definition of *ḥalalah* is restricted to a daughter of a priest and a
    *zonah* or divorcee (or of a high priest and a widow), or a *zonah*
    or divorcee herself if she has had relations with another priest (or
    a widow who has had relations with a high priest) (Maimonides,
    *Issurei Bi'ah* 19:1- 2). The halakhic definition of *zonah*, in turn,
    is not a "prostitute" in the ordinary sense of the word, but is either
    (1) a non-Israelite woman, or (2) an Israelite woman who has had
    relations with a man whom she is forbidden to marry (*Issurei Bi'ah*
    18:1-2).
4.  Note that Shadal's Italian translation of this phrase, *una donna
    ripudiata dal marito*, may be rendered either as "a woman repudiated
    [or 'divorced'] by her husband," or as "a woman divorced from
    her husband." In order to have the translation conform with the
    commentary, the second alternative has been given here in the
    English.

# Shadal on Leviticus

Mendelssohn in his introduction, *Or la-Netivah*[5]—*ha-tappuaḥ ne'ekhal me-Reuven* ("the apple was eaten by Reuben")—is not the way of Hebrew or its cognate languages. Rather, when the speaker knows who the eater was, he says *Reuven akhal et ha-tappuaḥ* ("Reuben ate the apple"), but if he does not know who the eater was, then he says *ha-tappuaḥ ne'ekhal* ("the apple was eaten," using a conjugation [*nif'al*] that indicates the reception of action), without mentioning the agent. Thus, the [passive] conjugations that indicate the reception of action are known as conjugations that do not identify the agent, for the early grammarians knew that it is not the way of Hebrew or its cognate languages to mention the agent in the ablative [e.g., "...by Reuben"], and they knew that if one were to say (as in *Kerem Ḥemed* vol. 7 [1843], p. 100) *ahuv mimmenni me'od*, the import of these words would be, "He is loved much more than I am," and not at all "He is very dear to me" [i.e., "He is much loved by me"].[6]

Rather, it is known that the word *min* [sometimes shortened to a prefix *me-* or *mi-*] is employed to indicate a causative factor, as in *me-ḥatat nevi'eha* ("It is because of the sins of her prophets"—Lam. 4:13); similarly, it was said, "And no more will all flesh perish by means of the waters of the flood [*mi-mei ha-mabbul*]" (Gen. 9:14). Another similar example is *nivle'u min ha-yayin* ("they are confused because of wine"—Isa. 28:7), not that the wine is the agent [i.e., the phrase should not be

---

5. *Or la-Netivah* (Berlin, 1783) was Mendelssohn's introductory pamphlet to his *Netivot ha-Shalom*. The last section of this pamphlet reviewed the grammatical principles that governed the larger work's Bible translation and commentary.

6. Shadal is citing an anonymous article in which he himself is the subject of both praise and criticism. (Elsewhere, Shadal identifies the nameless author as R. Solomon Judah Loeb Rapoport; see *Iggerot Shadal*, vol. 8, p. 1104.) Among other things, the author says, "Indeed Luzzatto is... *ahuv mimmenni me'od* [obviously the author means "much loved by me"], and is in fact deserving of being loved by any reader of his enlightened and beneficial books, but nevertheless he is a creature of clay like any other man...." Note that Shadal, in pointing out this author's grammatical error, is at the same time aiming a sarcastic barb at him, as if to say, "This person, in his own clumsy way, is admitting than I am loved much more than he is!"

# Emor

translated as "they are confused *by* the wine"]. The proof of this is the subsequent phrase, *ta'u min ha-shekhar* (ibid.), which must mean "they stagger *because of* strong drink," because the verb *ta'u* ("they stagger") is not in the passive. Likewise, *mi-keshet ussaru* ("their hands are bound for fear of the bow"—Isa. 22:3), which does not mean "they are bound *by* the bow," for a bow may strike or kill, but it does not bind.

Gesenius, in his *Thesaurus* [Leipzig, 1835, vol. 1] (p. 803), cites both of these verses from Isaiah to prove the existence [in Hebrew] of the ablative following the passive, but this is erroneous. He brings as further proof the phrase *ke-gibbor mitronen mi-yayin* (Ps. 78:65), which he interprets as meaning "like a mighty man who is overcome by wine (*victus a vino*)," but even if one assumes, like him, that the root *run* is used here in the sense of "overcoming," as in Arabic, it would make no sense to any linguist, or to anyone who has a discerning ear for Hebrew speech, to understand from the words *mitronen mi-yayin* that wine has overcome a person; to the contrary, the phrase is properly understood to mean "like a man who is mightier than wine," that is, one who has overcome wine.

In addition, this scholar cites the phrase *et nishberet mi-yammim be-ma'amakei mayim* (Ezek. 27:34). While it is true that this is a difficult verse, it is still extremely unlikely that *nishberet mi-yammim* means that the city [of Tyre] has been "broken by the seas," for previously (v. 26) it says that "the east wind has broken you in the heart of the seas," not that the seas broke it. Besides, what would it mean to say that it was "broken by the seas in the depths of the waters"? Therefore I say that this verse is opaque and one cannot use it for purposes of comparison.[7]

We also find the verse, "...like the slain that lie in the grave, whom You remember no more; *mi-yadekha nigzaru*" (Ps. 88:6), but this does not at all mean that "they are cut off *by* your hand." Rather, the meaning is elucidated by its companion phrases:

---

7. Shadal's own commentary on Ezekiel offers no comment on this phrase. Many English translations render *nishberet mi-yammim* as "broken by the seas"; *Metsudat David* and Malbim interpret the word *mi-yamim* as "because of the seas."

- *nigzarti mi-neged einekha* ("I am cut off from before Your eyes"—Ps. 31:23);
- *ki nigzar me-erets ḥayyim* ("for he was cut off out of the land of the living"—Isa. 53:8);
- *ki nigzar mi-beit YHVH* ("for he was cut off from the house of the Lord"—2 Chron. 26:21)

—each of which [indicate that the word *nigzar*] denotes a separation and a distancing, and that the prefix *mem* in *mi-yadekha* is like the *mem* that appears in *mi-neged einekha, me-erets ḥayyim,* and *mi-beit YHVH,* and that it relates back to the place from which there is a distancing [i.e., it means "from," not "by"]. Thus, the meaning [of the phrase *mi-yadekha nigzaru*] is as Mendelssohn translates and as R. Joel Brill comments, "they will not feel Your blows or Your strong hand"; or else it is as Gesenius interprets it, "they are far removed from Your help." This is similar to the Aramaic translation, *me-appei shekhintakh itpalagun* ("they are separated from before Your presence").

Know that the roots *gazar, garaz,* and *garash* are all "brothers," and thus we find the phrase *nigrashti mi-neged einekha* ("I am cast out from before Your eyes"—Jonah 2:5), with a *shin* [as opposed to the *zayin* in the parallel phrase *nigzarti mi-neged einekha* in Ps. 31:23]. Here, too [Lev. 21:7], in the phrase *gerushah me-ishah,* the prefix *mem* does not connect a passive party to an active party [i.e., the phrase does not mean "divorced *by* her husband"]; rather, it indicates the place from which there is a distancing, that is, "a woman who is separated and distanced *from* her husband."

Another example that we find is *ha-nishkaḥim minni ragel* (lit. "they [i.e., the waters of a stream] are forgotten from the foot"—Job 28:4), but it is not the foot that is forgetting [i.e., this does not mean "forgotten *by* the foot"]. Rather, the meaning is as Ibn Ezra explained, that they are forgotten *because of* "the foot," that is, as a result of being stepped through by many people. In other words, the stream has dried up and people walk through it, to the extent that its place can no longer be recognized.

We do find the following:

- "It is of the Lord [*me-YHVH*] that a man's footsteps are established" (Ps. 37:23);
- "The words of the wise... are given from one Shepherd [*me-ro'eh eḥad*] (Eccl. 12:11); and in the Aramaic of Daniel and Ezra:
- "I have made a decree [*minni sim te'em*]" (Dan. 3:29, Ezra 4:19); and
- "Until I have made a decree [*ad minni ta'ma yittesam*]" (Ezra 4:21).

It seems to me that all of these are [euphemistic] usages that convey honor and greatness, and that the speakers' intention in these verses was not to make the noun or pronoun preceded by *me-* or *min* into the actual agent; that is, the speakers did not precisely mean to say that the decree was promulgated *by* the king or that a man's footsteps were established *by* God. Rather, the speakers intended to say that the matter issued "from his presence," in the manner of:

- "The word has come forth from the Lord [*me-YHVH*]" (Gen. 24:50);
- "May my judgment go out from before You [*mi-l'fanekha*]" (Ps. 17:2);
- "Let a royal edict issue from him [*mi-l'fanav*]" (Esther 1:19);
- "An order is hereby issued from me [*min kodomai*]" (Dan. 6:27).

But even when the intention is not to speak in a manner conveying greatness or honor, it is unlikely that in Hebrew, the passive party would be connected to the active party with a *mem* prefix; see the comments below on the phrases *ve-ha-arets te'azev mehem* (Lev. 26:43) and *kol ḥerem asher yoḥoram min ha-adam* (Lev. 27:29).

Since the verse "It is of the Lord that a man's footsteps are established, though he desires his way [*ve-darko yeḥpats*]" (Ps. 37:23) has come to our attention, I will express my opinion about it, for in my view its meaning is quite simple, yet the commentators have gone far afield. I think the meaning of this verse is exactly the same as that which is written in Prov. 15:9, "A man's heart devises his way; but the Lord directs his steps." The phrase here, *ve-darko yeḥpats*, corresponds to "A man's heart devises his way [*lev adam yeḥashev darko*]"; there is no missing *bet*, as Ibn Ezra thought.[8] The meaning is that man is a master of free will, and he is the one who desires and chooses his own way and who devises in his heart what he will do, but the completion of his action does not depend on his own power, but is in the hand of Heaven, for "it is of the Lord that a man's footsteps are established." If the way that he is going is not correct in the eyes of the Lord, his footsteps will not be established, and he will be unable to complete his way and fulfill his devisings.

**21:8. "And you must regard him as sacred, for he presents the bread of your God; he must be sacred to you, for holy am I, the Lord, Who makes you holy.**

**21:9. "And the daughter of a priest, who dishonors herself by fornicating, dishonors her father; she must be burned.**

*who dishonors herself* (ki teḥel). Perhaps the root ḥalal ("to dishonor") is from kalal ("to be light" or "lightly esteemed"); likewise, anything that is ḥol ("common, profane") can be said to be kal ("light"), the opposite of nikhbad ("honorable") [from the root kavad, "to be weighty"].

**21:10. "But the priest who is superior to his brothers, he upon whose head will have been poured the oil of anointing, and who will have been installed to don the vestments [that are exclusive to the high priest], will not make his head disheveled, nor will he rend his garments [he will not do any act of mourning].**

**21:11. "Nor shall he come close to any dead person, nor shall he render himself impure (even) for his father or for his mother.**

**21:12. "And from the temple he shall not go forth; otherwise he would dishonor the temple of his God; for he has upon him the diadem of the oil of anointing of his God. I am the Lord.**

---

8.    Ibn Ezra understood Ps. 37:23 to mean, "It is of the Lord that a man's footsteps are established, and He delights in his way." Accordingly, he interpreted the phrase ve-darko yeḥpats (ודרכו יחפץ) as if it said ובדרכו יחפץ.

**21:13.** "He shall take to wife a woman in her virginity.

**21:14.** "Widow, or divorcee, debased woman, or harlot—these he shall not take; but he shall take to wife a virgin of his class.[9]

**21:15.** "Otherwise he would render his offspring profaned among his class [fallen from the priestly rank], for I, the Lord, have declared him holy."

**21:16.** And the Lord spoke to Moses, saying:

**21:17.** "Speak to Aaron, saying: Any of your progeny, (and so) for all the ages to come, who has some defect must not approach to present the bread of his God.

**21:18.** "Whoever (I say) has a defect must not approach: a blind man, or a lame man, or one who has a crushed nose, or some part that is too long.

**21:19.** "Or one who has a broken leg, or a broken arm.

**21:20.** "Or a hunchback, or one who is gaunt, or bleary-eyed, or scabby, or herpetic, or herniated.

***bleary-eyed*** *(tevallul).* The Hebrew resembles *shablul*, otherwise known as *ḥiliz* or *ḥillazon* ("snail"), a creeping thing that emits slime. Likewise, the eye of the person referred to here drips slime.

***herniated*** *(mero'aḥ ashekh).* The Hebrew is derived from *revaḥ* and *revaḥah* [i.e., "spread out"]; so translated Saadiah Gaon. According to others, *mero'aḥ ashekh* means one who has a crushed testicle, from *meru'aḥ* ("smearing, spreading") (e.g.. "let them spread it [*ve-yimreḥu*] on the boil," Isa. 38:21), and *eshekh*, which is a word for "testicle." Gesenius agreed with this interpretation and said that this is the meaning of *eshekh* in Syriac also; that it is from the root *shakhah*, which in the

9. See Lev. 21:1 and the accompanying comment and footnote.

# Shadal on Leviticus

Ethiopian language means "to indicate"; and that testicles were called by this term [*eshekh*] because witnesses used to testify [by swearing] upon their male organs, thus the Latin *testis* ("witness," "testicle").[10]

**21:21. "Whoever of the progeny of Aaron the priest has some defect shall not come near to present the sacrifices to be burned to the Lord; he has an imperfection; he must not come near to present the bread of his God.**

**21:22. "He will be able (however) to eat of the bread of his God, (that is) of the most holy things, and of the (other) holy things.**

**21:23. "But he must not go to the door-curtain or come near the altar, for he has an imperfection; otherwise he would profane the things that are holy to Me, for it is I, the Lord, Who have declared them holy."**

**21:24. Moses spoke [expounded all of this] to Aaron and to his sons, and to all the children of Israel.**

**22:1. And the Lord spoke to Moses, saying:**

**22:2. "Speak to Aaron and to his sons, so that they employ the necessary respect with the holy things of the children of Israel, (the things, that is) that they consecrate to Me; otherwise they would dishonor My holy name. I am the Lord.**

**22:3. "Say to them: For all the ages to come, whoever of your progeny comes near the holy things, consecrated by the children of Israel to the Lord, having upon him some impurity of his, that individual will go extinct from My presence. I am the Lord.**

---

10. This etymological theory has been called into question by modern linguists; see, for example, Editors of the *American Heritage Dictionaries, Word Histories and Mysteries* (2004), s.v. "testis," p. 282.

**22:4.** "Any one of the progeny of Aaron who is leprous or who has blennorhea must not eat of the holy things until he is pure, as well as one who has touched any (individual who is) impure through a dead person, or anyone from whom has issued a flow of seed—

**22:5.** "Or one who has touched some swarming thing from which he could contract impurity or some person from whom he could contract impurity, through whatever uncleanness that may be his—

**22:6.** "One who has touched one of these will be impure until night, and he shall not eat of the holy things without having bathed his body in water.

**22:7.** "The sun having set, he will be pure; then he will be able to eat of the holy things, for this is his bread.

**22:8.** "An animal that has died of itself or has been torn to pieces he shall not eat, for it would render him impure. I am the Lord.

**22:9.** "They shall observe My prescriptions, so that they do not incur sin for these [that is, for the holy things] and have to die for them, profaning them. It is I, the Lord, Who have declared them holy.

*so that they do not incur sin for these* (alav, lit. "for it"). For the holy food that he eats (mentioned above in v. 7: "then he will be able to eat of the holy things, for this is his bread.")

*and have to die for them.* In sin.

*profaning them (ki yeḥalleluhu,* lit. "profaning it"). The holy food.

**22:10.** "And no stranger may eat a holy thing; the resident foreigner who has established residence with a priest, as well as the hireling (of the priest), shall not eat a holy thing.

**22:11.** "When, however, a priest makes acquisition of an individual [that is, of a non-Israelite slave] purchased with his money, he will be able to eat of it; and every (slave) born in his house will be able to eat of his bread [even of holy things].

*When, however, a priest makes acquisition, etc.* The wife of a priest may eat of *terumah* [the priestly "tribute"], though this is not mentioned in the Torah. They [the Rabbis] derived this from the phrase [in this verse] *kinyan kaspo* ("purchased with his money"), but in my opinion, the female is included with the male.[11]

**22:12.** "When the daughter of a priest becomes the wife of a stranger [not a priest], she will not be able to eat of the sacred tributes.

**22:13.** "But when the daughter of a priest is a widow or divorced, and does not have offspring, and returns to her paternal house as in her childhood, she will be able to eat of the bread of her father, but no stranger shall eat of it.

**22:14.** "But when someone eats a holy thing by error, he will repay the priest for the holy thing, with the addition of a fifth.

**22:15.** "Let (the priests) not profane the holy things of the children of Israel, (the things, that is) that they will contribute to the Lord [in other words, they should not let them be eaten by one who is not a priest].

*Let (the priests) not profane (ve-lo yeḥallelu) the holy things of the children of Israel.* They are to treat the holy things with honor and reverence, and to let anyone who touches them know that they are holy, so that a stranger should not err and eat them unintentionally. They are not to treat them in a profane manner, so that anyone who so desires

---

11. The legal derivation from *kinyan kaspo* is found in *Yevamot* 66a and *Torat Kohanim* (*Sifra, Emor, Paresheta* 5:1); the wife is deemed *kinyan kaspo* because she may be acquired in marriage by means of the husband's payment of money to her. However, Shadal takes the broad view that the permission granted to the male members of the priestly clan to eat *terumah* impliedly includes the female members (except as provided in v. 12).

would eat of them, for if they were to do so, they would cause the children of Israel to bear a great sin [see next v.]; that is, the priests would be the ones who would cause strangers to sin by eating holy things unintentionally.[12]

**22:16. "Otherwise they would cause them to bear a great sin, these [non-priests] eating their holy things, for it is I, the Lord, Who have declared them holy."**

*they would cause them (ve-hissi'u otam) to bear a great sin.* The priests would cause the children of Israel to bear a great sin by having them eat holy things.[13]

**22:17. And the Lord spoke to Moses, saying:**

**22:18. "Speak to Aaron and to his sons, and to all the children of Israel, and say to them: When someone of the house of Israel, or of the foreigners dwelling in Israel, wishes to present a sacrifice of his, that is, any vow of his, or any donation, that may be offered to the Lord in a burnt offering—**

**22:19. "It must be such that it will be accepted for you; (that is) immaculate, male, of the bovine, ovine, or caprine species.**

*It must be such that it will be accepted for you (li-r'tsonekhem,* lit. "for your acceptance"). You shall bring it so that it will be accepted; see Rashi [who interprets *li-r'tsonekhem* as meaning, "Bring a thing that is fitting to effect propitiation [*ratson*] for you. And which animal is this? Immaculate, male, etc."].

---

12. *Contra* Nachmanides, who understands the unstated subject of *ve-lo yeḥallelu* to be "the children of Israel," i.e., "Let the children of Israel not profane the holy things that they will contribute."
13. *Contra* Nachmanides and Rashi, who interpret *ve-hissi'u otam* to mean, "They [the children of Israel] would cause themselves" to bear a great sin.

**22:20.** "Do not present any animal that has some defect, for it would not be of satisfaction (to God) for you [to your benefit].

**22:21.** "So, too, when one offers to the Lord a sacrifice of contentment, having made a vow or by donation, of large or small cattle, it must be immaculate so as to be accepted; it must not have any imperfection.

**22:22.** "An animal that is blind, or lame, or mutilated, or warty, or scabby, or herpetic—these you shall not offer to the Lord, and you shall not place any of them on the altar in a sacrifice to be burned to the Lord.

*blind (avveret).* The Hebrew is the feminine form, not of *ivver* [the usual masculine term for "blind"], but of *avvir*, which is used in Aramaic. The word follows the model of *tsaddeket*, the feminine form of *tsaddik*. Rashi, who understood *avveret* as a noun ["blindness," rather than "blind"], sensed that if this were so, the next term should have been *shever* ["a broken limb," rather than *shavur*, "lame"], and thus he was constrained to interpret the phrase as meaning, "It must not have *avveret* (noun), and it must not be *shavur* (adjective)."

*and you shall not place any of them on the altar, etc.* Do not say, "Since this is not a burnt offering but a sacrifice of contentment, most of which is eaten by the owners, why should it matter if it has a blemish?" For this reason the verse continues, "and you shall not place any of them on the altar in a sacrifice to be burned to the Lord"—it is improper for the tallow and the blood that are burned for the honor of the Lord [even in the case of a sacrifice of contentment] to be from a blemished animal (Isaac Pardo).

**22:23.** "And an animal of the large or small cattle, having some part overly developed and some other too little developed, may be brought as a donation, but in (payment for) a vow it will not be accepted.

**22:24.** "And an animal [that has its testicles] crushed, or battered, or removed, or cut, you shall not offer to the Lord, and in your country you shall not do these [that is, do not castrate any living thing].

**22:25.** **"And not even (purchased) from one of another nation may you present any of these in a sacrifice to your God, for they have their mutilation in themselves; they have a defect; they will not be accepted for you."**

*And not even (purchased) from one of another nation* (*u-mi-yad ben nekhar*, lit. "and from the hand of one of another nation"). It seems to me that the correct interpretation is the one that Wessely rejected [i.e., "purchased from a non-Israelite"], for since it says, "In your country you shall not do these [i.e., castrate an animal]," it is implied that it is permissible to buy castrated animals from non-Israelites for purposes of consumption, working the ground, riding, and so forth, and it might have been inferred that it was even permissible to bring such an animal as a sacrifice, so therefore it says that this is forbidden.[14]

What brings me to insist on this interpretation is the fact that the verse ends with the phrase *lo yeratsu lakhem* ("they will not be accepted *for you*"), which implies that it is an Israelite who is bringing the sacrifice. Wessely sought to overcome this by saying that they [i.e., offerings of castrated animals] would have been accepted *for them* [i.e., for non-Israelites who bring such offerings], since God's sanctuary is in our midst and nations come from the ends of the earth to bow before God the King and offer him sacrifices, [but if you Israelites allow them to bring offerings of blemished animals, it will not be accepted *for you*, that is, it will not be accounted as a merit for you.] This is nonsense, however, for the expression *lo yeratsu lakhem* is only a parallel to *ve-nirtsa lo* ("and it will be accepted for him," Lev. 1:4) and refers back only to the offeror of the sacrifice. Nevertheless, it is an undoubtedly valid law [see *Temurah* 7a] that it is forbidden for us to offer an animal that has had its testicles crushed, battered, etc., even on behalf of a foreigner, for it says, "And

---

14. Wessely rejects this interpretation on the ground that it should have been obvious that it would make no difference if the castration was done by the Israelite bringing the sacrifice or by someone else. Instead, Wessely maintains that this verse prohibits non-Israelites themselves from offering a castrated animal in the Israelite sanctuary, for it might have been thought that they should be permitted to do so because they were not subject to the prohibition against castrating an animal, and because they considered such animals a delicacy.

an animal [that has its testicles] crushed, or battered... you shall not offer to the Lord."

**22:26. And the Lord spoke to Moses, saying:**

**22:27. "A bovine, ovine, or caprine animal, as soon as it is born, must remain seven days beneath its mother; and from the eighth day onward it can be accepted in a sacrifice to be burned to the Lord.**

**22:28. "Whether of the large cattle or of the small, you shall not slaughter on one same day the mother and its offspring.**

***Whether of the large cattle or of the small*** *(ve-shor o seh).* The words *seh* and *seita* (each one meaning "a sheep or goat") are not found in Aramaic or Syriac, but are found in Hebrew and Arabic, and they mean (as I commented on the phrase *shor seh khesavim ve-seh izzim*, Deut. 14:4) an individual animal of the small cattle [*tson*], either one of the sheep or one of the goats. In Aramaic there is no word for an individual animal [that does not differentiate] whether the animal is of the sheep or of the goats, and so in that verse [Deut. 14:4], Onkelos was compelled to make a [differentiating] change in his translation, and he translated *seh khevasim* ("an individual of the sheep") as *immerin di-reḥelin* and *seh izzim* ("an individual of the goats") as *gadyan de-izzin*. In the present verse, however, he did not translate *seh* as *reḥela* ("sheep, ewe"), so that the word should not be understood as excluding goats, and therefore he chose to use the word *seita*, even though it is not Aramaic. Nevertheless, the word is fitting in this context, because it includes both species.

At the time that I wrote the book *Ohev Ger*, I did not understand this matter, just as the author of the book *Ya'er* did not understand it, and I cited his astonishment over Onkelos' translation.[15] The *Me'ammer* then criticized me and said that Onkelos chose not to use the word *reḥela* because it is exclusively feminine, and that he chose the word *seita*

---

15. As stated in *Ohev Ger*, p. 62 (Cracow edition), the author of *Ya'er* (a 1451 commentary on Onkelos) asserted that seita was not an Aramaic word, and he theorized that the original reading of Onkelos' translation of *seh* was *reḥela*.

because it includes both the male and the female, in order to have his translation conform with the main point of the law.[16] This, however, is a gross error, for [in the phrase *oto ve-et beno*, translated here as "the mother and its offspring" but lit. "him and his son"] the word *beno* [although masculine] includes both male and female offspring, but the word *oto* [also masculine]—like the words *shor* and *seh* ("large cattle," "small cattle")—refers here only to the mother, not the father. That is why Onkelos made a change and translated *shor* as *torta* ("cow"), in the feminine, and who would say that *torta* includes both the male and the female? Were it not for the fact that Onkelos wanted to have the word *seh* include both sheep and goats (as is my opinion now), it would indeed have been proper for him to translate it as *reḥela*, which is specifically the term for the female sheep.[17]

***you shall not slaughter on one same day.*** [The purpose of this command is] not for the sake of exercising mercy upon the animal per se, but to reinforce the sense of compassion in our hearts and to keep us far from cruelty.

**22:29. "And when you make a sacrifice of thanksgiving to the Lord, you must make it so that it becomes acceptable for you.**

---

16. According to the *Me'ammer*, the "main point of the law" is that it is forbidden to slaughter the "mother" on the same day as the "son" or the "daughter," and that the use of the gender-neutral *seita* for the parent brings out this meaning. The *Me'ammer* also questions the assertion that *seita* is not an Aramaic word.
17. The normative halakhic view is that the main focus of the prohibition of *oto ve-et beno* is on the slaughtering of the mother animal and her offspring, since the paternity of the offspring is generally in doubt. Where the paternity is known for certain, there is a dispute among the Tannaim as to whether it is forbidden to slaughter the father and his offspring on the same day (*Ḥullin* 78b-79a). According to to Maimonides (*Mishneh Torah, Sheḥitah* 12:11) and the *Shulḥan Arukh* (*Yoreh De'ah* 16:2), this should not be done, but the act carries no penalty. Rashi, however (in his comment on the present verse) takes the view that it is permitted to slaughter the father animal and his offspring on the same day.

# Shadal on Leviticus

*so that it becomes acceptable for you.* And when does it become acceptable? When you have others eat of it, so that none of it is left over until the morning.

**22:30. "It must be eaten on the same day; you shall not leave any of it over until the next day. I am the Lord.**

**22:31. "You shall observe My commandments and carry them out. I am the Lord.**

**22:32. "And do not profane My holy name; rather, act so that I become recognized as holy among the children of Israel; it is I, the Lord, Who have declared you holy—**

**22:33. "Who have brought you out of the land of Egypt, to be your God. I am the Lord."**

**23:1. And the Lord spoke to Moses, saying:**

**23:2. "Speak to the children of Israel, and say to them: The solemn occasions of the Lord, which you will proclaim days of holy convocation [religious meeting], these (I say) are My solemn occasions.**

*The solemn occasions of the Lord (mo'adei YHVH),* **which you will** *proclaim days of holy convocation (mikra'ei kodesh).* See Isa. 1:13.[18]

---

18. There, commenting on the phrase *kero mikra* ("make convocation"), Shadal says that this refers to a court's public announcement of holidays and new months, whether by the blowing of the shofar or by vocal announcement. On the other hand, Shadal expresses the view that the term *mikra kodesh* ("holy convocation") denotes assembly and gathering, and is synonymous with *mo'adei YHVH* ("the solemn occasions of the Lord"). He also cross-refers to his comment here.

In Rashi's comment, it seems to me that the word *melummadin* should be *no'adin*; see *Torat Kohanim*.[19]

As for the meaning of this verse, it seems to me (reading against the accents) that *mikra'ei kodesh* ("days of holy convocation") should not be connected to the preceding phrase *asher tikre'u otam* ("which you will proclaim"), but to the subsequent phrase *elleh hem mo'adai* ("these are My solemn occasions"). That is to say, "The solemn occasions of the Lord (days of gathering for God's name) are *mikra'ei kodesh* (days of holy convocation) that you will proclaim (establish and announce)." So it may be inferred from v. 4 below, "These are the solemn occasions of the Lord, days of holy convocation [*mikra'ei kodesh*], that you will proclaim in their time."[20]

**23:3. "Six days labor will be done, and the seventh is a day of great rest, a holy convocation; you shall not do any work; it is a Sabbath to the honor of the Lord, in all your habitations.**

**23:4. "These are the solemn occasions of the Lord, days of holy convocation, that you will proclaim in their time.**

**23:5. "In the first month, on the fourteenth of the month, toward night, (there will be made the) paschal sacrifice to the Lord.**

**23:6. "And on the fifteenth of the same month is a feast of unleavened breads to the Lord; seven days you shall eat unleavened breads.**

---

19. Rashi's comment on this verse, as it appears in most editions, reads as follows: "Make solemn occasions so that the Israelites should become *melummadim* ("trained, practiced") in them." Shadal's suggested reading would have the phrase mean "so that the Israelites should assemble in them." Such a reading would adhere more closely to the source of Rashi's comment, *Torat Kohanim* (*Sifra*, *Emor*, *Parsheta* 9:1), which says, "Make the solemn occasions so that all of Israel can observe them [*she-ya'asu otam*]," i.e., by declaring a leap year if the Jews in exile need more time to travel to Jerusalem.
20. However, Shadal's translation conforms to the accents, which place the major disjunctive [*etnahta*] at the word *kodesh*.

**23:7. "On the first day there will be a holy convocation for you; any servile work you shall not do.**

**23:8. "You shall present for seven days sacrifices to be burned to the Lord. On the seventh day, then, (there will be made) a holy convocation; you shall not do any servile work."**

**23:9. And the Lord spoke to Moses, saying:**

**23:10. "Speak to the children of Israel, and say to them: When you have entered into the land that I am about to give you and you reap its harvest, you shall bring to the priest a sheaf [according to the tradition: barley flour of the measure of an *omer*] of the first fruits of your harvest.[21]**

**23:11. "He will present the sheaf before the Lord, so that it may be accepted of him to your benefit. On the day after the festival will the priest present it.**

***On the day after the festival*** *(mi-moḥorat ha-shabbat,* lit. "on the day after the Sabbath"). The author of the *Kuzari* [Judah ha-Levi] (3:41) says that it should likely be conceded to the Karaites that *mi-moḥorat ha-shabbat* refers to the Sabbath of Creation [i.e., the seventh day of the week], but that some of the judges and the Sanhedrin thought that the Torah mentioned the Sabbath only by way of example, and that the people had the authority to begin putting the scythe to the crops [see

21. The Hebrew word translated here as "sheaf" (Ital. *manipolo*) is *omer*. In his comment on Lev. 23:9, Rabbi David Zvi Hoffmann cites Shadal's translation with its bracketed addition, and he expresses the view that the word *omer* actually has three different meanings: (1) a sheaf of barley; (2) a unit of measure equal to a tenth of an ephah; and (3) a special name for the offering described here, denoting a "gift of tribute."

Deut. 16:9] on any day that it wished; thus, they (the judges and the Sanhedrin) established that the beginning of the harvest should be on the second day of Passover.[22]

Know that all the lengthy verbiage of Ibn Ezra on this verse is nothing but sleight of hand, and that the [unstated] main point of his reasoning is in accordance with the view of the author of the *Kuzari*, that the "Sabbath" mentioned here is the actual Sabbath, but that the Torah mentioned the Sabbath day merely by way of example, and that we have the authority to present the Omer on the day we wish; this is the meaning of the word *li-r 'tsonekhem*, according to Ibn Ezra in his riddle.[23]

**23:12. "On the day that you present the sheaf, you will make into a burnt offering to the Lord an immaculate lamb born within the year—**

---

22. The Karaites read this verse literally and held that the Omer offering should always be brought on a Sunday, but the Rabbanite view (*Menaḥot* 66a) is that it is brought on the day after "the holiday." The *Kuzari* 3:41 states as follows: "Now, suppose we allow the Karaite interpretation of the sentence 'From the morrow of the Sabbath till the morrow of the Sabbath' (Lev. xxiii. 11, 15, 16) to refer to the Sunday. But we reply that one of the judges, priests, or pious kings, in agreement with the Synhedrion and all Sages, found that this period was fixed with the intention of creating an interval of fifty days between 'the first fruits of the harvest of barley and the harvest of wheat,' and to observe 'seven weeks,' which are 'seven complete Sabbaths.' The first day of the week is only mentioned for argument's sake in the following manner: should the day of 'putting the sickle to the corn' be a Sunday, you count till Sunday. From this we conclude that should the beginning be on a Monday, we count till Monday. The date of putting the sickle, from which we count, is left for us to fix. This was fixed for the second day of Passover, which does not contradict the Torah..." (trans. Hirschfeld, pp. 173-174).
23. The verse states that the priest will present the Omer offering *li-r 'tsonekhem* ("so that it may be accepted of him to your benefit"). Ibn Ezra's comment rephrases this as, "You will present it *bi-r 'tsonekhem*," which seems to mean "according to your will," i.e., when you choose.

# Shadal on Leviticus

**23:13.** "With its flour offering, of two tenths (of an *ephah*) of fine flour kneaded with oil, to be burned to the Lord in a propitiatory aroma, and with its libation of a quarter of a *hin* of wine.

**23:14.** "And bread [of the new harvest], or parched grain, or fresh grain, you shall not eat until the aforementioned day, (not) until you have brought the sacrifice of your God: an everlasting statute, for all the ages to come, in all of your habitations.

**23:15.** "You shall number then from the day after the festival, from the day (that is) that you have brought the sheaf of presentation, seven weeks, which are to be complete.

**23:16.** "You shall number fifty days, thus arriving at the day after the seventh week, and then [that is, on the fiftieth day] you shall present to the Lord a new flour offering [of new wheat].

***You shall number... at the day after the seventh week*** *(ad mi-moḥorat ha-shabbat tisperu).* The Hebrew should be accented עַד מִמָּחֳרַת הַשַּׁבָּת הַשְּׁבִיעִת תִּסְפְּרוּ in accordance with Rashi's opinion; see his comment.[24]

***thus arriving at*** *(ad,* lit. "until") ***the day after the seventh week.*** You shall number fifty days until you arrive at the day after the seventh week, and then you shall present a new flour offering.

**23:17.** "From your habitations [that is, from the harvest of your land] you shall bring two breads of presentation, of two tenths (of an *ephah* between them both); they will be of fine flour, and they will be baked leavened; they are first fruits (offered) to the Lord.

---

24. A more literal translation of the first part of this verse would be, "Until the day after the seventh week, you shall number fifty days." Rashi says that this should be understood to mean, "Until the day after the seventh week—which is the fiftieth day—you shall number." Shadal's proposed accentuation, which sets off the word *ha-shevi'it* ("seventh") with a lesser disjunctive tevir rather than the traditional greater disjunctive *zakef katon,* would facilitate Rashi's interpretation.

**23:18.** "And together with the bread you shall present seven immaculate lambs, born within the year, and one young bull, and two rams, which will be made into a burnt offering to the Lord, with their respective flour offerings and libations, to be burned in a propitiatory aroma to the Lord.

**23:19.** "You shall also make a young goat into a sacrifice of aspersion, and two lambs born within the year into sacrifices of contentment.

**23:20.** "The priest will make a waving of them before the Lord, together with the breads of the first fruits, which together with the two lambs will be holy to the Lord, to the (exclusive) use of the priest.

**23:21.** "You shall proclaim the aforementioned day, which will be for you a day of holy convocation, on which you will not do any servile work—an everlasting statute in all your habitations, for all the ages to come.

**23:22.** "And when you reap the harvest of your land, you shall not finish the extremities of your field in reaping, nor shall you gather (from the ground) the fallen ears; to the poor person and to the foreigner you shall abandon them. I am the Lord your God."

**23:23.** And the Lord spoke to Moses, saying:

**23:24.** "Speak to the children of Israel, saying: In the seventh month, the first of the month will be for you a day of rest, to be remembered [proclaimed] by means of the sound (of the horn), (a day of) holy convocation.

*to be remembered [proclaimed] by means of the sound* (zikhron teru'ah). Cf. "Proclaim [*hazkiru*] that His name is exalted" (Isa. 12:4). The meaning is, by this means everyone was to know that this day was the New Year. Similarly, in the Jubilee year they would sound the horn [*shofar*] to make it known that it was the Jubilee. In order to avoid mistaking the proclamation of the Jubilee year for that of any other year, we were commanded to sound the horn for the Jubilee year on Yom Kippur [Lev. 25:9].[25]

**23:25. "No servile work shall you do, and you shall present sacrifices to be burned to the Lord."**

**23:26. And the Lord spoke to Moses, saying:**

**23:27. "But the tenth of this seventh month is a day of expiation; a holy convocation it will be for you, and you shall afflict your persons [by fasting], and you shall present sacrifices to be burned to the Lord.**

---

25. In an 1863 exchange of letters with Rabbi Elia Benamozegh (1823-1900), Shadal expressed in more depth his views on the significance of sounding the *shofar*. Benamozegh, a devotee of Kabbalah, wrote to Shadal, "Tomorrow [Rosh Hashanah] you will hear the Shofar and I will hear it. What will this sound say to you?" (*Lettere dirette a S. D. Luzzatto da Elia Benamozegh* [Livorno, 1890], p. 73; see also R. Gianfranco Di Segni, "Le polemiche fra rabbini non sono certo una novità," Kolòt, 9/16/2010.) Shadal responded, "I will tell you that the trills of the Shofar were (as I believe) commanded by God to put into public notice (at a time when no calendars were printed) the beginning of the year, just as on the tenth day of the year, with the same Shofar, the arrival of the Jubilee year was brought into universal awareness. If today such sounds have lost their [original] purpose, they still preserve (as do so many ceremonies) the immense value of reminding us of our ancient political existence, and they revive in us the feeling of nationality, which—without so many small but repeated reminders—perhaps might have become extinct among us, as it did among all the other ancient nations. Those trills excite in me clear ideas, profound sensations, the most edifying reflections. The miracle of our existence animates me, it encourages me to endure in the struggle against Spinoza, against all the supposedly enlightened ones, and to risk everything, whatever may occur, in defense of a cause that has been victorious until now and that will certainly remain victorious." He goes on to say that an example of the "simple" Judaism that he favors is "to sound the horn, or to hear it sounded, without engaging in mystical Cavanot [meditations], but with the sole Cavanà [intention] of fulfilling a Divine precept, which is holy for us for the simple reason that it was imposed upon us by God." (*Epistolario italiano, francese, latino*, pp. 1032-1033,1035).

# Emor

**But** *(akh).* See below on v. 39.

**and you shall afflict your persons.** See above on Lev. 16:29.

**23:28.** "And you shall not do any work on the aforementioned day, for it is a day of expiation; a holy convocation it will be for you, on which it will be propitiated for you before the Lord your God.

**23:29.** "For which reason any individual who does not afflict himself on the aforementioned day will go extinct from his people.

**23:30.** "And any individual who does work on the aforementioned day—I will cause that person to be destroyed from the midst of his people.

**23:31.** "You shall not do any work, a perpetual statute for all the ages to come, in all your habitations.

**23:32.** "A day of great rest it is for you, and you shall afflict your persons. On the ninth of the month, in the evening, from one evening to the other, you shall celebrate your rest."

**On the ninth of the month, in the evening.** This part of the verse is to be construed, "On the ninth of the month, in the evening, you will have your day of great rest," with the added explanation, "from one evening to the other, you shall celebrate your rest." This is in accordance with the accents, but if the word *ba-erev* ("in the evening") were accented with a *revia* [instead of the stronger disjunctive *zakef katon*], it would be more proper, for in that case the text would not be elliptical, but instead it would be understood as follows: "On the ninth of the month in the evening (that is, from one evening to the other) you shall celebrate your rest." Perhaps the accentuator wanted the phrase "from one evening to the other," etc., to apply to all the festivals, as per Abravanel [and therefore he made the phrase stand alone]. Undoubtedly, all the festivals are celebrated "from one evening to the other," but this was specifically added here with respect to Yom Kippur on account of the fast, so that it should be known that one is obligated to fast for 24 complete hours.

209

# Shadal on Leviticus

**23:33.** And the Lord spoke to Moses, saying:

**23:34.** "Speak to the children of Israel, saying: On the fifteenth of the same seventh month is the festival of the huts, (which lasts) seven days, to the honor of the Lord.

**23:35.** "On the first day (there will be) a holy convocation; any servile work you shall not do.

**23:36.** "For seven days you shall present sacrifices to be burned to the Lord. On the eighth day, then, there will be for you a holy convocation, and you will present sacrifices to be burned to the Lord; it is a day of congregation [in the Temple]; any servile work you shall not do.

**23:37.** "These are the solemn occasions of the Lord, which you shall proclaim days of holy convocation, on which (you will have) to present sacrifices to be burned to the Lord, burnt offerings, flour offerings, (other) sacrifices, and libations, according to the law of every single day.

**23:38.** "Besides the (sacrifices of) the Sabbaths of the Lord, and besides your gifts, and besides all your vows, and besides all your donations that you wish to give to the Lord.

**23:39.** "But on the fifteenth of the seventh month, when you bring in the produce of the land, you shall celebrate the festival of the Lord seven days: the first day (will be) a day of rest, and the eighth day a day of rest.

*But (akh).* In connection with Yom Kippur [above, v. 27] it is written *akh* because of the obligation of affliction, which has no parallel among the holidays, while in connection with the Festival of the Huts [*Sukkot*] it is written *akh* because of the obligations of the palm branch [*lulav*] and the hut [*sukkah*], which have no parallel among the other solemn occasions.

210

**23:40.** "And you shall provide yourselves for the first day from the fruits of the stately tree [citron], the branches of palms, the branches of myrtle, and river willows; and you shall rejoice before the Lord your God seven days.

**23:41.** "You shall celebrate [this festival of the huts] as a festival of the Lord seven days out of the year, an everlasting statute for all the ages to come; you shall celebrate it in the seventh month.

**23:42.** "In the huts you shall dwell seven days; all the natives [and hence landholders] in Israel shall dwell in the huts.

**23:43.** "So that your descendants may know that in huts I made the children of Israel dwell, when I brought them out of the land of Egypt [that is, so that they should not become arrogant because of the abundant harvest, but should remember their ancient misery and recognize their prosperity as coming from God]. I am the Lord your God."

**23:44.** And Moses set forth to the children of Israel the solemn occasions of the Lord.

**24:1.** And the Lord spoke to Moses, saying:

**24:2.** "Command the children of Israel, that they bring you clear, virgin olive oil [see Exod. 27:20] for illumination, to make a lamp burn daily.[26]

**24:3.** "Outside the door-curtain (situated before the ark) of the Law, in the tent of congregation, Aaron will arrange it (so that it burns) from evening to morning, before the Lord, daily, an everlasting statute for all the ages to come.

---

26. In Shadal's translation of and commentary on Exod. 27:20, which closely parallels the present verse, he explains that the word *katit* ("virgin") is an adjective modifying *shemen* ("oil") and means "extracted with one simple pressing of the olives."

**24:4.** **"He will arrange the lights on the pure [shining] candelabrum, before the Lord, daily.**

**24:5.** **"And you will take of the fine flour, and you will bake it into twelve cakes; each one will be of two tenths (of an *ephah*).**

**24:6.** **"And you will place them in two orders [one cake above the other], six to an order, on the pure table, before the Lord.**

*on the pure table.* That which Rashi wrote, that the supporting pillars [*senifin*] must not raise the bread above the table top, means that the lowest cake in each order was not to rest upon the canes [*kanim*], but upon the table itself; see *Menaḥot* 97a.[27]

**24:7.** **"And you will put upon [or alongside] each order translucent frankincense, which will serve the bread as an accompanying fragrance, to be burned to the Lord.**

**24:8.** **"Every Sabbath day (the priest) will present it [this bread] before the Lord, constantly, (receiving it) from the children of Israel by an everlasting pact [law].**

**24:9.** **"And it will belong to Aaron and to his sons, and they will eat it in a holy place; for it is for them a most holy thing (to receive) from the things to be burned to the Lord, an everlasting statute."**

---

27. In *Menaḥot* 97a, the *kasot* and *menakkiyyot* mentioned in Exod. 25:29 are identified, respectively, as *senifin* ("supports") and *kanim* ("canes" or "rods"), which rested on notches in the supports and bore the cakes of the bread of presentation [*leḥem ha-panim*]. Subsequently it is stated that the lowest cakes of each order did not need canes, because they rested upon the table itself. It should be pointed out that Shadal himself, in translating and commenting on Exod. 25:29, understands the *kasot* and *menakkiyyot* to be types of libation vessels; he says, "The explanations given by the Rabbis and Rashi for these vessels [and the others mentioned in this verse] appear to conform with what existed in the Second Temple, but not with what existed in the desert."

**24:10. Now a man born of an Israelite woman, but the son of an Egyptian man, and living among the children of Israel, went forth; and this Israelite woman's son and an Israelite man [that is, on his father's side as well] came to fighting in the camp.**

*Now a man born of an Israelite woman, etc.* After completing the commandments that are for the purpose of God's honor (the sacrifices, the festivals, and the laws of the priests), the Torah concludes [this section] with the penalty for one who curses the Name of God, which is the polar opposite of everything commanded heretofore. Until this point there had been no command about this (for the admonition *elohim lo tekallel* [lit. "Do not curse God," Exod. 22:27] means "Do not curse the judges"), as it could not have been imagined that an Israelite would curse the Name, and the Torah would never have admonished against this if it had not so happened that a son of an Egyptian man had committed this abomination. Once this incident occurred, the admonition followed, and it was written here in order to conclude all that pertains to the holiness of the Name.

**24:11. And the son of the Israelite woman uttered the (sacred) Name, and he blasphemed, and he was brought to Moses. His mother was named Shelomith, daughter of Dibri, of the tribe of Dan.**

**24:12. And they put him in a place of custody, so that it would come to be declared to them by order of the Lord (how he should be treated).**

**24:13. And the Lord spoke to Moses, saying:**

**24:14. "Let the blasphemer be brought out of the camp, and let all those who were hearers [of the blasphemy] place their hands on his head, and let all the congregation stone him.**

*and let all those who were hearers place their hands on his head.* As if to say, "Your blood is upon your head"; see Rashi [who, citing *Sifra*, gives this interpretation and adds that the hearers would mean

213

to say, "We are not culpable for your death, for you brought it upon yourself"]. Similarly, with respect to the sacrifices, one who places his hand on the head of his sacrificial animal puts his sin upon it, as the high priest does upon the head of the goat that is sent into the wilderness [Lev. 16:21]. Eventually this placing of the hands was extended to sacrifices of contentment [*shelamim*], even though they were not offered to atone for sin. A. H. Mainster adds that even in the present case, the people were putting their sins on the head of the blasphemer, for if they had not brought him to justice, his sin would have been upon the entire congregation, or upon his hearers.

**24:15. "And to the children of Israel you shall speak, saying: Whoever blasphemes his God will bear the punishment of his sin.**

*Whoever blasphemes his God.* Without uttering the Tetragrammaton.

**24:16. "And one who blasphemes the name of the Lord [the Tetragrammaton] will be put to death; he will be stoned by all the congregation. Whether a foreigner or a native, when he blasphemes the (holy) Name, he will be put to death.**

*And one who blasphemes the name of the Lord.* If he blasphemes the Tetragrammaton (Ibn Ezra).[28]

**24:17. "And if someone strikes (kills) any individual of the human race, he will be put to death.**

*And if someone strikes any individual of the human race.* Even a foreigner. After prescribing the death penalty against the blasphemer, who was the son of an Egyptian man,[29] the Torah makes it known that

---

28. Ibn Ezra explains that unlike a blasphemer who refers to God by the more generic name *Elohim* (which may refer merely to "angels" or "judges"), one who blasphemes the four-letter Name of God leaves no doubt as to his intention.
29. In the version of this comment that appears in the Columbia X 893 L 9765 manuscript, the following is inserted at this point: "and perhaps he blasphemed because an Israelite struck him, and other Israelites came to that Israelite's aid...."

one who strikes any member of the human race, even a foreigner, will be put to death, for the foreigner is not to be thought of as if he were a beast. Rather, "One who strikes a beast will pay for it, and one who strikes a person will be put to death" (below, v. 21). So also, "when someone inflicts on his neighbor a bodily wound" [then *lex talionis* applies; below, v. 19]; this law concludes with the statement, "just as he will have inflicted a wound on another person, so will be done to him" (v. 20). The entire section closes with, "just as it will be for the foreigner, so for the native" (v. 22) (some of this appears in Ibn Ezra's comment).

**24:18. "And one who strikes a brute animal will pay for it: animal for animal.**

**24:19. "And when someone inflicts on his neighbor a bodily wound, as he did, it will be done to him.**

**24:20. "Break for break, eye for eye, tooth for tooth; just as he will have inflicted a wound on another person, so will be done to him [but in Num. 35:31, ransom is forbidden in the case of homicide; thus in the case of a bodily wound, monetary compensation is permissible].[30]**

---

30. Shadal takes the view that according to the text's plain meaning [*peshat*], monetary compensation was permissible but not mandatory. See his comment on the phrase "Eye for eye" in Exod. 21:24, where he says, "This teaches that anyone who injures his fellow is to be given the same defect that he gave... [However, the] Rabbis interpreted this to mean that he pays a monetary penalty (*Bava Kamma* 83b). From what is written, 'And do not accept a ransom for the life of a homicide, who is guilty of death, but he must be put to death' (Num. 35:31), there is clear proof that the Torah permitted the taking of a monetary ransom in the case of other injuries that do not involve death... This is one of the things that the Torah left to the judges, for if indeed there would be a rich person who did not mind losing his money and who took pleasure in injuring others, the judges would be able to impose the written penalty, 'eye for eye.'"

See also my footnote ad loc.: "Modern scholarship echoes Shadal's view: 'The central claim of the new research on talionic systems is that revenge coexisted with the option of compensation. Revenge was not phased out gradually, but was a central component

**24:21.** "One who strikes a beast will pay for it, and one who strikes a person will be put to death.

**24:22.** "You shall have one single law: just as it will be for the foreigner, so for the native; for I, the Lord, am your God."

**24:23.** Moses spoke to the children of Israel, and they brought the blasphemer outside the camp, and they stoned him. The children of Israel did as the Lord commanded Moses.

---

of the whole idea of compensation' (Kaius Tuori, "Revenge and Retribution in the Twelve Tables: Talio esto Reconsidered," *Fundamina*, vol. 13, pp. 140-145 (2007)). The normative halakhic view, as expressed in *Bava Kamma* 84a, is that the phrase 'eye for eye' cannot be taken literally." (*Shadal on Exodus*, p. 337, n. 12.) Nevertheless, the Talmud does record that Rav Huna (ca. 216-ca. 297 C.E.), although not invoking "eye for eye," advocated cutting off the hand of one who habitually struck others, and that he actually imposed such a penalty (*Sanhedrin* 58b).

# Behar

*The land's Sabbath • The Jubilee: "Proclaim liberty" •*
*"When a brother of yours becomes poor" •*
*"My servants they are"*

**25:1. The Lord spoke to Moses on Mount Sinai, saying:**

**25:2. "Speak to the children of Israel, and say to them: When you have entered into the country that I am about to give you, the land must rest a Sabbath to the Lord.**

*the land must rest a Sabbath to the Lord.* The commandment of the Sabbatical year [*shemittah*] resembles the commandment of the [weekly] Sabbath, for just as the purpose of the Sabbath is to reinforce in the hearts of the people the belief that they are a holy nation, so the commandment of the Sabbatical year will induce the belief in their hearts that their land, too, is a holy land, since it rests during this year as God rested on the seventh day (see Abravanel's words in *Naḥalat Avot*, ch. 5, on the *mishnah* that begins "Exile comes to the world," for they are pleasing).[1]

---

1.  There, expressing the view that the land of Israel is a chosen land, just as the people of Israel are a chosen people, Abravanel states that the purpose of both the people's Sabbath day and the land's Sabbatical year is to commemorate God's resting on the seventh day

# Shadal on Leviticus

Just as God, when the people were in the wilderness, would give them a two-day supply of food on the sixth day, so also when they were in their land, He would order his blessing for them in the sixth year so that its produce would suffice for the Sabbatical year. Moreover, the [people's awareness of] the holiness of the land would be a powerful inducement to keep the people far from contaminating and desecrating the land with abominable practices. In addition, an inevitable result of the land's resting would be that the servants and animals would rest from a portion of their labors, and this would parallel the resting of servants and animals on the Sabbath day. Since the produce of that year would be ownerless, this would provide compassion for the poor and would equalize the rich and the poor, bringing low the rich person's pride and reminding that person that all human beings are equal. So also the Sabbatical cancellation of debts would be a source of compassion and grace for the poor.

Just as the people, besides their resting on the seventh day, were provided with other special days on which to rest and to rejoice in God's name, so the holy land, besides the Sabbatical year, was given the Jubilee year. The Jubilee would equalize the rich and the poor as would the Sabbatical year and the Sabbath day, by means of the cessation of the labor of the land as well as the ownerlessness of the produce. There would also be the return of lands to their original owners and the freeing of servants, constituting great compassion for the poor and greatly reinforcing the equality of the state's people.

It should be taken into consideration that just as the Jubilee year occurs once in a cycle of seven Sabbatical years, so the annual holidays add up to [approximately] one seventh of the number of the year's Sabbath days, which are more than 49 but never as many as 65. The holy convocations total seven days: the first and seventh days of Passover, the one day of Shavuot, the one of the New Year, the one of Yom Kippur, the first day of Sukkot, and Shemini Atseret.

---

of Creation, "as if that land, in its exalted state of holiness, for all its inability to speak, is testifying on this occasion as to the goal of the nation of Israel's resting." The unit of time best suited for the land's testimony, says Abravanel, is not the day but the year, on account of the annual agricultural cycle. He adds that the chosen land was entitled to its own Sabbatical rest, and that the people would suffer exile if they oppressed the land by depriving it of its rest.

**25:3. "Six years will you sow your field, and six years will you prune your vine, and you will gather its produce.**

**25:4. "But in the seventh year the land will have a Sabbath of rest, a Sabbath to the honor of the Lord; your field you shall not sow, and your vine you shall not prune.**

**25:5. "The harvest that is born to you spontaneously [from fallen grains] you shall not reap, and the grapes of your uncultivated vines you shall not pick; it will be for the land a Sabbatical year.**

*your uncultivated grapes* *(innevei nezirekha).* See Clericus, Mendelssohn, Rosenmueller, and Gesenius.[2]

**25:6. "The [produce of the] Sabbath of the land will be yours to eat of, yours (that is) and that of your male slave, and of your female slave, and of your hireling, and of your sojourner, who are dwelling with you.**

*and that of your male slave, and of your female slave.* In the *parashah* of *Mishpatim* (Exod. 23:11) it says that "the indigent of your people" are allowed to eat of it, and here it adds slaves and sojourners, who are not from the children of Israel. Know that in Rashi's comment on the phrase "and of your hireling, and of your sojourner," it is written in a manuscript in my possession, and in the 5278 edition [a *ḥumash* produced in 1518], *af ha-goyim* (not *ha-gerim*), and so it appears in *Torat Kohanim (Sifra, Behar, parsheta alef).*

**25:7. "And (also) to your animal, and to the wild beasts existing in your country, it will be permitted to eat all of its produce.**

2.  Gesenius' *Lexicon*, s.v. *nazir*, says that the term originally denoted an ascetic who did not shave his hair, and by extension referred to a vine that was not pruned. Similarly, Mendelssohn's *Biur* on this verse (alternative view) explains that unpruned vines are called *nezirim* because their untrimmed twigs or shoots resemble the unshaven hair of the human *nazir*. Clericus and Rosenmueller's comments refer to the "hair of the vine."

# Shadal on Leviticus

*And (also) to your animal, and to the wild beasts, etc.* The Sabbatical year serves as a reminder that the land is God's and that from His hand it comes to us; that we are strangers and sojourners with Him; and that we should not take pride in our wealth, since everything comes from His hand. Every seventh year the land returns to its Owner, the Lord God, and hence that year is called "a Sabbath to the Lord," and its produce is for the rich and poor alike; for the foreigner, the native, the slave, and the sojourner alike; and even for the animals and beasts, for all are equal before Him.

**25:8. "You shall number, then, seven hebdomads[3] of years, (that is) seven years seven times; and when the course of the seven hebdomads of years will have given you forty-nine years—**

**25:9. "In the seventh month, on the tenth of the month, you shall sound a loud horn; on the day of expiation you shall sound the horn in all your land.**

**25:10. "You shall consecrate the fiftieth year, and you shall proclaim liberty in the country to all its inhabitants. That will be for you a Jubilee, and every one of you will return to his possession, and every one will return to his own family.**

*Jubilee (yovel).* This term was in use, before the giving of the Torah, among the peoples that worshipped Baal; the Torah says "That will be for you a Jubilee" as if it were known what this was. It seems to me that this is a compound word, *Yo Bel*, for *yah, yahu, yau,* and *yo* all represent a cry of joy (see my interpretation of the name YHVH),[4] while Bel is the name of a pagan god, like Baal (בעל) but with the slurring of the *ayin* sound. It seems that the pagans used to call out this exclamation on their joyful holidays. Similarly, among the Greeks and Romans, *Io Paean* and

---

3.  "Hebdomad" (Italian *ebdomada*) is a Greek-derived word denoting a group of seven things.
4.  In his commentary to Gen. 2:4 and Exod. 15:3, Shadal expresses the view that the Tetragrammaton YHVH is a compound of *yahu,* a cry of joy, and *wah,* a cry of woe, reflecting God's unique essence as the one Worker of Good and Evil.

*Io Bacche* were cries of joy that were used on holidays and other special occasions; these were compounds of *Io*, a joyful cry, and a second word that was the name of a god.[5] The Torah sanctified the joy and commanded that this time be one of redemption and liberty for the poor who had been forced to sell their inherited land, or even their own bodies as well; in that year, besides, the produce of the land was to be for all its inhabitants equally, and the rich and poor were to be equalized together.

Targum Jonathan (Josh. ch. 6), the Talmud (*Rosh Hashanah* 26a), and Rashi interpreted *yovel* as "ram," but there is no proof for this in Scripture, and *keren ha-yovel* ("the horn of the *yovel*," Josh. 6:5) means only the horn that was blown to celebrate the Jubilee. Later on the expression developed *shoferot ha-yovelim* ("Jubilee horns," Josh. 6:4ff), and still later, *bi-m'shokh ha-yovel* ("when the horn sounds," Exod. 19:13) [that is, the word *yovel* itself took on the meaning of "horn"]; see Gesenius.[6]

**25:11. "This (that is), the fiftieth year, will be for you a Jubilee; you shall not sow, and you shall not reap its products born spontaneously, and you shall not pick its uncultivated vines.**

**25:12. "For that year is a Jubilee; holy it will be for you; from the field itself you may eat of its crops [without bringing them into your own granaries].**

---

5.  Paean was "a surname of Apollo, derived from the word *paean*, a hymn which was sung in his honour, because he had killed the serpent Python, which had given the people cause to exclaim *Io Paean!* The exclamation of Io Paean! was made use of in speaking to the other gods, as it often was a demonstration of joy." (John Lempriere, *Bibliotheca Classica* (London, 1840), p. 521). "Io Bacche" was one of the "hideous shrieks and shouts" featured during Greek festivals of Bacchus, the god of wine (ibid., p. 254).

6.  In his *Lexicon*, s.v. *yovel*, Gesenius says that this is an onomatopoetic word signifying "a joyful sound," and that the syllable *jo* ("yo") is found in the sense of "crying out" in various European languages, as for example the German *jodeln* ("to yodel"). He goes on to say, "The Chaldee Targumist and the Jewish doctors absurdly translate *yovel* a ram, and *keren yovel* a ram's horn, nor are the conjectures of the modern writers any better..." (trans. Tregelles).

**25:13.** "In this year of the Jubilee, every one of you will return to his possession.

**25:14.** "And when you make a sale [of some farmland] to your neighbor, or you make a purchase from your neighbor, you must not abuse one another.

**25:15.** "You shall buy from your neighbor, calculating how many years have passed after the Jubilee [to evaluate them to your benefit]; and he will sell to you calculating the years of harvest [that remain before the Jubilee, of which he sells you the income].

**25:16.** "The greater the number of these years will be, the greater the disbursement you will make to him; and the lesser the number of the years will be, the less you will pay him; for (only) a number of harvests is that which he sells you.

*the greater the disbursement you will make to him* (tarbeh miknato). The purchaser is being addressed, for at the end of the verse it says "that which he sells you." It is quite astonishing that Rashi [commenting on the phrase *tarbeh miknato*] wrote, "You may sell it [*timkerennah*] at a high price"; in a Prague edition it says, "He may sell it [*yimkerennah*]," and this is correct.[7]

---

7. Nehama Leibowitz (*Gilyonot*, 1954) cites Shadal's comment, challenges her readers to explain Shadal's "astonishment," and asks them, "How might it be possible to defend Rashi's reading and set aside his astonishment?" To answer this question, it might first be noted that the phrase *tarbeh miknato* may be translated, contra Shadal, as "you [i.e., the seller] may increase its price." See Rosenbaum and Silbermann (*Leviticus*, Appendix, p. 197): "Rashi seems to suggest that the first part of the verse refers to the seller who, if many years intervene between the time of the sale and the Jubilee, is allowed to sell the field at a high price, and the second part to the purchaser who, in view of the small number of years that intervene, may offer a low price for it. He could have of course referred the whole verse to the purchaser, when the translation would be: according to the multitude of years thou shalt increase the price (i.e. pay a higher price for the field) and according to the fewness of the years thou shalt diminish

**25:17.** **"You shall not abuse one another, but fear your God; for I, the Lord, am your God.**

*You shall not abuse one another.* It seems to me that the reason for this admonition is that since the purchaser has been cautioned [as to what he should expect to pay], this is added so that people should not think that the seller is free to sell at an excessively high price (Shalom Simeon Modena).

**25:18.** **"You shall carry out my statutes, and my laws you shall observe and carry out; and (then) you will endure on your land in tranquility.**

**25:19.** **"The land will give its produce, and you will enjoy of it to the fill, and you will endure on the land in tranquility.**

**25:20.** **"And if you say, 'What will we eat in the seventh year, whereas we will not sow, and we will not gather our harvests?'—**

**25:21.** **"I will decree for you My blessing in the sixth year, which will produce a harvest (sufficient) for three years.**

*for three years.* Half the sixth year, all of the seventh, and half the eighth (see Rashi [who comments that they would sow in Marḥeshvan of the eighth year and reap five months later in Nisan]), for part of a year is called a year.

**25:22.** **"And you will sow in the eighth year, and you will eat of the old crops. Until the ninth year, until (that is) the arrival of its harvest (of the eighth), you will eat of the old.**

---

the price thereof. But since the preceding verse speaks of both the seller and the purchaser, Rashi preferred to divide this verse also in the same way." Nevertheless, Shadal might have argued that such a division would be unnatural, and that the entire verse should be construed as addressing the same party (the purchaser) throughout.

# Shadal on Leviticus

***Until the ninth year.*** See Rashi [who says that this means until the Sukkot holiday of the ninth year, when the harvest of the eighth year is brought into the people's homes].

**25:23. "The land, however, must not be sold absolutely [for always], for to Me belongs the land, and you are with me (like) foreigners and sojourners.**

**25:24. "And in all the country of your possession you shall accord to the land (the possibility of) redemption.**

***you shall accord to the land (the possibility of) redemption.*** This refers to the text that follows below. This "redemption" [*ge'ulah*] was to be accomplished with money, unlike what was to occur during the Jubilee, which was simply a return of land without a redemption (Rashi, Rashbam, Mendelssohn). Compare, "You were sold for nought, and you shall be redeemed [*tigga'elu*] without money" (Isa. 52:3); that is, just as your sale was not accomplished by the usual method, since it was for nothing, so your redemption will not be done in the usual way.

**25:25. "When (that is) an impoverished brother of yours sells of his possession, his *go'el* [redeemer, that is, one to whom, by reason of his consanguinity, this right belongs], the one closest to him, may come and redeem that which his brother [kinsman] will have sold.**

**25:26. "One, however, who does not have a *go'el* [that is, one who does not have a relative who is able or willing to disburse the necessary sum], but comes into the ability and has enough to redeem his (farmland)—**

**25:27. "He will evaluate the years of his sale [that is, he will calculate the value of the years enjoyed by the purchaser, dividing the sum paid by the number of the years from the sale to the Jubilee, and multiplying the quotient by the number of the years enjoyed], and he will pay back the surplus to the one to whom he sold, and it will return to his possession.**

*the surplus.* The money exceeding the value of the crops that the purchaser consumed.

**25:28.** **"If, however, he does not have enough to make such a restitution, that which he has sold will remain in the hand of the purchaser until the year of the Jubilee, and it will come out of it in the Jubilee, and (the seller) will return to his possession.**

**25:29.** **"When, however, one sells a dwelling house in a walled city, his right of redemption will last until the end of the year of the sale; throughout a year it may be redeemed.**

*When, however, one sells a dwelling house, etc.* Redemption causes harm to the purchaser; thus the Torah instituted a [permanent right of] redemption [only] with respect to an inherited field, so that a person should not remain without a field from which to sustain himself, but with respect to houses in a walled city, upon which one's life does not depend—since one who has a field can dwell on it and build himself a house there—the Torah conferred a redemption right for one year only. Hence the purchaser, after a year has passed from the time of his purchase, may make expenses to improve his house, which he would not have done if the seller could redeem it in any year. However, houses in unwalled villages are as necessary [to their owners] as fields, and therefore such houses have a permanent right of redemption [v. 31 below]; see the *Me'ammer.*[8]

---

8.  In his comment on v. 31, the *Me'ammer* points out that houses within walled cities are usually owned by artisans or merchants who would, in general, benefit economically by selling their houses permanently. In some cases, a temporary shortage of money might induce such owners to sell, but they are granted only a one-year right of redemption, because otherwise the purchasers would be discouraged from making the type of home improvements that are expected in a city. On the other hand, "houses in unwalled villages" [*batei ha-ḥatserim*] are located in open fields and serve as shelters for farmers and vineyard keepers, and therefore such houses are subject to the same permanent right of redemption as the fields themselves.

# Shadal on Leviticus

**25:30.** "But if it is not redeemed before an entire year has passed, the house situated in a walled city will remain absolutely with the purchaser, for all the ages to come; it will not come out [of his hands] in the Jubilee.

*in a walled city (ba-ir asher lo ḥomah).* Rashi aptly commented (as it appears in some editions) that the word *lo* [which is written as לֹא] was directed [by the Masoretes] to be read as לוֹ [so that the phrase *ba-ir asher lo ḥomah* is made to mean "in a city that has a wall"], since the latter word is pronounced similarly to the written word לֹא, but that in truth this word ought to have been read as *lah* (לה, the feminine form of לוֹ), since it refers back to the feminine noun *ir*.[9]

**25:31.** "The houses in the villages not surrounded by a wall, however, will be regarded as belonging to the field of the country; they may be redeemed, and in the Jubilee they will come out [of the hands of the purchaser].

**25:32.** "As to the cities of the Levites, to the houses, that is, of the cities possessed by them, the Levites will have a perpetual right to redeem them.

*the Levites will have a perpetual right.* Since they do not have fields or vineyards, the houses in the cities of their possession are necessary to them, like the houses in the unwalled villages that belong to other Israelites.

**25:33.** "And if another acquires it from the Levites, the sold house, and (any part of) that city of their possession [where it is not redeemed by the Levites themselves] will come out in the Jubilee [from the hands of the purchaser]; for the houses of the cities of the Levites, they are their land property in the midst of the children of Israel [that is, Palestine had to be divided among all the tribes except for that of Levi, who had to be assigned only a few cities with a very small surrounding area].

---

9. Modern editions of Rashi include this comment, though it sometimes appears in parentheses.

226

***And if another acquires*** *(yig'al*, lit. "redeems") ***it from the Levites.***
If one of the Levites (Levi B) redeems a house from an Israelite who
bought it from Levi A, then Levi B should not think that it will remain
in his hands forever inasmuch as the tribe will not lose out; rather, in the
Jubilee the house will come out of the hands of Levi B, the redeemer, and
will return to the hands of Levi A, the seller.[10]

***the sold house, and (any part of) that city of their possession*** *(memkar*
*bayit ve-ir aḥuzzato)*. The conjunctive *vav* [in the word *ve-ir*] introduces
an explanatory phrase; in other words, this means "the sold part of the
city of their possession."[11]  Apparently the alternative view cited by
Ibn Ezra ["Even if the redeemer is another Levite"] accords with my
explanation, which is also that of Mendelssohn.

The Latin translation (Vulgate) renders the first part of the verse as,
"If they are *not* redeemed." According to this reading, the sequence of
this section is as follows:

- v. 29:  Houses within a walled city have a one-year period of
redemption.
- v. 30:  If they are not redeemed within a year, they may no longer be
redeemed, and even in the Jubilee year they do not come out of the
purchaser's hands.
- v. 31:  However, houses within unwalled villages are treated the
same as fields, and they may be redeemed after a year; if they are
not redeemed, they come out of the purchaser's hands in the Jubilee.
- v. 32:  The houses of the Levites are their possession, and they carry
a permanent right of redemption like the houses in unwalled villages.
- v. 33:  And if they are not redeemed, they come out of the purchaser's
hand in the Jubilee.

10. Shadal's translation does not conform with his comment; see the
final footnote on this verse.
11. Shadal's translation, which understands the conjunctive *vav* literally
as "and," once again does not conform with his comment, according
to which the phrase might have been translated, "the sold house, that
is, the sold part of the city of their possession."

Similarly, Rashbam sensed that the meaning was "if it is not redeemed," and therefore he explained the phrase as referring to a situation in which one wishes to redeem but does not have the means to do so.[12]

**25:34. "Likewise the surrounding field of their cities may not be sold, for it is a perpetual property for them.**

*the surrounding field of their cities.* According to the plain meaning, the Levites were forbidden to sell their surrounding field, because it was very small.[13]

**25:35. "When a brother of yours becomes poor, and he is found nearby you with faltering resources [close to falling into indigence], you must sustain him and act so that he may live, whether he is with you as a stranger [living with his own family] or as a sojourner [entering into the service of some house].**

*as a stranger (ger) or as a sojourner (ve-toshav).* See *Ohev Ger* [pp. 62-63 in the Cracow edition], where I explicated this phrase in accordance with Onkelos' translation [in some editions], *yedur ve-yitotav,* i.e., "let him be a *ger* and let him be a *toshav,* and let him live with you." But this is a difficult interpretation; instead, perhaps the meaning is "whether he is a *ger* (who has a wife and children), or whether he is a *toshav* (who is by himself), let him live with you."

---

12. R. David Zvi Hoffmann, whose understanding of this verse is the same as that of Shadal's comment, says that the emendation of critics such as Ewald and Dillmann, who read the first part of the verse as "if it is not redeemed from the Levites," is unnecessary and in fact incorrect. Hoffmann also disagrees with those (including Rashi) who say that *yig'al* in this verse does not mean "redeem" but "acquire"; he is thus effectively disagreeing with Shadal's translation of the verse.
13. However, according to *Sifra* (followed by Rashi), this verse is construed to mean that if a Levite dedicated his field to the Temple [*hekdesh*] and did not redeem it, and then the Temple treasurer sold it to a third party, the Levite could redeem it at any time.

25:36. "You must not take from him interest or increase, but you shall fear your God, and act so that your brother may live with you.

25:37. "Your money you shall not give him at interest, and your food you shall not give him for (having from it) an increase.

25:38. "It is I, the Lord, your God, Who brought you out of the land of Egypt, to give you the land of Canaan, to be your God.

25:39. "And when a brother of yours becomes poor nearby you, and sells himself to you, you must not hold him in servitude as a slave.

25:40. "He will be with you as a hireling, or as a sojourner [entered into the service of a family], and he will serve by you until the year of the Jubilee.

25:41. "Then he will go forth from your house, together with his children, and he will return to his family, and he will reenter into his paternal possession.

25:42. "For they are My servants, whom I have brought out of the land of Egypt; they may not sell themselves so as to become slaves.

25:43. "You must not lord it over him with rigor, but you shall fear your God.

25:44. "But the male slave and the female slave that you will have, who are of the surrounding nations, from whom you may purchase male and female slaves—

25:45. "And also of the children of the sojourners dwelling with you, you may purchase, or (individuals) of their family, begotten in your country [and sold by their own parents], these will be your property.

25:46. "These you will hold as hereditary property, to pass on to your children after you; you will have service of them in perpetuity. But with regard to your brothers, the children of Israel, you must not lord it over one another with rigor.

**25:47.** "And when a foreigner or sojourner comes into ability nearby you, and a brother of yours becomes poor near you, and he sells himself to the foreigner dwelling by you, or to a descendant of the family of a foreigner—

***or to a descendant*** *(le-eker).* The word *eker* denotes "root" [*ikkar, shoresh*] (Ibn Ezra), and means a person from the root of a foreigner's family; that is, even if this person is born in the land of Israel, do not leave a Hebrew servant in his hands, since he is from a family of foreigners, and he himself is a gentile born of gentiles, though as one who was born in the land of Israel he is not referred to as a "foreigner" [*ger*] (the late Jacob Hai Pardo). According to A. H. Mainster, however, this is an individual who is from a family of foreigners and sojourners, but who "uprooted" himself [*ne'ekar*] from them and became a full convert; even though he is considered Jewish for all purposes, do not leave a Hebrew servant in his hands.

**25:48.** "After having been sold, there will be redemption for him; one of his brothers will redeem him.

**25:49.** "Either his uncle or his cousin will redeem him, or some (other) blood relative of his, of his family, will redeem him; or (he himself) will come into ability and redeem himself.

**25:50.** "(But in the act of selling himself) he will calculate with his purchaser (the time that will pass) from the year in which he sells himself until that of the Jubilee, and the purchase money will be (fixed) after the years have been calculated. His service with him must be like that of a hireling [that is, not for life, but for so much per year].

***until that of the Jubilee.*** One who sells himself to a non-Israelite does not go forth in the sixth year, for the Torah permitted one who wished to sell himself for more than six years to sell himself to a foreigner dwelling in the land of Israel.[14] However, in the Jubilee year even he goes free, for the Jubilee was a year of liberty in the land for all its inhabitants, and it would not be proper for even one of them not to return to his home then. The Torah wished to equalize the entire nation as one, as friends, and such equality would not be realized if one person remained in servitude.

***His service with him must be like that of a hireling*** *(ki-y'mei sakhir yihyeh immo,* lit. "as the days of a hireling he will be with him"). Similar to "for (only) a number of harvests is that which he sells you" [above, v. 16, referring to the Sabbatical year's limitation on land sales]. He is sold to him not as a permanent bondman, but only until the Jubilee for a fixed amount of years, and he is with his master only as in the days of a hireling, i.e., as if he were hired by him for a definite period. The word *ki-y'mei* (lit. "as the days of") is the equivalent of *ke-vi-y'mei* ("as *in* the days of"); see Exod. 11:4.[15]

**25:51. "(Then) if there are still many of those years [contemplated in the contract], according to those he will make return, to redeem himself, of the money with which he was purchased.**

---

14. In the version of this comment that appears in the Columbia X 893 L 9765 manuscript, Shadal adds here that the six-year limitation on a Hebrew's servitude to a Hebrew master was intended not for the servant's benefit, but in order to prevent the master from becoming arrogant and to remind him that all Israelites were equal. The Torah did not find it necessary to teach these lessons to a non-Israelite master, Shadal says, and besides, if such a master were not able to purchase the servant for more than six years, he would not purchase him at all, or he would do so for a lower price.

15. In his comment on that verse, Shadal interprets the phrase *ka-ḥatsot ha-lailah* ("near midnight") as the equivalent of *ke-va-ḥatsot ha-lailah*, and he supplies a list of similar expressions throughout the Bible, including several instances of *ki-y'mei* as the equivalent of *ke-vi-y'mei.*

**25:52.** "And if few of the years remain to arrive at that of the Jubilee, he will put them [equally] to calculation; according to his years [those, that is, that he would still have had to serve] he will pay him for his own redemption.

**25:53.** "He will be with him as an annual hireling, and you must not permit him to lord it over him with rigor.

*as an annual hireling, etc.* The style of the Torah is to state the gist of the matter at the beginning of a section and to repeat it at the end, in order to reinforce its impression upon one's soul. Thus, in vv. 15 and 16 above, it says, *"He will sell to you calculating the years of harvest* [that remain before the Jubilee]. The greater the number of these years will be, the greater the disbursement you will make to him; and the lesser the number of the years will be, the less you will pay him; *for (only) a number of harvests is that which he sells you."* Here, too, its says first, *"His service with him must be like that of a hireling.* (Then) if there are still many of those years... And if few of the years remain...," and afterwards it says once more (as an admonition to the court), *"He will be with him as an annual hireling"* (vv. 50-53). The Torah then completes the admonition to the court by saying, "You must not permit him to lord it over him with rigor." All of this pertains during the time of his service, which is until the Jubilee, and afterwards it adds that if the Jubilee has arrived and he has not been redeemed, then he goes free in the Jubilee, and this, too, is an admonition to the court.

**25:54.** "And if he cannot redeem himself with these rules, he will go forth (free) in the year of the Jubilee, together with his own children.

**25:55.** "For it is to Me that the children of Israel are servants; My servants they are, whom I brought out of the land of Egypt. I, the Lord, am your God."

*For it is to Me that the children of Israel are servants.* In Rashi's comment it is written, "Anyone who enslaves them below [on earth] enslaves them, as it were, on high [*mesha'bdan mi-le-ma'alah*]."

However, in *Torat Kohanim* [*Sifra* 9:4, the source of this comment], it is written, "...he is considered as if he is enslaving on high [*mishta'bed le-ma'alah*]." The author of *Korban Aharon* [Aaron Ibn Hayyim] interpreted this to mean, "He is considered as if he is enslaving [*mesha'bed*] God Himself." In a manuscript of Rashi in my possession, it is written *mesha'bed mi-le-ma'alah*."[16]

**26:1. "You must not make idols for yourselves, nor erect for yourselves images and statues; and illustrated stones you shall not keep in your country, to prostrate yourselves upon them; for I, the Lord, am your God.**

***and illustrated stones*** *(ve-even maskit,* Ital. *e pietre effigiate).* Stones with depictions or portrayals (Rashbam, Ibn Ezra).

**26:2. "My Sabbaths you shall observe, and my temple you shall respect. I am the Lord."**

---

16. Chavel's edition of Rashi conforms with Shadal's manuscript, *mesha'bed mi-le-ma'alah.* Rosenbaum and Silbermann have the reading *mesha'bdo mi-le-ma'alah,* which brings out more explicitly the meaning of "enslaving Him."

# *Beḥukkotai*

*"If you follow my statutes..." • "But if you do not obey
me..." • Sevenfold punishments • "I will recall to memory
My pact with Jacob" • Donating a person's value •
Consecrating animals, houses, or fields •
"These are the precepts"*

**26:3.** "If you follow My statutes and observe My precepts, and carry them out—

**26:4.** "I will give you the rains in their time, and the land will give its crops, and the tree of the field will give its produce.

**26:5.** "The threshing will arrive (will last) for you until the grape harvest, and the grape harvest will overtake the sowing; and you will eat your bread to the fill, and you will dwell in tranquility in your land.

**26:6.** "I will put peace in the country, and you will be able to lie down without anyone disturbing you. I will make the savage beasts disappear from the territory, and the sword will not pass through your land.

# *Beḥukkotai*

26:7. "You will pursue your enemies, and they will fall before you by the sword.

26:8. "Five of you will pursue a hundred of them, and a hundred of you will pursue ten thousand of them; and your enemies will fall before you by the sword.

26:9. "I will turn toward you (in propitiation), I will make you proliferate and multiply, and I will maintain the alliance made with you.

26:10. "You will eat the old, the very old produce, and you will take out the old to make room for the new.[1]

26:11. "I will keep My seat in your midst, and never will it happen that My soul will reject you.

26:12. "Rather, you will have Me among you, and I will be your (protecting) God, and you will be My people.

26:13. "I am the Lord your God, Who brought you out of the land of Egypt, freeing you from being their slaves, and I broke the bars of your yoke, and I made you walk with your head held high.

26:14. "But if you do not obey Me, and you do not carry out all of these precepts—

26:15. "And if you despise My statutes, and if your soul rejects My laws, failing entirely to carry out My commandments, breaking (in sum) My pact [that is, the loyalty sworn to Me]—

26:16. "I, in equal measure, will treat you as follows: I will assign over you misfortune [the poor outcome of your labors], consumption

---

1. In the version of a portion of Shadal's Leviticus commentary that appears in the Columbia X 893 L 9765 manuscript, Shadal inserts a comment here on the word *noshan* ("the very old produce"): "This indicates duration, that the produce would not become spoiled."

**and fever [here, diseases of grains], that consume the eyes [in the vain hope of harvest] and destroy the soul; and you will sow your seed in vain, and (that little which it will produce) your enemies will eat it.**

*misfortune (behalah).* It seems to me that this is used in the same sense as in, "Therefore He made them end their days uselessly, and their years in distress [*ba-behalah*]" (Ps. 78:33); "They will not labor in vain, nor will they give birth uselessly [*la-behalah*]" (Isa. 65:23). Here, too, the reference is to plagues that would cause them loss in their agricultural labors, namely, "consumption" [*ha-shaḥefet*] and "fever" [*ha-kaddaḥat*], which are plagues of the grain, not of the body. This fits in with the subsequent phrases, "that consume the eyes and destroy the soul" (as the farmer expects to harvest but does not), and "you will sow your seed in vain"; afterwards it is added that even if the seed sprouts, their enemies will eat it.

The word *behalah* appears without the definite article prefix *ha-*, because it denotes a [general] thing that frustrates the people's hopes, after which the Torah specifies *ha-shaḥefet* and *ha-kaddaḥat*. The curses mentioned in the *parashah* of *Ki Tavo* (Deut. ch. 28) can be explained in a similar manner.[2] Ibn Ezra, too, mentions that "many say" that *ha-shaḥefet* and *ha-kaddaḥat* are two diseases of the seed, like *shiddafon* and *yerakon* (Deut. 28:22).

**26:17. "I will turn against you, and you will be left defeated before your enemies; those that hate you will lord it over you, and you will flee (even) without anyone pursuing you.**

**26:18. "And if with all that, you do not obey Me, I will continue to punish you sevenfold for your sins.**

2. In Shadal's comment on Deut. 28:22, interpreting the words *shaḥefet* and *kaddaḥat* in that verse, he cross-refers to the comment here and notes that two other maladies mentioned afterwards in Deut. 28:22, *shiddafon* and *yerakon* (which he translates as "smut" and "blight"), are understood by Rashi to be crop diseases, and that a third one, *ḥerev* (which might have been understood as "sword"), is the equivalent of *ḥorev* and indicates "dryness" that would harm crops.

# Beḥukkotai

**26:19.** "I will break down your proud arrogance [founded upon the fertility of the soil], and I will render your sky like iron, and your land like copper.

*I will break down your proud arrogance.* I will break that which is the cause of your arrogance.

**26:20.** "Your strength will be consumed in vain, and your land will not give its crops, and the trees of the country will not give their produce.

**26:21.** "And if you proceed against Me obstinately and do not wish to obey Me, I will add upon you (other) plagues, sevenfold, according to your sins.

*And if you proceed against Me obstinately (keri).* Naphtali Wessely [in *Netivot ha-Shalom*] interpreted this phrase to mean, "If, even in this evil event [*mikreh*] that has befallen you, you proceed against Me as you did previously." But under his interpretation, the main idea is missing, for the meaning of the verse according to this interpretation is, "If, notwithstanding these events and plagues that I have brought against you, you still proceed against Me [*telekhu immi*, lit. "you walk with Me"]"—but how then should the expression *telekhu immi* be understood, since it is akin to the expression "Noah walked with God" (Gen. 6:9)?

Mendelssohn interpreted *keri* as denoting "opposition," giving it the same derivation as *likrat* ("towards"), i.e., "if you proceed against My will," "if you make it your goal to do the opposite of what I desire." However, we do not find the word *likrat* used in the sense of opposition; to the contrary, we find, "He [Balaam] did not go, as in the other times, toward [*likrat*] the omens" (Num. 24:1); that is, he did not go after them. Besides, when he [Mendelssohn] came to the phrase, "I will proceed against you *ba-ḥamat keri*" (below, v. 28), his position collapsed,[3] for what is the meaning of "in the anger of opposition"? In fact, all anger [*ḥemah*] involves opposition, and thus he was forced to separate the two

---

3. Shadal's expression in the Hebrew original is *lo matsa yadav ve-raglav*, "he could not find his hands and feet."

connected words, and he translated *ba-ḥamat keri* as if it were written *be-ḥemah be-keri* ("in anger, in opposition").[4] This is not interpretation; rather, it is a distortion of the text.

If only I knew why these scholars repeatedly turned here and there to find for themselves strained and far-fetched ways of interpreting the word *be-keri*, when they were preceded by the eminent translator Onkelos, of blessed memory, the first in time and rank of the entire class of interpreters, who—on the basis of the received tradition in his hands—translated the word *be-keri* [into Aramaic] as *be-kashyu* ("with hardness"), and the words *ba-ḥamat keri* as *bi-t'kof regaz* ("with strengthened anger"), and these are interpretations that fit the plain meaning of the text without any difficulty at all. And if you ask how the meaning of "hardness" came to be associated with the word *keri*, I suggest that this was derived from the word *korah* ("beam"). Be that as it may, this word was undoubtedly known to our forebears by tradition from their forebears, and they knew that it indicated "hardness" (*Bikkurei ha-Ittim* 5589 [1828], p. 89).[5]

**26:22. "I will send against you the savage beasts, which will deprive you of children, and exterminate your animals, and reduce you to a small number, and your streets will remain deserted.**

**26:23. "And if after that you do not rectify yourselves toward Me, and you proceed with Me obstinately—**

**26:24. "I, too, will proceed toward you harshly, and I, too, will strike you sevenfold, for your sins.**

---

4.  Mendelssohn's German translation of the phrase in question in v. 28 is *so will ich euch im Zorn entgegen wandeln* ("so will I in anger walk against you").

5.  Shadal's entire comment here is taken from this source, an excerpt from an article of his explaining various Hebrew words including *keri* (pp. 82-90). In this article, he also expresses disagreement with Rashi's interpretation of *keri* as "irregularly" or "by chance," and with Menahem ibn Saruq's interpretation of the word as denoting "refraining" or "withholding."

**26:25.** "And I will cause to come against you a sword that will avenge the (violated) pact, and you will retreat into your cities, and I will send an epidemic in your midst, and you will have to give yourselves into the enemy's hand—

**26:26.** "(Reduced to extremes by hunger as well), I having broken for you the support of bread, so that ten women [that is, many families] will bake bread in a single oven, and will take it back by weight, and you will eat it without being satisfied.

*ten women.* From ten families (Ibn Ezra); see also Wessely and Reggio.[6]

**26:27.** "And if after that you do not obey Me, and you proceed toward Me obstinately—

**26:28.** "I will proceed toward you with obstinate anger, and I, too, will punish you sevenfold, for your sins.

**26:29.** "And you will eat the flesh of your sons, and the flesh of your daughters you will eat.

**26:30.** "I will destroy your altars, and I will exterminate your images, and I will cause your dead bodies to fall upon those [that is, the wreckage] of your idols, and My soul will reject you.

*those of your idols (pigrei gilluleikhem,* lit. "the dead bodies of your idols"). Perhaps this refers to animals that were worshiped, which would also die of hunger.

---

6. Wessely's comments on this verse (in *Netivot ha-Shalom*) state that "ten" is a number signifying "many" in biblical usage, and that the meaning of this curse is that the food shortage was to be so severe that each family retrieving their bread from the common oven would suspect that they would not receive their fair share if the portions were estimated, and so they would insist on weighing them. Reggio's commentary closely tracks these comments of Wessely.

# Shadal on Leviticus

**26:31.** "I will render your cities deserted, and your temples desolate, and I will not smell your propitiatory aromas.

**26:32.** "I Myself will render your country deserted, and your enemies who will occupy it will be left astounded at this.

**26:33.** "I will scatter you among the nations, causing you to be pursued by an unsheathed sword; and your land will be a desert, and your cities will be a desolation.

**26:34.** "Then the land will fulfill its rests, during all that time when it will be deserted, while you remain in the country of your enemies. Then the land will rest, and it will fulfill its Sabbatical years.

*Then the land will fulfill its rests, etc.* See v. 41 below. In a manuscript of Rashi in my possession it says, *"And it will fulfill:* to complete [*le-mal'ot*] its Sabbatical years" (with the reading of *le-mal'ot* instead of *la-melekh*).[7]

 **26:35.** "All the time in which it will be deserted, it will rest that which it did not rest in your Sabbatical years, when it was inhabited by you.

**26:36.** "And in those among you who remain, I will cause to enter a despondency of heart in the lands of their enemies, so that the sound of dry leaves will pursue them, and they will flee as one flees from the sword, and they will fall without anyone pursuing them.

*dry leaves (aleh niddaf).* In a manuscript of Rashi in my possession, it says *she-ha-ru'ah hodafto* ("[a leaf] that the wind pushes along"), i.e., it makes the leaf *niddaf*, which is the equivalent of *neh'daf* ("pushed, driven").[8]

---

7. In some editions (including that of Rosenbaum and Silbermann), Rashi's comment reads *ve-hirtsat la-melekh et shabbetoteha*, understood to mean, "The land will satisfy the King with regard to its Sabbatical years." Chavel's edition has the reading *lemal'ot*.
8. In standard editions (including those of Chavel and of Rosenbaum and Silbermann), Rashi's comment reads *she-ha-ru'ah dohafo*,

**26:37.** "They will stumble over one another, as if they had the sword at their backs, without anyone pursuing them; you will not be able (in sum) to raise your head in the face of your enemies.

**26:38.** "You will go wandering among the peoples, and the land of your enemies will devour you.

**26: 39.** "And those of you who remain will feel the pain of their own sins, in the lands of their enemies; and together with those, they will also feel the pain of the sins of their fathers.

*with those.* Together with their own sins.

**26:40.** "And they will confess their sins, and those of their fathers, of having been (that is) unfaithful to Me, and also (after being warned of the punishments) of having proceeded toward Me obstinately.

**26:41.** "And I too, proceeding toward them harshly, and causing them to go to the land of their enemies, (I will do this only) so that their obtuse heart will be humbled, and then their punishment will be finished.

*their punishment will be finished (yirtsu et avonam,* lit. "they will complete their punishment"). Compare, "Till he shall complete [*yirtseh*], as a hireling, his day" (Job 14:6). Otherwise, perhaps every instance of *yirtsu* and *tirtseh* occurring here [see also v. 34 above, where *tirtseh* is translated as "will fulfill"] should properly be vocalized with a *pataḥ* [i.e., *yartsu* and *tartseh*] so as to be in the *hif'il* (causative) conjugation, as in *ve-hirtsat et shabbetoteha* ("and it will fulfill its Sabbatical years,"

which likewise means "that the wind pushes along," but the alternate reading *hodafto* appears to be preferable, because it relates more directly to the word *niddaf*, from the root *hadaf*. The words *aleh niddaf* are commonly translated in English as "a driven leaf" but may also mean "a fallen leaf." Shadal's translation "dry leaves" (Ital. *fogliame secco*) is in conformance with his opinion that *aleh* may be construed as a collective noun, as in *aleh zayit* (Gen. 8:11), which he translates as "olive foliage" (see his comment there).

241

v. 34). *Hirtsah* [the *hif'il* infinitive form of the root *ratsah*, "to give satisfaction"] means "to pay" (just as *shillem* [which also means "to pay"] denotes "to make peace [*shalom*]," and thus *hirtsah* conveys the sense of "to placate"). In that case, the meaning of the phrase here would be that when their heart is humbled, then the payment for their sin will be complete (i.e., "they will have paid"). Similarly, the soil is obligated, as it were, to pay its Sabbatical years to God (see Mendelssohn on v. 34).[9]

**26:42. "And I will recall to memory My pact with Jacob; and also My pact with Isaac, and also My pact with Abraham I will remember, and the land I will remember.**

**26.43. "And the land, after their emigration, will remain abandoned, and it will fulfill its Sabbatical years, being deserted after their departure, and they [at the same time] will finish their penalty. For they despised My laws, and their soul rejected My statutes.**

*And the land, after their emigration, will remain abandoned (ve-ha-arets te'azev mehem).* The word *te'azev* is not directly connected to the word *mehem* [i.e., the phrase does not mean "will be abandoned by them"]. Rather, the verse is to be construed as follows: "The land, when it will be without them, will remain abandoned and will not be settled again." Those [e.g., Mendelssohn] who interpret the phrase to mean "the land will be abandoned by them," that is, "they will abandon it," have no taste for Hebrew speech. Instead, the prefix letter *mem* in the word *mehem* [lit. "from them"] denotes separation and distancing. The meaning is that after Israel is exiled from their land, no other nation will prosper upon it, and their land will not be inhabited as it was, but it will be abandoned after its separation from them, and it will fulfill its Sabbatical years. Similarly, the phrase *boh'shamah mehem* ("being deserted after their departure") does not mean that they will make it deserted [i.e., "being deserted *by* them"], but that the land will remain deserted after its separation from them.

---

9.  There, commenting on the word *tirtseh*, Mendelssohn explains that one who repays what he owes to another can be said to "make peace" or "appease" that person from asserting a legal claim against him.

***being deserted*** (*boh'shamah*). This is one of the rules of the [guttural] letters *alef, he, ḥet,* and *ayin,* that sometimes they are vocalized with a *sheva* that should properly have occurred in the preceding letter, and are preceded by a vowel that it should have had itself [i.e., the first two letters in the word *boh'shamah, bet* and *he,* have their vowels transposed, and thus the word properly would have been vocalized *be-hoshamah*]. For example:

- *la'ser* instead of *le'asser* (Deut. 26:12);
- *ba'ser* instead of *be'asser* (Neh. 10:39);
- *ma'zrim* instead of *me'azzerim* (2 Chron. 28:23);
- *maḥlemim* instead of *meḥallemim* (Jer. 29:8);
- *mah'lekhin* instead of *mehallekhin* (Dan. 4:34).

**26:44. "But despite all this, even when they find themselves in the land of their enemies, I will not reprove them and will not reject them so as to exterminate them and break the pact that I have with them; for I, the Lord, am their God.**

**26:45. "And I will remember in their favor the pact made with the elder ones, whom I brought out of the land of Egypt, before the eyes of the nations, to become their (protecting) God. I am the Lord."**

**26:46. These are the statutes, the precepts, and the laws that the Lord gave on Mount Sinai, by means of Moses, (as the basis for the pact) between Him and the children of Israel.**

**27:1. The Lord spoke to Moses, saying—**

**27:2: "Speak to the children of Israel, and say to them: When one utters a vow to give to the Lord the value of some person—**

***When one utters a vow*** (*ki yafli neder*). See Num. ch. 6.[10]

---

10. A parallel expression, *ki yafli lin'dor neder,* appears in Num. 6:2 in connection with one who makes a Nazirite oath. Although

# Shadal on Leviticus

*the value (erkekha, עֶרְכְּךָ).* The Hebrew is a doubled form [i.e., the basic form of the word is *erekh,* but the final letter *kaf* is doubled], like the words *ra'anan, sha'anan,* and *umlal* [in each of which the final letter is similarly doubled] (Rashbam). This serves to distinguish [the *erkekha,* which is] a fixed value, from any other type of value [*erekh*].

*the value of some person (be-erkekha nefashot).* The value of any person [*nefesh adam*] seems to be included, whether that of the donor himself (who says *erki alai,* "I obligate myself to donate my value") or that of someone else (in which case the donor says *erekh ploni alai,* "I obligate myself to donate the value of so-and-so") [see Maimonides, *Arakhin ve-Ḥaramin* 1:2]. Rashi interpreted the phrase to refer to one who vows to give *erekh nafsho* [implying that he means "his own value"], but this is inexact, and thus when he reaches the verse "But if the age is from five..." (v. 5 below), he was compelled to write, "Not that the person making the vow is a minor" [but instead, this is an adult who vows to donate the value of a minor]. If he had interpreted *be-erkekha nefashot* to mean one who vows to donate either his own value or that of someone else, Rashi would not have had to write such a comment. And in fact, the age group from five to twenty years includes one who has reached the age of thirteen and is no longer considered a minor; and such a person is able to take the vow of *erki alai.*

It should be noted that in a manuscript of Rashi in my possession, it is written, "[One who vows to donate *erekh nefashot,* 'the value of a life,' means] to say, 'I obligate myself to donate the value of something [i.e., an organ] that my life [*nafshi,* not *nafsho*] depends on,'" and this reading is correct.

---

Shadal's printed commentary contains no comment on that verse, the Columbia X 893 L 9765 manuscript includes a note indicating that the expression means "when one vows wondrously," as in *mafli la'asot* ("did wondrously," Judges 13:19). Shadal does not elaborate on this idea, but Ibn Caspi (on Lev. 27:2), takes the view that anyone who makes a vow "does wondrously," while the *Keli Yakar* (R. Solomon Ephraim Luntschitz), commenting on Num. 6:2, says that if a man vows to abstain from wine, he "does wondrously" (i.e., he goes above and beyond what is normal or necessary) because he is stronger than wine (i.e., he should be able to "hold his liquor" and avoid falling into sin through drink).

27:3. "The value of a male from the age of twenty years to that of sixty years, the value (I say) will be fifty silver shekels, according to the weight of the Temple.

27:4. "If, however, it is a female, the value will be thirty shekels.

27:5. "If, then, the age is from five to twenty years, the value of a male will be twenty shekels, and that of a female, ten shekels.

27:6. "And if it is from one month to five years, the value of the male will be five silver shekels, and of the female, the value will be three silver shekels.

27:7. "And from sixty years and upward, if it is male the value will be fifteen shekels, and for the female, ten shekels.

*And from sixty years.* Rashi's statement—"The man's value, when he becomes old, decreases more than a third, while the woman's value decreases only a third"—is to be understood as follows: the man's value, when he becomes old, lowers to less than a third; i.e., he is not worth even a third of what he was worth (for at first he was worth 50 shekels and now 15), but the woman's value lowers only to a third (i.e., at first it was 30, and now 10). In the Talmud (*Arakhin* 19a), it is said, "A female, when she ages, stands at one third, and... a male does not stand at even one third."

27:8. "And if he is too poor for (to be able to pay) the (fixed) value, he will present that individual [whose value he must pay] to the priest, who will evaluate him. The priest will evaluate him according to the ability of the one who made the vow.

27:9. "With regard, however, to some animal that may be made a sacrifice to the Lord, whatever the animal may be that one gives to the Lord will be holy.

# Shadal on Leviticus

***whatever the animal may be that one gives*** *(kol asher yitten mimmennu,*
lit. "all that he gives of it"). This phrase is to be understood [according
to the Halakhah] as Mendelssohn translated it, "that portion which he
devoted"; the Rabbis explained that if one said, "Let the leg of this
animal be a burnt offering" [then only that portion, and not the entire
animal, will be holy—*Arakhin* 5a]. However, according to the plain
meaning [as reflected in the translation here], Scripture is not speaking
about one who devotes part of an animal.

**27:10. "He must not exchange it, neither replacing a good one with a
bad one, nor a bad one with a good one; and if he replaces an animal
with another, that one and its replacement will be holy.**

***He must not exchange it, neither replacing...*** *(lo yaḥalifennu ve-lo
yamir oto,* lit. "he must not exchange it or replace it"). This [i.e., "he
must not exchange it or replace it"] is a general statement, after which
the details are specified: he must not replace a good one with a bad one
[*tov be-ra*] or a bad one with a good one [*o ra be-tov*]. According to the
accentuator [who can be said to have created a single phrase *ve-lo yamir
oto tov be-ra* by marking the word *be-ra* with a disjunctive *tipḥa*], it
appears that *temurah* is a change of good to bad, while *ḥilluf* is a change
of bad to good. There are supports for this:

- "They exchanged [*va-yamiru*] their glory for the likeness of an ox"
  (Ps. 106:20);
- "The sycamores are cut down, but cedars we will put in their place
  [*naḥalif*]" (Isa. 9:9);
- "But those who wait for the Lord will renew [*yaḥalifu*] their
  strength" (Isa. 40:31).

One verse presents a difficulty: "And he [Laban] changed [*ve-heḥelif*]
my wages ten times" (Gen. 31:7). But perhaps the meaning is that from
Laban's point of view, the changes were from bad to good, for he was
always seeking an advantage for himself.

  Now it is true that if the words *lo yaḥalifennu* are connected to *ra
be-tov,* the intervening word *o* ("or") would be superfluous, but in fact,

246

# Beḥukkotai

Moses our Teacher did not intend to divide the verse in accordance with the [conventional] accents. Rather, to bring out his intended meaning, it would have been proper to accentuate the words *lo yaḥalifennu ve-lo yamir oto* as follows:

לֹא יַחֲלִיפֶנּוּ וְלֹא יָמִיר אֹתוֹ

[thus setting off these words as a unified phrase, "he must not exchange it or replace it"]. Then he began the next part of the verse with words that refer back to the end of the immediately preceding phrase [*ve-lo yamir oto*], that is, with the words *tov be-ra* ("a good one with a bad one"), corresponding to the meaning of *yamir*, and then he went on to say *o ra be-tov* ("or a bad one with a good one"), corresponding to the meaning of *yaḥalifennu*.[11]

**27:11. "But if it is some impure animal, of which a sacrifice is not made to the Lord, he will present the animal to the priest.**

**27:12. "The priest will evaluate it, according to whether it is good or bad; the price that the priest assigns it, that will be (valid).**

***The priest will evaluate it,*** *etc.* The phrase "the price that the priest assigns it, that will be" is explained by Rashi to refer to other individuals who come to buy these animals from the Temple treasury [*hekdesh*], while "if he wants to redeem it" (next v.) refers back to the owners, with whom Scripture deals more strictly and adds a fifth to the redemption price, which is also the case with one who consecrates his house (v. 14) or his field (v. 16). But all of this is difficult in light of the plain meaning [of the present verse], for the Torah makes no mention at all of a Temple treasurer who sells consecrated things to anyone who may appear, and the implication of the verses is merely that one who consecrates anything that cannot be brought upon the altar must pay its value as soon as he

---

11. In Shadal's *Beit ha-Otsar*, vol. 2, pp. 187-188, he offers additional biblical verses to support the distinction between the verbs *heḥelif* and *hemir*, and he paraphrases the present verse as follows: "He must not exchange it [*lo yaḥalifennu*], a bad one with a good one, and he must not replace it [*ve-lo yamir oto*], a good one with a bad one."

makes the consecration, and that if he comes afterwards to redeem it, he must add a fifth of its value. Indeed, if he was not going to redeem it, why would he have paid its value in the first place? Would he not have turned over to the treasury the physical consecrated thing itself?

Therefore it seems to me that one who consecrated a thing would not deliver the physical thing, but he would keep it in his possession, taking special care of it and treating it in accordance with protocols of holiness that are unknown to us. A model for this would have been the second tithe [*ma'aser sheni*], which was called "holy" (below, vv. 30 and 31) and was eaten by the owners in Jerusalem. The Torah did not want a person to consecrate a thing that could not be brought upon the altar unless this would bring about some benefit to others, for it was not the will of the Torah that a person should think that he has done a holy act that was favored by his God (other than the sacrifices themselves, as for example when he would donate a burnt offering), if his act has not occasioned any benefit to others. Therefore the Torah commanded that as soon as a person consecrates a thing, he must give its monetary price to the House of God and the priests, and that afterwards the thing would remain in his possession under the laws of holiness. If he later wants to take it back into the secular domain, then he adds a fifth of its value and redeems it, and uses it as he wishes.

**27:13. "And if he wants to redeem it, he will add to it a fifth over the value.**

**27:14. "And when one consecrates his own house as a holy thing to the Lord, the priest will evaluate it, according to whether it is good or bad; as the priest evaluates it, so it [its price] will remain [fixed].**

**27:15. "And if the consecrator wants to redeem his own house, he will add to it a fifth of the money of the value, and it will remain his.**

**27:16. "And if one consecrates to the Lord some field of his hereditary possession, the value will be according to the sowing that it takes. A field with a capacity of a *homer* [ten *ephah*] of a sowing of barley will be valued at fifty silver shekels.**

248

**27:17.** "If he consecrates his field from the year of the Jubilee onward, this price will be valid.

**27:18.** "But if he consecrates his field after the Jubilee, the priest will make account of the money [that he will have to pay if he wants to redeem it] according to the years that remain until that of the Jubilee, and the [legal] price will undergo a subtraction [corresponding to the years passed since the previous Jubilee].

**27:19.** "And if the consecrator wants to redeem the field, he will add to it a fifth of the [legal] price, and it will remain his.

**27:20:** "And if he does not redeem the field, and likewise if he [the administration of the Temple treasury] has sold the field to another person, it may no longer be redeemed.

*And if he does not redeem the field, and likewise if he has sold the field to another person.* Here, too [as in v. 12 above], this has been interpreted to mean, "if the treasurer has sold it." But as for the treasurer, who mentioned his name? Besides, there is another difficulty: it would have been proper for the Torah to establish a time until which the treasurer would have to wait before selling, for otherwise no time at all would be left for redemption, since immediately after a person consecrated his field, the treasurer would hasten to sell it, and then the consecrator would no longer be able to redeem it.

According to my way of understanding,[12] Scripture's intended

---

12. Here Shadal's commentary is obviously in direct conflict with his text translation. In this instance, it cannot be said that the commentary represents a change of opinion that occurred after he wrote the translation in 1858, because precisely the same comment had already appeared in his earlier work *Ha-Mishtadel* (1846). A clue to Luzzatto's thinking may be provided by an additional comment of his on the present verse that appears in the Columbia X 893 L 9765 manuscript: "The Rabbis' interpretation was, 'if the treasurer has sold it.' But according to the plain meaning, it seems to me that if the consecrator does not redeem the field within a certain time (perhaps within a year), but instead, after having consecrated it, he sells it so as to be able to redeem it with the proceeds of the sale, 'it may no longer be redeemed.'" It is possible that, notwithstanding

meaning is that if the consecrator has not redeemed his field—that is, he has not paid for it with the added fifth—but nevertheless wants to take it out of consecration, so that he does not have to treat the field in accordance with protocols of holiness, and for this purpose he sells the field to another person, then the Torah penalizes him by preventing him from redeeming it from the purchaser; rather, the field remains in the hands of the purchaser until the Jubilee, and afterwards, when it comes out of the purchaser's hands in the Jubilee, it will be "holy to the Lord" (below, v. 21); it will not return to the purchaser, but it will be retained by the Temple treasury and become a permanent possession of the priests. If the consecrator had not sold the field, then it would have come out of its state of holiness at the time of the Jubilee, and the owner would have been able to derive benefit from it as he would from any other hereditary possession of his (and so it would seem from vv. 17 and 18 above, for otherwise, why would the redemption price have been calculated according to the years remaining until the Jubilee?). But now that he has misappropriated the field [from the Temple treasury] and sold it, he forfeits it permanently from the Jubilee onward.[13]

---

his own opinion based on the "plain meaning" [*peshat*], Shadal deliberately chose to adhere to the normative Rabbinic view in his text translation.

13 R. David Zvi Hoffmann, in his comment on the present verse, rejects this view (attributing it to various modern Bible critics), saying that no one but the Temple treasurer had the legal right to sell the Temple's property, and that if anyone else purported to sell it, such a sale would be null and void, and anyone who benefited from it would be guilty of misappropriation. How then, Hoffmann asks, could the Torah have permitted the purchaser to retain the field until the Jubilee? One way of answering this objection might be to adopt an alternative approach given by Jacob Milgrom: this verse is speaking of an owner who consecrates his field *after* he sells it, thereby indicating that he does not want the land back from the purchaser when the Jubilee comes (*Leviticus: A Book of Ritual and Ethics*, p. 329). In such a case, (1) the purchaser would be within his rights if he retained possession of the field until the Jubilee; and (2) the transfer of the field to the Temple and the priests after the Jubilee would not constitute a penalty to the owner (for he would have done nothing deserving of a penalty), but would instead honor his implied wish that the field remain in the Temple's realm permanently as if he had declared it *ḥerem* (see next v.).

**27:21.** "And when the field comes out [of the hands of the purchaser] in the Jubilee, it will be holy to the Lord, like a field consecrated under the name of *ḥerem*[14]; it will become a hereditary possession of the priests.

**27:22.** "And if one consecrates to the Lord a field bought by him, not belonging to his hereditary fields—

**27:23.** "The priest will make him the account of the proportional value [equal to or less than the legal value, according to the years that remain] until the year of the Jubilee, and he will then pay the price as a holy thing to the Lord.

**27:24.** "Then in the year of the Jubilee, the field will return to the power of the one from whom he bought it, to the one (that is) to whom belongs the hereditary possession of that land.

**27:25.** "Every appraisal will be (made) in shekels of the temple. The shekel will be twenty *gerah*.

**27:26.** "But a firstborn of an animal, which has been recognized as such [and therefore holy] to the Lord, may not be consecrated by anyone; whether of the large or of the small cattle, it already belongs to the Lord.

**27:27.** "If it is of an impure animal, it will be ransomed according to its value with the addition of a fifth; and if it is not redeemed, it will be sold for its value.

*If it is of an impure animal.* This refers to one who consecrates the firstborn of a donkey (as per Ibn Ezra and Wessely).[15] According to

14. Left untranslated by Shadal, this word has been rendered by others as "proscribed, "devoted," or "set apart."
15. *Contra* Rashi, who takes the view that the animal referred to in the present verse is not a firstborn, because the only impure animal whose firstborn must be redeemed is a donkey (Exod. 13:13, as interpreted in *Bekhorot* 5b), and in that case the redemption is with

my way of understanding, the phrase "it will be ransomed [*u-fadah*] according to its value" means that the owner pays the value, as any other person who consecrates a thing would do, but in this case he must add on a fifth without accomplishing a redemption that would restore the animal to the secular realm. This fifth is paid only for the purpose of removing the animal from the extra degree of sanctity that the owner added onto the animal when he consecrated it; by paying the value plus a fifth, he removes this second degree of sanctity, and the animal returns to its first degree of sanctity, which is that of a firstborn. Then, if the owner does not redeem it—that is, if he does not ransom it with a lamb [as required by Exod. 13:13]—the animal is sold for its value, i.e., the priests sell it to third parties,[16] and the owner loses his money, just as he would [under Exod. 13:13, which states,] "and if you do not want to redeem it, you shall kill it."

A remaining difficulty is the phrase "and if it is not redeemed [*yigga'el*]," for the standard redemption [*ge'ulah*] is only by means of money, and one who gives a lamb is called a *podeh* ("ransomer"), not a *go'el* ("redeemer"). Perhaps in this case, the person is commanded to "redeem" the animal not with a lamb, but with a second additional payment of a fifth, and if he does not redeem it by paying this second fifth, then the animal "will be sold for its value."

Now all that I have said with regard to the consecrated thing remaining in the hands of the consecrator, who would treat it in accordance with protocols of holiness [see the comment on v. 12, above], would have applied to an impure animal, a house, or a field. However, a pure animal would have been brought to the altar as a sacrifice, and a human being who was "consecrated" [by another] and whose value was paid to the Temple treasury was apparently not subject at all to a law of

---

a lamb given to a priest, not with the payment of the animal's value to the Temple treasury.

16. In the version of a portion of Shadal's Leviticus commentary that appears in the Columbia X 893 L 9765 manuscript, the following comment on the phrase "will be sold for its value" is inserted: "Because the Temple treasury cannot derive any benefit from it, in light of the provision, 'Do not cause to work the firstborn of your bovine animals...' (Deut. 15:19), they sell it and it goes out into the secular realm (Judah Aryeh Osimo)."

holiness, for one person cannot be subordinated to another, such that Reuben would be able to impose some obligation upon Simeon without his consent (Tevet 5602 [1841/42]).

**27:28. "But any consecration that one makes to the Lord under the name of *ḥerem*, of anything that belongs to him, whether of persons [that is, non-Israelite slaves], of animals, or of the fields of his patrimony, will not be able to be sold or redeemed. Every *ḥerem* belongs, as a most holy thing, to the Lord [and thus to the priests].**

*But any consecration... under the name of* ḥerem. This refers to one who consecrates one of his Canaanite slaves, animals, or inherited lands under the name of *ḥerem* ("proscription"). Every *ḥerem* is given to the priests, who cannot sell it to others (in the manner of [a consecrated impure animal, which may be] "sold for its value"—above, v. 27). The owner, too, is not permitted to redeem it, for the *ḥerem* is a most holy thing [*kodesh kodashim*], and no one other than a priest may derive benefit from it.

**27:29. "Any person who has been declared *ḥerem* [that is, by decree of some supreme authority, as in Joshua ch. 6] may not be ransomed; he must be put to death.**

*Any person who has been declared* ḥerem *(kol ḥerem asher yoḥoram min ha-adam).* This is a different matter, not a *ḥerem* consecrated to Heaven, for it is not said to be "to the Lord"; rather, this is one who must be destroyed and killed. This is not something that may be accomplished by any individual person, for it is not said [as it is in v. 28 above] *asher yaḥarim ish* (lit. "that a man may declare *ḥerem*"), but *asher yoḥoram* ("who has been declared *ḥerem*"). Rather, this is a matter that is entrusted to the nation as a whole or to its leaders, who may issue a decree as an emergency measure (even if the regular law does not so provide) and say, "One who does such and such will be declared *ḥerem*." This is in accordance with Nachmanides and Wessely.[17]

---

17. Both of these commentators say that such a *ḥerem* may be decreed by the king or the Sanhedrin. Wessely notes that all the inhabitants

# Shadal on Leviticus

Rosenmueller interprets the phrase *asher yoḥoram min ha-adam* as the equivalent of *asher yaḥarim ish*, as if any Israelite individual would be permitted to declare *ḥerem* his children and the members of his household. This is a gross error, resulting from the notion that a Hebrew speaker [who wished to say, "The apple was eaten by Reuben"] would say *ha-tappuaḥ ne'ekhal me-Reuven* (see above at Lev. 21:7). However, the phrase *min ha-adam* refers not to the active party but to the passive party: [i.e., *kol ḥerem asher yoḥoram min ha-adam* does not mean "anyone who is declared *ḥerem* by a person," but] "anyone *from among* the human race who is declared *ḥerem*." The active party is left unidentified, because it is not just any individual, but one who has the authority to make such a declaration, i.e., the nation as a whole or the king or a judge. But the idea that one of the common people would be permitted to declare *ḥerem* his children or the members of his household is one that goes against the ways of the Torah of Moses. We see that in several places, the Torah cries out against the abominable practices of nations that sacrifice their children, and we see that it transferred the law of *ben sorer u-moreh* [the right to have one's "perverse and rebellious son" put to death] to the court (Deut. 21:18-21). In addition, we see that when someone strikes his non-Israelite slave, and he dies under the master's hand, the slave will be avenged with the master's death (Exod. 12:20).[18] Blessed be He Who separated us from those who go astray, and Who gave us His Torah, the Torah of truth, whose ways are ways of pleasantness, and all its paths are peace.

**27:30. "And every tithe (of the crops) of the land, whether of sown produce, or of the fruit of the trees, belongs to the Lord; it is a holy thing to the Lord.**

**27:31. "And if one wants to redeem something from his tithe, he will add a fifth to it.**

---

of the city of Jericho (except for Rahab and her household) were declared *ḥerem* by Joshua (Josh. 6:17).

18. In his comment ad loc., Shadal notes that under Roman law, "the master had the authority to put his slaves to death by any cruel or unusual means, and for any reason at all."

**27:32.** "Likewise, every tithe of the large and small cattle, (that is) every tenth among the animals that pass under the staff, will be holy to the Lord [they would have nine of every ten animals pass, one by one, through a narrow doorway; they would be counted, and every tenth one would be marked with a staff dipped in a red color].[19]

**27:33.** "(The owner) must not examine whether it is good or bad; that is, he must not replace it; and if he replaces it, that one and its replacement will be holy, neither may they be redeemed."

**27:34.** These are the precepts that the Lord commanded Moses for the children of Israel in Mount Sinai.

# חזק

---

19. This procedure is prescribed in Mishnah *Bekhorot* 10:7.

# APPENDIX

Shadal's choice to focus on the *peshat*, or "plain meaning" of the biblical text, rather than to pursue esoteric, hidden inferences, is consistent with his conviction that Judaism is "a religion without mysteries." This statement is found in his letter to a friend, Giuseppe Almeda, along with other observations about the essentials of "Mosaism." My annotated translation of this letter from the original Italian appeared in *Ḥakirah*, vol. 10, pp. 225-241 (2010). With only a few minor changes, this article is reproduced here as follows.

## *A Letter to Almeda: Shadal's Guide for the Perplexed*

## Translator's Introduction

"One who has the erudition, the knowledge, and the time must lend me aid." With these words, a troubled Jewish man named Giuseppe Almeda appealed for guidance in his search for religious truth. The erudite scholar who answered this *cri de coeur* in 1839 was Samuel David Luzzatto (1800-1865), known by his Hebrew acronym Shadal.

# Shadal on Leviticus

Who was Giuseppe Almeda? An Internet search yields a bit of information. I have been able to ascertain that he lived in Trieste, the cosmopolitan Italian seaport that was then part of the Austrian empire. The databases of the Museum of the Jewish People at Beit Hatfutsot further disclose that he was a shipping insurance promoter, that his family (originally De Almeida) came from Portugal, and that he lived from 1800 to 1861.[1] Thus he was not only Shadal's fellow *triestino,* but also his close contemporary.

As to who Shadal was, there is of course no mystery. He was the leading Jewish writer, educator, thinker, and Bible scholar of nineteenth-century Italy. It was only natural that Almeda should have turned to him for spiritual aid, as the two men were in fact part of a circle of friends.[2] The letter in which Almeda's questions are presented appears as number 185 in the *Epistolario italiano francese latino* (Padua, 1890), the posthumous collection of Shadal's correspondence in Italian, French, and Latin. (His Hebrew letters are collected in the better-known, two-volume *Iggerot Shadal.*)

Almeda starts by explaining his state of mind concerning religion. His Judaic education had been *quasi nulla,* "almost nil," and he had come to favor a pared-down belief in God, the immortality of the soul, and a "practical morality." But then he began to wonder whether this would be enough of a spiritual legacy to pass down to his children. Conversion to Christianity appeared to be a tempting choice, but ultimately he could not bring himself to take such a step: "No, my God! This I will never do... Because I was born into Judaism, I must persist in it." The alternative, as he saw it, was to "seek within" the Jewish religion, "to the greatest extent possible, conviction and truth." Hence his appeal to Shadal.

---

1. See "ALMEDA Origin of Surname," https://dbs.anumuseum.org.il/skn/en/c6/e217676/Family_Name/ALMEDA.
2. See Tullia Catalan, "La 'primavera degli ebrei.' Ebrei italiani del Litorale e del Lombardo Veneto nel 1848-1849," *Zakhor* 6 (2003): 41 n. 23, citing Angelo Cavalieri, *Giuseppe Almeda: memorie* (Trieste, 1868). Catalan's article makes mention (pp. 48-49) of the Almeda-Shadal correspondence of 1839. Almeda's name is included among the "Signori Associati" listed at the end of Shadal's early work on Hebrew grammar, *Prolegomeni ad una grammatica ragionata della lingua ebraica* (Padua, 1836).

# Appendix: A Letter to Almeda

The next part of Almeda's document consists of five sets of questions, dealing with: (1) Jewish beliefs; (2) worship; (3) practices, ceremonies, and prohibitions; (4) morality; and (5) Jewish Reform. The content and tone of the questions make it obvious that Almeda had to be convinced that traditional Judaism could speak to his spiritual yearnings. Not only Christianity, but also the nascent Reform movement seemed to offer at least as good a model in many respects. And yet it seems that deep down, he wanted to be convinced by tradition.

Shadal's answer takes the form of a letter in Italian, numbered 186 in the *Epistolario* and dated March 6, 1839. He opens by expressing "the warmest esteem for the candor of a truly righteous and virtuous soul, and for the wise and judicious mind, of which [Almeda's] writing offers the most undoubted proof, and at the same time declaring my awareness of the honor of the trust that he has shown me." Shadal goes on to answer nine of Almeda's questions—the eight contained in the section on Jewish beliefs, plus the one question concerning the Jewish system of morality. If Shadal ever specifically answered the rest of Almeda's queries, the results do not appear elsewhere in the *Epistolario*. However, the nine answers provide not only a basic response to Almeda's searchings, but also an overview of Shadal's distinctive take on Jewish tradition.

The questions that Shadal dealt with are as follows:

1.  Is there a canonical book that clearly enumerates the cardinal points of the Jewish faith?
2.  Must one believe to be equally true the precepts, the miracles, and the events recorded in the Bible?
3.  Would a Jew who practices the rites and ceremonies, but does not believe in the revelation of Moses, be worthy of salvation in the mind of true believers?
4.  Does the immortality of the soul, and the rewards and punishments of the life hereafter, constitute a basic Jewish belief?
5.  Will the resurrection of the dead be political, religious, or both? Will it be universal?
6.  Is the resurrection not an inconceivable mystery, on the order of the mysteries maintained by Christians?

# Shadal on Leviticus

7.  Can the Jewish religion become universal?  And if it cannot, how can Judaism be called divine?
8.  How is it that to all of these questions, religious and learned persons have given inconsistent answers?
9.  Do Jews receive a moral education purely as Jews, and not as subjects of the government of their respective countries?

In the course of answering these questions, Shadal expresses a number of ideas that he often returns to in his other writings.  Among these are: (1) "Moses did not dictate articles of faith, because God does not command belief, that is, He does not command that which cannot be commanded"; (2) rather, God requires practices, ceremonies, and prohibitions that foster personal virtue and social wellbeing; (3) God chose the Jews as spiritual custodians because they had already accepted the idea of monotheism from their ancestor Abraham; and (4) Jewish morality is grounded upon a sense of compassion, on the one hand, and the fear of Divine retribution, on the other.

Written in Shadal's characteristically vigorous and literary style, the letter to Almeda displays the writer's broad familiarity with secular as well as religious literature.  His responses quote not only the Bible and the Talmud, but also a Stoic Greek philosopher, two Italian poets, and a contemporary Prussian statesman.  Both Almeda's spiritual angst and Shadal's reply seem, in some ways, surprisingly modern.  In particular, one remark by Shadal leaps out to the present-day reader:  lamenting the fact that people tend to shed their morality as soon as they acquire "some glory by means of various personal gifts," Shadal sardonically observes that "no vice is sufficient to destroy the reputation of a distinguished artist or a celebrated writer."

Although relatively brief, Shadal's letter to Giuseppe Almeda is a remarkable addition to the genre of Jewish religious literature of which some more famous examples are Maimonides' *Guide for the Perplexed* and Samson Raphael Hirsch's *Nineteen Letters,* the latter of which was published only three years before Shadal's work.  I am indebted to my friend Shimon Steinmetz for alerting me to the availability of the

# Appendix: A Letter to Almeda

*Epistolario* online, thus enabling me to discover the letter to Almeda and to make it familiar to an English-speaking audience.[3]

Here, then, are my translations of an excerpt from Almeda's request and the entire response by Shadal, both documents headed by the titles that they were given in the *Epistolario*.

## Questions Presented by
## Giuseppe Almeda of Trieste to S. D. Luzzatto

Although I was born in the bosom of Judaism, my religious education was almost nil. The ceremonies, the prayers that I saw performed or that I did myself left no deep or intimate impression on me; I felt no serious conviction in my soul.

Having reached the age of reason... I came to be—thanks to the serious meditations of the German philosophers and the modern eclectic-French school—intimately convinced of the existence of God, then of the immortality of the soul, and then of the true bases of morality: duty and virtue.

Now I am halfway down the path of life, and I am coming to consider whether these convictions, these beliefs, this internal cult of God and truth, are sufficient to discharge my obligations on this earth, and whether practical morality and the worship of the heart are all that the Almighty asks of one who seeks Him out sincerely... Besides which, I am a father... And some day perhaps I will be reproached for not having initiated [my children] in that which could have given them consolation and resolve throughout the hardships of life...

I see the Christian imbibe his religion with his mother's milk and absorb it into his blood, to the extent that reason most often comforts him in his faith. In contrast, I see the Jew more and more disbelieving the more he seeks to delve into science. What should I do? Abjure the faith of my fathers? But I am not convinced of that which I am close to embracing; I can merely glimpse it, sensing in it a material usefulness. Yet a general aversion, perhaps born of prejudice, awaits one who renounces his own religion.

---

3. *The Epistolario* can be found at http://books.google.com/books?id=jkw-AAAAYAAJ. I also thank Shimon for his valuable suggestions for improving this article.

# Shadal on Leviticus

And how can I resolve solemnly to profess a faith that condemns to eternal perdition those who gave me life?

No, my God! This I will never do; an urgent voice from my conscience tells me that this is Your will. Because I was born into Judaism, I must persist in it; nor can there be any fault in doing so.

After this, what remains for me? To seek within it, to the greatest extent possible, conviction and truth.

For this purpose I lack the erudition, the knowledge, the time. And yet the matter is sacred, important, essential. One who has the erudition, the knowledge, and the time must lend me aid, and it is for this reason that I have resolved to put into writing some questions in this regard, requesting, of one who is willing, to answer them one by one. Not without reason have I first introduced a few ill-chosen words as to my profession of faith and the state of my soul, for it matters greatly to the one who will respond to know how the questioner thinks about certain underlying matters, not so much for the sake of the substance of the answers as much as for the form they should take...

## To Giuseppe Almeda, Trieste

The page that introduces the proposed questions does not explicitly request any response, any explication; rather, it is presented for the sole object of serving as guidance, not for the substance of the answers to be given, but for the form that they are to take. Thus it is that I—expressing for the proponent the warmest esteem for the candor of a truly righteous and virtuous soul, and for the wise and judicious mind, of which his writing offers the most undoubted proof, and at the same time declaring my awareness of the honor of the trust that he has shown me—pass on immediately to respond to the questions. I do so even though I know that, in order to make the answers understood by the one who will read them as well as they are by the one who writes them, they ought to have been prefaced with lengthy discourses tending to substitute new groups of ideas for the existing ones, [taking into account] the great and unique source of divergence in human judgments, and the principal cause of the great diversity of ways of seeing and hearing that are displayed among the various individuals of the human race.

# Appendix: A Letter to Almeda

**1. Is there a canonical book that is recognized without controversy as being obligatory, in which the cardinal points of our faith are clearly enumerated?**

All of the books of the Holy Scriptures are commonly regarded as having infallible authority. The Pentateuch alone is unquestionably obligatory. However, neither it nor the other books of Scripture enumerate, or even mention, points of faith. The first one who enumerated them was Maimonides, and the motive that induced him to do so will be seen in the discussion of question 3, below. Moses did not dictate articles of faith, because God does not command belief, that is, He does not command that which cannot be commanded. He assigns grave punishments for many religious transgressions, but He never makes mention of the sin of disbelief, nor does He condemn antireligious speech, except for seduction to idolatry (since it leads to material acts condemned by the law) and blasphemy, or cursing aimed against the nation's God, which was thus an act of *lèse-majesté* [an offense against the Sovereign].

The succeeding prophets, and the ancient Rabbis, animated by the same spirit as Moses, never make mention of articles of faith. Scripture detests the atheist, but the atheist of depraved conduct. "The vile one says in his heart: 'There is no God'; they have committed wicked and abominable actions" (Psalm 14:1).

On the other hand, Moses did not institute a religion; rather, on the bases of one that already existed, he raised the edifice of a state and of a body of legislation. For if by "religion" we mean various beliefs concerning one God or more, and some sentiments of filial devotion and some acts of homage toward such God or gods, the Israelites prior to Moses professed a religion. Moses presented himself to them in the name of the God of their forebears, not in the name of a God unknown to them. He did not repeat to them a catechism that they already knew; and it was only for the sake of posterity that he expounded it implicitly in the history that he left to us from the times previous to his.

There we see Abraham, Isaac, Jacob, and their descendants believing in One God, Master of heaven and earth, Distributor of just rewards and punishments, Whose Providence watches over the well-being of his devotees. We see them believing in miracles, angels, revelations in wakefulness and sleep, and giving thought to the place where their bodies should be buried (probably believing in resurrection). We see them praying to God in their distress, and also on behalf of others. We see them rendering to God thanks for favors received, by means of sacrifices. The way of God, which Abraham taught to his descendants, consisted in the exercise of humanity and justice (Genesis 18:19). The sole required ceremony was circumcision. An ancient, but spontaneous, practice among them was that of not eating the ligament that attaches the femur to the acetabulum.[4]

---

4. Shadal is referring, of course, to the *gid ha-nasheh*, the part of Jacob's body that was injured in his fight with the angel (Gen. 32:25-33). In his commentary on these verses, Shadal takes the position that Jacob's thighbone (femur) was dislocated in the struggle when the ligament that attached it to the socket of the hip bone (acetabulum) gave way. Such an explanation is contrary to the halakhic view, according to which the *gid ha-nasheh* is the sciatic nerve. In a footnote to my translation of the commentary (Daniel A. Klein, *The Book of Genesis: A Commentary by Shadal (S. D. Luzzatto)* (Northvale, NJ: Jason Aronson, 1998) 316 n. 6), I sought to reconcile this surprising discrepancy by distinguishing between the halakhic practice and Shadal's literary interpretation of the narrative. However, after seeing Shadal's letter to Almeda, I was compelled to modify my approach. Accordingly, in the republished version of my translation (*Shadal on Genesis: Samuel David Luzzatto's Interpretation of the Book of Bereshit* (New York: Kodesh Press, 2019) 377 n. 6), I say that although Shadal indeed maintained that the "spontaneous" (i.e., uncommanded) pre-Mosaic custom was not to eat the ligament of the head of the femur, he would have recognized that the prohibition as subsequently codified was transferred, for whatever reason, to the sciatic nerve. See *Ḥullin* 100b for the proposition that the practice of not eating the *gid ha-nasheh* was not a mitzvah until it was promulgated at Sinai (although Rashi's comment ad loc. seems to take the view that the practice itself started at Sinai).

It should be noted that not only Shadal, but classical exegetes such as Rashbam and even, on occasion, Rashi, "permitted themselves to interpret texts according to the simple sense even when it stands in opposition to the conclusion which is demanded by the *derashah* of the passage, and that they saw no contradiction in

# Appendix: A Letter to Almeda

On the basis of this religion, Moses raised his Republic, his legislation. At the time that the Israelite people were brought into possession of the promised land, God so chose to organize the people by means of civil and criminal legislation, to which religion was given as a base. Moses, the chosen organ of the Divine will, does not teach a new religion, but inculcates in the Israelites that of their ancestors. He does not announce any new dogma, but imposes new practices, new ceremonies, new prohibitions, with which it pleased God to render both fixed and public that cult which had originally been individual and spontaneous. He does not teach a new morality, but dictates a code that does no more than develop and sanctify the principles of humanity and justice that Abraham taught.

The Mishnah, the supremely authoritative text of Rabbinic Judaism, enumerates [in *Sanhedrin* 10:1] three classes of persons who are condemned to deprivation of future blessedness, and they are: one who says that the Resurrection of the Dead is not (taught) in the Torah, one who says that the Torah is not from Heaven, and the Epicurean (*apikores*). Rabbi Akiva adds, one who reads esoteric books (according to some, the Apocryphal books) and one who recites over a plague (as a remedy) the text of Exodus 15:26. Abba Shaul adds, one who pronounces the Tetragrammaton. About this Mishnah text, I would observe that if those ancient scholars had meant that a person can be condemned for his beliefs, they would have said "one who denies the Resurrection of the Dead," not "one who says that the Resurrection of the Dead is not in the Torah"; and instead of specifying the "Epicurean," they would have said

this" (Yeshayahu Maori, "The Approach of Classic Jewish Exegetes to Peshat and Derash and Its Implications for the Teaching of Bible Today," trans. Moshe Bernstein, *Tradition* 21 (1984): 3). Further, it should be emphasized that like those exegetes, "Shadal did not intend to deny the authoritativeness of the Rabbinic halakhah or to determine that on the basis of his interpretations, one ought to conduct one's practice and to turn aside from the established halakhah. Like them, he regarded himself as subject to the halakhah accepted by the Rabbis" (Shmuel Vargon, "S. D. Luzzatto's Critique of Rabbinic Biblical Exegesis Which Strays from the Plain Sense of the Bible," *Jewish Studies Internet Journal* 2 (2003): 101, http://www.biu.ac.il/JS/JSIJ/2-2003/Vargon.pdf) (my translation from the Hebrew).

"one who denies God." Besides, it would be hard to understand how Akiva and Abba Shaul placed alongside these three cardinal misbeliefs three physical acts. All of this impels me to conclude that these scholars never thought to enumerate points of faith, nor did they believe to be condemned those who do not believe; rather, they intended to declare as deprived of future blessedness (that is, not condemned to eternal suffering, but deprived of resurrection): (1) those violators of the law who, instead of pleading in their own defense human or individual frailty, claim that the Pentateuch does not teach of the Resurrection, thus after death there is nothing to hope for or fear, thus anything that pleases is lawful; (2) those who, in other words, allege the non-divinity of the Torah; and finally (3) the Epicurean, that is, not the merely theoretical atheist, but the practicing one.

***2. Must one believe to be equally true the precepts, the miracles, and the events recorded in the Holy Scriptures? What I mean is, must one hold to an equal standard of belief the dogma of the Unity of God proclaimed by Moses, the miracle of the Red Sea, and the law of not eating forbidden foods?***

Speaking precisely, true things are all equally true; one such thing cannot be truer than another. On the other hand, the precepts demand observance, not belief; to "believe in" a precept is not a very clear expression, and even less so the question whether one must hold to an equal standard of belief the dogmas, the miracles, and the precepts. One believes or does not believe a dogma; one believes or does not believe a miracle; but a precept is either observed or not observed. However, one believes or does not believe in the Divine provenance of a precept. If, then, the sense of the question is whether one must have equal faith in the divinity of the precepts, in the miracles, and in the dogmas, I respond in the first place that in Mosaism, faith is not commanded, and in the second place that whoever is persuaded of Mosaism is equally persuaded of the precepts, miracles, and dogmas contained in the Pentateuch. If, however, by "believing in the precepts" one means giving them importance, I respond that the observance of the precepts being a commanded thing, and the dogmas and miracles not being commanded things, these are things of different natures, and one cannot make comparisons or contrasts among them. But if it is asked whether violation of the precepts constitutes a desertion from Mosaism equal to the denial of the dogmas and the miracles, I respond: violation out of weakness, passion, or the like, no; violation due to denial of the divinity of the precepts, yes.

*3. With respect to a Jew who, having arrived at the truth of natural religion, practices the rites and ceremonies out of a love for order, but does not have faith—on account of either ignorance or error—in the revelation of Moses, would such a person be worthy of salvation in the mind of true believers? (See question 5 under "Reform").*[5]

I say yes. Maimonides, the originator of the opinion to the contrary, did not draw it from the sources of Judaism, but rather from those of Aristotelianism, which taught that because the soul is not a substance, but a faculty, man acquires immortality through knowledge of the metaphysical truths, and that whoever does not know them does not have a soul and is a beast. This past year I set this fact out clearly, and I drew upon myself a crusade on the part of believers and nonbelievers alike—a result that every sincere friend of the truth and of the *juste milieu* [the middle way, "golden mean"] must expect.[6]

---

5. The question to which Almeda refers (and to which Shadal does not respond in this letter) asks whether there is a danger that if certain laws and practices were to be abolished by reformers, the entire idea of revelation would be lost and the Jewish religion would be reduced to a form of pure Deism. Shadal's opinion of the Reform movement was clearly expressed elsewhere. For example: "Some Israelites, eager to exonerate themselves from the religious practices connected with Judaism, and wishing to do so with a sort of legality, so as not to have to be regarded as impious transgressors of the Law of God, mask their project of totally abolishing the Mosaic law under the specious name of Reform" (letter to A. J. Fürst, Sept. 1, 1843, in *Epistolario*, 424-425.)

6. Shadal is evidently referring to his article in the Prague periodical *Kerem Ḥemed* 3 (1838): 61-76, in which he criticizes Maimonides on several grounds, one of which is his adoption of the Aristotelian concept of the soul (see in particular p. 67). The article in question did indeed stir up much controversy; for example, about five weeks after writing the letter to Almeda, Shadal broke off his friendship

# Shadal on Leviticus

*4. Does the immortality of the soul, and the rewards and punishments of the life hereafter, constitute a solemn, universal, and indestructible belief of Mosaism? Is it deduced from the Holy Scriptures, and if so, from where? Why is there no august ceremony that makes mention of it at the point of one's death? Why do people pray so confusedly for the dead if, as I have heard, such prayer is not an essential point? If prayers for ourselves have value, why can they not be equally effective for a substance that continues to exist?*

The immortality of the soul is solemnly expressed in Ecclesiastes 12:7 ["And the dust returns to the earth as it was, and the spirit returns to God who gave it"]. Rewards after the resurrection are clearly announced in Daniel 12:2 ["And many of them that sleep in the dust of the earth shall awake, some to everlasting life, and some to reproaches and everlasting abhorrence"]. That belief in the resurrection existed among the ancient Israelites can also be deduced from the poetical allusion that Isaiah makes to it in 26:19 ["But your dead shall live, my dead bodies shall arise—awake and sing, ye that dwell in the dust—for Your dew is as the dew of light, and the earth shall bring to life the shades"].

That the Israelites at the time of Moses believed in the immortality of the soul can be perceived beyond doubt from the law that forbids consultation with the dead. Moses implicitly teaches of a blessedness beyond this life when he narrates that Abel's sacrifice was pleasing to God, and that Abel was murdered soon after, as well as when he says that Enoch was faithful to God and was taken by God before he reached even half the usual lifespan of his times.

However, for purposes of sanction in his laws, Moses announced rewards that were earthly, natural, verifiable in this life, and such a sanction was much more effective than one that would have been drawn from heavenly rewards, supported by faith alone.

Words of comfort relating to immortality are offered by the rabbi at the bedside of every dying person, and upon the coffin of every deceased. A religion without mysteries could not suggest any other

with Rabbi Solomon Judah Rapoport as a result of this and related scholarly disputes (see, for example, Morris B. Margolies, *Samuel David Luzzatto: Traditionalist Scholar* (New York: Ktav, 1979), 151).

ceremony, much less an august ceremony. The dead are not prayed for, because it is believed that God rewards or punishes everyone according to his actions, not according to those of any other person. I can pray for my sick child, because his death or illness affects me as well; it is not so for my deceased father, because he must be treated according to his own merits, and his punishments that are unknown to me do not affect me. Nevertheless, some ancient Rabbis taught that leaving behind a well-raised and pious child is ascribed by God to the parent's merit, and thus the prayers and good works of the child are of benefit to the parent's soul. And this doctrine is most praiseworthy for its salutary effects.

*5. Will the anticipated regeneration be political, religious, or both? Will it be universal? Is normative Rabbinism, the keeper of this belief, unanimously in agreement as to its nature?*

The anticipated regeneration will be political for the Jews and religious for the universality of the human race, the entirety of which will embrace not Judaism but monotheism. So the prophets and the ancient Rabbis unanimously teach.

*6. Is the resurrection of the dead not an inconceivable mystery? And if it is, why criticize the irrational mysteries that Christians maintain? For it costs no more to believe that one dead man will return to life after a thousand years or two than to believe that a million dead people will return to life at some future time.*

The resurrection is not inconceivable. The body is not destroyed, but is dissolved. Could the Creator not gather together its particles, or incorporate them into a new body like the first? The resurrection of Jesus does not constitute part of the mysteries of Christianity; that is, it is not one of the inconceivable dogmas that some might criticize.[7]

---

7. The Roman Catholic Church does in fact refer to "the mystery of the Resurrection"; see, for example, *New Catholic Encyclopedia* (McGraw-Hill, 1967), s.v. "Resurrection of Christ." However, the term "mystery," in this context, may mean nothing more than an incident in the life of Jesus that is deemed to have special significance to Christians (see *Random House Dictionary* (1966) s.v. "mystery").

# Shadal on Leviticus

*7. Can the religion of Moses become universal? And if it cannot, and if the Jews, as I believe, do not maintain this pretension, how can Mosaism be called divine, revealed by the Creator Himself? For it is repugnant to reason to believe it to be among the truths proclaimed by God Himself, without also believing that all humankind will at some time taste of this heavenly manna.*

Mosaism will never become universal, but its fundamental principle—that is, monotheism—can indeed become universal. It is precisely for this purpose that God chose the Jewish people, that is, so that it might become the custodian of these truths and the organ by which they might be propagated among all the nations. The Jewish people was chosen because it was the only one that had already known and professed these truths through the teaching of its ancestors. Revelation to any other, polytheistic, people would have been fruitless, for without the advance conviction of the unity of God, any revelation, no matter how indisputable, would leave in its wake a doubt that some other day, some other god might reveal himself and impart different and contrary doctrines.

*8. How is it that to all of these questions, I receive answers that are inconsistent one from another, from persons who are religious and learned?*

Precisely because Judaism has no articles of faith and leaves full freedom to the thinker, making only material actions binding. True Religion is not the science of divine matters (a science that is too far above the reach of man); it is an intimate belief, a filial devotion, that extends itself in the acts of a spontaneous and indeterminate cult, as in the case of the Judaism that preceded Moses, or—as in the case of Mosaism—in practices and observances that are determined by law. The goal of such law is not that God may become known and worshipped by us, as if He were in need of our homage, but rather: (1) to keep alive in our minds the

---

What Shadal appears to be maintaining is that the resurrection is not a doctrine that can be understood only by an initiated elite. Note that in his response to question 4, he makes a similar claim for Judaism in general, calling it "a religion without mysteries."

idea of God and of Providence, the only idea that is capable of keeping us constantly attached to virtue; and (2) to accustom us to keep a rein on our desires and to undergo privations patiently, an indispensable attitude for rendering us superior to the passions and the temptations of vice. As [the Stoic philosopher] Epictetus said, if one would keep to heart two words, he would be blameless: *sustine et abstine* ["sustain and abstain"; "bear and forbear"].

Jeremiah reposes the glory of humankind in the sound knowledge of God, that is, he says, in the knowledge that God is that Being Whose acts are universal compassion, benevolence, and justice; for these, concludes the prophet—introducing God Himself as the speaker— "these are the things that I desire (that people should do)" (Jer. 9:23). This text manifestly proves, in the first place, that the knowledge which God wants us to have of Him has, as its object, not His honor but our betterment. He does not say that God is great, powerful, terrible, but that He is beneficent and just; nor does He content Himself in explaining the concept that we should have of God, but He adds, "These are the things that I desire"; that is, the knowledge of God is not desired for its own sake; compassion, humanity, and justice are what He desires; it is important to know Him so as to practice the virtues that He loves; "these are the things that I desire," says God, not a sterile knowledge of Me. In the second place, this text proves that our betterment and perfection, desired by God, consist of the social virtues: compassion, humanity, justice; that these are the things desired by God, and the only things for which He wishes to be known and worshipped by us.

**9. Do Jews receive—purely as Jews, and not as subjects of this or that government that has thought of it—a moral education? With what standards? With what book? What is the moral education of a Jew in the Levant that still preserves the entire teaching of Mosaism?**

Those Jews who have the benefit of being trained from infancy by religious parents or teachers receive, in whatever region in which they live, the best of moral educations, that of the Bible, of the Talmudic books, and of example. The sincerely religious Jew is the same in all countries and all eras; European or Asiatic, in the Middle Ages or in the nineteenth century, he is a model of virtue. His morality is the fruit of the two principles that dominate within him, one disinterested and the other interested, and these are the sense of compassion and the fear of God.

The disinterested sense of compassion, of sympathy, inborn in humankind, but too often suffocated by egoism and by calculating reason, is warmly nourished and reinvigorated by the Jewish religious upbringing, that is, by the books of the Bible and Talmud, and by the example set by religious trainers. In every age, humanity and compassion have comprised the glory of the Jewish people. The Syrians, after having lost a battle, said to their king (I Kings 20:31), "We know, by reputation, the kings of Israel to be compassionate." The Rabbis of the Talmud said, "One who has no compassion is not of the descent of Abraham" (*Beitsah* 32a). Indeed, the shame of all the ancient legal systems, torture, is an unknown thing to Jewish legislation, whether Mosaic or Rabbinic; it was practiced only by Herod, a king of foreign origin, despiser of all things Jewish and imitator of the Romans in everything. A commonplace maxim of the Talmud is, "Love your neighbor as yourself; even for a convicted criminal, select the least harsh form of death" (e.g., *Sanhedrin* 45a). Even causing pain to animals is, according to the Talmudic sages, forbidden by the Divine law. Nowadays, here in Italy, it is not uncommon to see tenant farmers call themselves fortunate when the holdings that they cultivate pass into the hands of a Jew.

The fear of God, an interested sense, the other foundation of Jewish morality, exercises its salutary influence where the disinterested sense of compassion would not suffice, suffocated by interest and need. Belief in an eye that sees, an ear that hears, a book in which everything is recorded, an avenging hand to which all resistance is vain—this belief is inculcated by all the Prophets, by all the Rabbis, by all good instructors of Judaism.

What other principles could morality possess? I mean to say a sincere morality which, issuing forth from the heart of the teacher, is capable of reaching the bottom of the student's heart—not a useless morality of pure ostentation. Honor, the great basis of the morality of civilization, governs a person on the world's scene, and abandons him as soon as he thinks himself invisible, or as soon as he acquires some glory by means of various personal gifts, for no vice is sufficient to destroy the reputation of a distinguished artist or a celebrated writer.

The idea of social utility is too easily defeated by the idea of personal utility. The sense of justice is nothing more than an emanation from the sense of compassion; like the latter, it needs to be nourished and invigorated, and being, like the latter, disinterested by its nature, it often gives way in the face of individual utility and need, where it is not sustained by the interested idea of reward and punishment. The dignity of the rational being, the categorical imperative of the conscience, the sense of duty, are not felt by everyone. As for those Jews who receive a moral education from their respective governments, what other morality do they learn from them if not the Jewish one, that of the Holy Scriptures? Is the evangelical morality anything other than the biblical? If it contains any new principle, it is that of the damnation of unbelievers, the basis of all intolerance, and the doctrine of the "Keys" [the power of the Church to forgive sins], the basis of [the often abused authority to grant] indulgences. Christianity is certainly a worthy foundation for public civility and morality, but this is only thanks to the biblical morality that it teaches. The equalization of humankind, in that we are all the children of One Father, is a doctrine of the Pentateuch.

Being born in the bosom of a civilized or barbarous nation does not modify the morality of the Jew, but the varying degree of morality of the peoples who surround him in the various regions of his dispersion can render him more or less devoted to them. If in Asia and Africa he is less so than in Europe, that would stem not from a difference in his moral education, but from the eternal laws of the human heart, according to which:

> *Amar chi t'odia, ell'è impossibil cosa;*
> *Nè con altro che amore amor si merca.*[8]

The moral education of civilization can render the Jew more attached to honor, that is, to the appearance of virtue, but never more attached to virtue itself. And if civilization seizes away from him his ancestral

---

8. These are lines from two different Italian poets. The first, by Vittorio Alfieri (1749-1808), means, "To love one who hates you, that is an impossible thing." The second, by Pietro Metastasio (1698-1782), means, "With nothing else but love is love dealt."

education, it can only weaken or destroy his religious principles, for which it hardly possesses an equivalent to substitute. If religion was once useful for refining barbarous peoples, it is now necessary in the development of an advanced civilization, in which:

> With the development of the intellectual powers, with the increase and perfection of all the objects that delight the inclinations of the senses, there is an increase of brutal desires, sensual passions, a yielding to unjust tendencies, the skill of achieving an interested goal at the expense of the rights of one's fellow man, and such crimes multiply and proceed at an equal pace with the development of such powers. (Ancillon, *Du juste milieu,* vol. II, p. 29.)[9]

March 6, 1839

---

9. Johann Peter Friedrich Ancillon, *Du juste milieu, ou du rapprochement des extrêmes dans les opinions* ["The Middle Way, or Of the Reconciliation of Extremes in Opinions"] (Brussels: Société Belge de Librairie, 1837), a French translation from the original German. Ancillon (1766-1837) was a Prussian historian and statesman. The excerpt in question was quoted by Shadal in French.

# Sources Cited by Shadal

## *Scholars and Commentators*

**Abravanel, (Don) Isaac** (1437-1508). Classic Torah commentator, philosopher, and statesman, born in Lisbon.

**Arnheim, Heymann** (1796-1869). Prussian rabbi, educator, and Hebraist. Wrote translation of and commentary on Book of Job (Glogau, 1836); was one of the translators of Leopold Zunz's edition of the Bible, *Die vier und zwanzig Bücher der Heiligen Schrift* (Berlin, 1838). Translated the Pentateuch, *Die fünf Bücher Moses nebst den Haftaroth* (Prague, 1855).

**Basevi, Joseph Shabbetai** (Giuseppe Sabato, 1823-1884). Student of Shadal, born in Padua; ordained in 1847. Served as rabbi in Sabbioneta, Spalato, and Padua.

**Brill, Joel** (1762-1802). Author of a Hebrew commentary printed with Mendelssohn's German translation of the Book of Psalms (Berlin, 1791).

**Forster, Johann Reinhold** (1729-1798). German traveler and naturalist. *Liber singularis de Bysso Antiquorum* (London, 1776).

**Frizzi, Benedetto** (Benzion Raphael Kohen, 1756-1844). Italian physician, engineer, and scholar from Ostiano. Founded one of the first

# Shadal on Leviticus

Italian medical journals (1790-91). Wrote *Dissertazione sulla lebbra degli Ebrei* (Trieste, 1795), a study of the Biblical "leprosy" in light of the medical knowledge of his time.

**Gesenius, Heinrich Friedrich Wilhelm** (1786-1842). German Orientalist, lexicographer, and biblical scholar; professor of theology at University of Halle. Among his works are *Hebräisches und chaldäisches Handwörterbuch über das Alte Testament* (Leipzig, 1815), translated by Samuel Prideaux Tragelles as *Gesenius' Hebrew and Chaldee Lexicon to the Old Testament Scriptures* (London, 1846); a later edition was translated as *A Hebrew and English Lexicon of the Old Testament,* ed. Brown, Driver, and Briggs (1907). Also wrote *Thesaurus philologicus criticus linguae Hebraeae et Chaldaeae veteris testamenti* (Leipzig, 1835), and an Isaiah translation and commentary (Leipzig, 1820-1821, 1829).

**Grego, Abraham** (1817-1858). Student of Shadal, from Verona; participated in some of the revolutionary events of 1848.

**Homer** (eighth century B.C.E.). Reputed author of the Greek epic poems, the *Iliad* and the *Odyssey.*

**Ibn Ezra, Abraham** (1089-1164). Classic Torah commentator, poet, grammarian, and philosopher, born in Tudela, Spain. Although Shadal often expresses criticism of Ibn Ezra's attitude and writing style, he frequently cites and often adopts Ibn Ezra's views in his Torah commentary.

**Igel, Eliezer Elijah** (Lazar Elias, 1825-1892). Student of Shadal, born in Lemberg (Lvov); ordained in 1847. In a letter to R. Samson Raphael Hirsch in Nikolsburg, dated August 8, 1849, Shadal said that Igel was seeking to serve the Jewish community of Teschen, Moravia, and he recommended him in the warmest terms (*Iggerot Shadal*, vol. 2, pp. 1063-1064). Although Igel apparently never went to Teschen, he became district rabbi of Czernowitz in 1854 and later chief rabbi of Bukovina, in which positions he succeeded in maintaining peace between the local Orthodox and Reform factions.

**Jablonski, Paul Ernst** (1693-1757). German Hebraist and Egyptologist; wrote *Opuscula quibus liingua et antiquitas Aegyptiorum* (1804-1813).

# Shadal on Leviticus

**Josephus Flavius** (c. 38 C.E.-c. 100 C.E). Jerusalem-born historian in Rome; played a controversial part in the Jewish War of 66-70 C.E. Among his works is *Jewish Antiquities*, a history of the Jews from Bible times written in a Hellenistic style.

**Landau, Moses** (1788-1852). Head of the Prague Jewish community, grandson of R. Ezekiel Landau. Wrote a German translation and Hebrew commentary on several books of the Bible (1834-38).

**Linnaeus, Carolus** (Carl von Linné, 1707-1778). Swedish botanist who established the binomial system of scientific nomenclature.

**Maimonides, Moses** (*Rambam*, R. Moses ben Maimon, 1135-1204). Renowned halakhic authority, philosopher, and physician, born in Córdoba, Spain. Criticized by Shadal for adopting the world-view of Aristotelian philosophy, which valued the mind over the heart.

**Mainster, Abraham Hai** (1816-1882). Student of Shadal, born in Verona; ordained in 1841. Rabbi of Viadana, Rovigo, and Verona.

**Mendelssohn, Moses** (*Rambeman*, R. Moses ben Menahem, or Moses of Dessau, 1729-1786). German Jewish philosopher and Bible translator; his *Netivot ha-Shalom* (1780-1783), a German translation of the Torah printed in Hebrew characters, was accompanied by the *Biur*, a Hebrew commentary written in collaboration with Solomon Dubno, Naphtali Herz Wessely (see below), Naphtali Herz Homberg (see below at *Korem*), and Aaron Jaroslaw.

**Mizrahi, Elijah** (*Re'em*, c. 1450-1526). Leading halakhic authority of Ottoman Empire, born in Constantinople. Wrote supercommentary to Rashi (Venice, 1527).

**Modena, Shalom Simeon** (Pacifico, 1830-1910). Student of Shadal, born in Modena. Director of the Talmud Torah of Alexandria, Egypt, 1884-1892.

**Nachmanides** (*Ramban*, R. Moses ben Nahman, 1194-1270). Classic Torah commentator, halakhic authority, and philosopher, born in Gerona, Spain.

# Shadal on Leviticus

**Olper, Samuel Solomon** (1811-1876). Student of Shadal, born in Rovigo; ordained in 1838. One of the few Italian rabbis to advocate Reform. Rabbi of Venice, 1838-1848; member of the revolutionary Assembly of Venice in 1848. Later served as rabbi in Florence, Casale, and Turin.

**Onkelos** (second century C.E.). Proselyte who translated the Pentateuch into Aramaic, reportedly under the guidance of R. Eliezer ben Hyrcanus and R. Joshua ben Hananiah. Some scholars maintain that the name is a corruption of Aquila (second century C.E.), a proselyte who translated the Bible into Greek. Onkelos's translation (Targum) is the subject of Shadal's *Ohev Ger*.

**Osimo, Judah Aryeh** (Leone, 1815-1869). Student of Shadal, born in Montagnana; ordained in 1841. Rabbi of Padua, 1867-1869.

**Pardo, Isaac** (1824-1892). Student of Shadal, born in Leghorn; ordained in 1847. Chief Rabbi of Verona. A manuscript consisting of his transcription of Shadal's lectures, modifying the transcription previously made by his brother, Jacob Hai Pardo (see below), was utilized in the 2015 Bassi edition of *Perush Shadal la-Torah*.

**Pardo, Jacob Hai (Vita)** (1818-1839). Student of Shadal, brother of Isaac Pardo (see above); born in Ragusa (Dubrovnik). Wrote commentary on part of Micah at age 18, published by Shadal as a first supplement to his *Avnei Zikkaron* (Prague, 1841).

**Rashbam** (R. Samuel ben Meir, 1080-1158). Classic Torah commentator and Tosafist, grandson of Rashi (see below). His commentary, to a greater extent that Rashi's, strictly adhered to the *peshat*, or plain meaning of the text.

**Rashi** (R. Solomon Yitshaki, 1040-1105). The preeminent classic Torah commentator, born in Troyes, France.

**Reggio, Isaac Samuel** (1784-1855). Italian rabbi of Gorizia; played a key role in formation and organization of the Istituto Convitto Rabbinico (Collegio Rabbinico) of Padua and helped to secure Shadal's professorship there. Wrote Torah commentary with Italian translation, *Torat ha-Elohim* (Vienna, 1821).

# Shadal on Leviticus

**Rosenmueller, Ernst Friedrich Karl** (1768-1835). German Orientalist, theologian, and exegete; included exegetical notes by Shadal, in French, on Isaiah as an introduction to his own Isaiah commentary (Leipzig, 1835). Rosenmueller's *Scholia in Pentateuchum* (Leipzig, 1828), was relied upon heavily by Shadal as a source of information and commentary.

**Rosh** (R. Asher ben Yehiel, c. 1250-ca. 1328). A leading halakhic authority in his native Germany and later in Spain. Student of Rabbi Meir of Rothenburg and father of Rabbi Jacob Ba'al ha-Turim. Author of *Hilkhot ha-Rosh*, an abstract of the practical Halakhah, which has been printed with most editions of the Talmud.

**Saadiah Gaon** (882-942). Leader of Babylonian Jewry, Talmudist, philosopher, and grammarian, born in Egypt; wrote commentary on and Arabic translation of Bible.

**Scheuzer, Jean-Jacques** (Johann Jacob Scheuchzer, 1672-1733). Swiss naturalist, author of *Physica Sacra* (Augsburg and Ulm, 1731-1735), translated as *Physique Sacrée, ou Histoire-Naturelle de la Bible* (Amsterdam, 1732), a multi-volume work finding correspondences between the Bible and the then current state of scientific research.

**Sforno, Ovadiah** (c. 1475-c. 1550). Classic Torah commentator, Talmudist, and physician, born in Cesena, Italy.

**Valmont de Bomare, Jacques Christophe** (1731-1807). French botanist and naturalist; wrote *Dictionnaire Raisonné Universel d'Histoire Naturelle* (Paris, 1764-1768).

**Virey, Julien-Joseph** (1775-1846)French naturalist and anthropologist. His *Histoire des moeurs et de l'instinct des animaux* (Paris, 1822) appeared in an Italian translation, *Storia dei costumi e dell'instinto degli animali* (Pavia, 1825).

**Wessely, Naphtali Herz** (1725-1805). Poet, linguist, and exegete, born in Hamburg; wrote the commentary to Leviticus (edited by Moses Mendelssohn) in *Netivot ha-Shalom* (Berlin, 1782). His commentary attempts to reconcile the plain meaning [*peshat*] with comments in the Talmud and Midrashim. Mendelssohn shortened Wessely's work, added interpretations of passages that he had left unexplained, and added comments where their opinions differed.

## *Works Cited by Title Only*

***Ba'al ha-Turim.*** Torah commentary by R. Jacob ben Asher (1270?-1340), author of the classic halakhic work *Arba'ah Turim.*

***Bikkurei ha-Ittim.*** Literary-scientific periodical published in Vienna (12 volumes, 1821-1832, later volumes 1844 and 1845).

***Kerem Ḥemed.*** Scholarly periodical published in Vienna, Prague, and Berlin (9 volumes, 1833-1856).

***Korem.*** Commentary on the Torah by Naphtali Herz Homberg (1749-1841), an extreme exponent of Haskalah; printed after *Ha-Mishtadel* and *Botser Olelot* in the 1846 edition of *Netivot ha-Shalom.*

***Kuzari.*** Defense of Judaism, written in Arabic (1140) by Judah ha-Levi (before 1075-1141).

***Korban Aharon.*** Commentary (Venice, 1611) on *Sifra (Torat Kohanim)* by Aaron Ibn Hayyim (1545-1632). a Biblical and Talmudic commentator, who was born in Fez and died in Jerusalem.

***Me'ammer.*** Torah commentary (Prague, 1833-1837) by Wolf Meir (Mayer) (1776-1850), instructor of Hebrew language and Bible at the German-Jewish Hauptschule (high school) in Prague. The commentary is also included in the 1862 Prague edition of Mendelssohn's *Netivot ha-Shalom.*

***Netivot ha-Shalom.*** See Moses Mendelssohn (above).

***Sefer ha-Zikkaron.*** Supercommentary to Rashi on the Torah (completed in Tunis, 1507; published in Leghorn, 1845, under the editorship of S. D. Luzzatto) by Abraham ben Solomon ha-Levi Bukarat (late fifteenth-early sixteenth century), exegete and poet in Malaga and Tunis.

***Sefer Mitsvot Gadol.*** Compilation of the positive and negative precepts,

# Shadal on Leviticus

by Moses of Coucy (France, 13th century), first published some time before 1480.

***Siftei Hakhamim.*** Supercommentary on Rashi (1680) by Shabbetai Bass of Prague (1641-1718), publisher and bibliographer.

***Tosefot Yom Tov.*** Mishnah commentary, supplementing that of R. Ovadiah Bertinoro, by R. Yom Tov Lipmann Heller (1579-1654) of Moravia.

## *Early Manuscripts and Printed Works (Untitled)*

***5278 edition.*** Identified by Shadal only with the Hebrew letters *resh ayin ḥet*, indicating the year 5278 (1518). Evidently a printed *Ḥumash*, with Rashi and Targum Onkelos.

***5351 Ḥumash.*** Identified by Shadal with the Hebrew letters *shin nun alef*, indicating the year 5351 (1591), and as originating in Venice and containing three Targumim.

## *Shadal's Own Works*

***Ohev Ger.*** A study of the methodology of Onkelos the proselye (*ger*) in his translation of the Torah; Vienna, 1830; second edition, Cracow, 1895.

## Translator-Editor's References

Abrahams, Israel. "Samuel David Luzzatto as Exegete." *Jewish Quarterly Review* 57:83-100 (1966).

Arnheim, Heymann. *Die fünf Bücher Moses nebst den Haftaroth.* Prague, 1855.

Benstein, Jeremy. *Hebrew Roots, Jewish Routes: A Tribal Language in a Global World.* Millburn, N.J.: Behrman House, 2019.

Bouglé, Célestin. *Essays on the Caste System*, trans. D. F. Pocock.

Cambridge: Cambridge University Press, 1971.

Chavel, Hayyim Dov (Charles), ed. *Perushei Rashi al ha-Torah*, 3rd ed. Jerusalem: Mosad ha-Rav Kook, 5743 (1983).

Cohen, Mordechai Z. "A Talmudist's Halakhic Hermeneutics: A New Understanding of Maimonides' Principle of Peshat Primacy." *Jewish Studies, an Internet Journal*, vol. 10, pp. 257-359 (2012),.

Davis, Mark S. "Crimes Mala in Se: An Equity-Based Definition." 17 Criminal Justice Policy Review 270 (Sept. 2006).

Deutscher, Guy. *The Unfolding of Language.* New York: Henry Holt and Co., 2006.

Di Segni, Gianfranco. "Le polemiche fra rabbini non sono certo una novità." *Kolòt*, 9/16/2010.

Douglas, Mary. *Leviticus as Literature.* Oxford: Oxford University Press, 1999.

Editors of the American Heritage Dictionaries, *Word Histories and Mysteries: From Abracadabra to Zeus.* Boston: Houghton Mifflin Co., 2004.

Ehrlich, Arnold B. *Mikra ki-Pheschuto*, Part 1. Berlin: Poppelauer, 1899.

Firth, John; Conlon, Christopher; and Cox, Timothy, eds. *Oxford Textbook of Medicine* (6th ed.). Oxford: Oxford University Press, 2020.

Frandsen, Paul John. *Incestuous and Close-Kin Marriage in Ancient Egypt and Persia: An Examination of the Evidence.* Copenhagen: Museum Tusculanum Press, 2009.

Freud, Sigmund. *A General Introduction to Psychoanalysis* (1920), trans. Joan Riviere. New York: Pocket Books, 1953.

Frizzi, Benedetto. *Dissertazione sulla lebbra degli Ebrei.* Trieste, 1795.

Gesenius, Heinrich Friedrich Wilhelm. *Gesenius' Hebrew and Chaldee Lexicon to the Old Testament Scriptures*, trans. Samuel Prideaux Tregelles. London, 1853.

Goldstein, Alec. *A Theology of Holiness.* New York: Kodesh Press, 2018.

Grzybowski, Andrzej; Nita, Małgorzata. "Leprosy in the Bible." *Clinics in Dermatology* 34(1):3-7 (Jan.-Feb. 2016).

Heller, Richard M.; Heller, Toni W.; Sasson, Jack M. "Mold: 'Tsara'at,'

Leviticus, and the History of a Confusion." *Perspectives in Biology and Medicine* 46(4):588-591 (Autumn 2003).

Hirsch, Samson Raphael. *Judaism Eternal*, vol. 1, trans. I. Grunfeld. London: Soncino Press, 1956.

Hoffmann, David Zvi. *Das Buch Leviticus*. Berlin: Poppelauer, 1905. Hebrew version: *Sefer Vayikra*. Jerusalem: Mosad Harav Kook, 1976.

Judah ha-Levi. *Judah Hallevi's Khitab al-Khazari*, trans. Hartwig Hirschfeld. London: George Routledge & Sons; New York: E. P. Dutton & Co., 1905.

Klein, Daniel A. *Shadal on Exodus: Samuel David Luzzatto's Interpretation of the Book of* Shemot. New York: Kodesh Press, 2015.

———. *Shadal on Genesis: Samuel David Luzzatto's Interpretation of the Book of* Bereshit. New York: Kodesh Press, 2019.

———. "Unconventional but Not Unorthodox: Shadal's Approach to the Oral Torah." *La Rassegna Mensile di Israel,* Vol. 84 Iss. 1-2, pp. 47-68 (2018).

Klein, Ernest. *A Comprehensive Etymological Dictionary of the Hebrew Language for Readers of English.* Carta Jerusalem and University of Haifa, 1987.

Lempriere, John. *Bibliotheca Classica.* London, 1840.

Leibowitz, Nehama. *New Studies in Vayikra (Leviticus),* trans. Rafael Fisch and Avner Tomaschoff, vols. 1 and 2. Jerusalem: Eliner Library, World Zionist Organization, Department for Torah Education and Culture in the Diaspora, 1993.

Levy, B. Barry. *Fixing God's Torah: The Accuracy of the Hebrew Bible Text in Jewish Law.* New York: Oxford University Press, 2001.

Lockshin, Martin. "*Peshat* vs. *Halakha* Dilemma: Shadal and Tradition." TheTorah.com (2016). http://thetorah.com/article/peshat-vs-halakha-dilemma-shadal-and-tradition

Luzzatto, Samuel David. *Beit ha-Otsar*, vol. 2. Przemysl, 1888.

———. "Breve Prospetto della Legislazione Mosaica." *L'Educatore Israelita*, 1st year, 2nd ed. (1853), pp. 291-295.

———. *Epistolario italiano francese latino*. Padua, 1890.

———. *Ha-Mishtadel*. Vienna, 1846-47.

# Shadal on Leviticus

———. *Iggerot Shadal.* Przemysl and Cracow, 1882-94.

———. *Il Pentateuco volgarizzato e commentato (Ḥamishah Ḥumshei Torah Meturgamim Italkit u-M'forashim Ivrit).* Padua: Francesco Sacchetto, 1871-76.

———. *Index raisonné des livres de correspondance de feu Samuel David Luzzatto.* Padua, 1878.

———. *Mehkerei Ha-Yahadut.* Warsaw: Ha-Tsefirah, 1912/13; Jerusalem: Makor, 1970.

———. *Perush Shadal la-Torah,* ed. Yonatan Bassi. Jerusalem: Carmel, 2015.

——— and *continuatori. La Sacra Bibbia volgarizzata.* Rovigo, 1872.

Margolies, Morris B. *Samuel David Luzzatto: Traditionalist Scholar.* New York: Ktav, 1979.

Milgrom, Jacob. *Leviticus: A Book of Ritual and Ethics.* Minneapolis: Fortress Press, 2004.

Preuss, Julius. *Biblical and Talmudic Medicine*, trans. Fred Rosner. New York: Ktav, 1971; reprinted, New York: Sanhedrin Press, 1978; reprinted, Rowman & Littlefield, 2004. (Originally *Biblisch-talmudische Medizin*, Berlin, S. Karger, 1911.)

Rosenbaum, M., and Silbermann, A. M. *Pentateuch with Rashi's Commentary.* New York: Hebrew Publishing Co., 1934.

Roth, Cecil. *Venice.* Philadelphia: Jewish Publication Society, 1930.

Rudavsky, David. "Samuel David Luzzatto and Neo-Orthodoxy." *Tradition,* vol. 7 no. 3, pp. 21-44 (Fall 1965).

Shapiro, Marc B. "Maimonides' Thirteen Principles: The Last Word in Jewish Theology?" *The Torah U-Madda Journal,* vol. 4, pp. 187-242 (1993).

Shoham-Steiner, Ephraim. *On the Margins of a Minority: Leprosy, Madness, and Disability Among the Jews of Medieval Europe,* trans. Haim Watzman. Detroit: Wayne State University Press, 2014.

Slifkin, Natan. *The Camel, the Hare and the Hyrax.* Zoo Torah, 2011.

———. *The Torah Encyclopedia of the Animal Kingdom, vol. 1: Wild Animals.* Biblical Museum of Natural History / Maggid Books / OU Press, 2015.

Stevanović, Lada. *Laughing at the Funeral: Gender and Anthropology in the Greek Funerary Rites.* Belgrade: Serbian Academy of Sciences and Arts, 2009.

# Shadal on Leviticus

Student, Gil. "Shadal and the Orthodox Canon." Torah Musings (January 11, 2016). http://www.Torahmusings.com/2016/01/shadal-and-the-orthodox-canon/.

Trachtman, Chaim. "Tzaraat as Cancer." TheTorah.com (2016). https://thetorah.com/article/tzaraat-as-cancer.

Tuori, Kaius. "Revenge and Retribution in the Twelve Tables: *Talio esto* Reconsidered." *Fundamina,* vol. 13, pp. 140-145 (2007).

Vargon, Shmuel. "Samuel David Luzzatto's Critique of Rabbinic Exegesis Which Contradicts the Plain Meaning of Scripture" (Hebrew). *Jewish Studies, an Internet Journal,* vol. 2, pp. 97-122 (2003).

Wolf, Arthur P. *Incest Avoidance and the Incest Taboos: Two Aspects of Human Nature.* Stanford, Cal.: Stanford University Press, 2014.

## *Translator-Editor's Manuscript Sources*

*Columbia X 893 L 9765.* An undated manuscript, possibly in Shadal's hand, containing notes in Italian and Hebrew for translation of and commentary on Leviticus ch. 23-27, Numbers ch. 5-26, and Deuteronomy ch. 1-26. In Columbia University's Rare Book and Manuscript Library.

*Lutzki 672.* An undated manuscript, possibly in Shadal's hand, containing notes in Italian and Hebrew for translation of and commentary on Exodus and Leviticus. Catalogued by Moses (Morris) Lutzki (1895-1976), cataloguer of Hebrew manuscripts for the Jewish Theological Seminary of America (JTS) and professor of bibliography at Yeshiva University. In the JTS Library.

# PRIMARY SOURCE INDEX

# Shadal on Leviticus

| | | | |
|---|---|---|---|
| 22:8, | 116 | 5:16, | 50 |
| 22:10, | 63 | | |
| 22:27, | 213 | 6:9-11, | 45 |
| | | 6:19, | 51, 77 n. 8 |
| 23:11, | 219 | 6:21, | 112 |
| | | 6:22, | 72 |
| 24:10. | 86 n. 2 | 6:23, | 95 |
| 25:29, | 212, n. 27 | 7:7-9 | 69, 70 |
| | | 7:12, | 69 |
| 27:20, | 211 | 7:18, | 167 n. 1 |
| 29:24, | 78 | 8:33, | 94 |
| 29:36, | 81 | | |
| 29:37, | 68 | 9:1, | 94 |
| 29:44, | 91, n. 8 | 9:3, | 94, 95 |
| 29:46, | 91, n. 8 | 9:7, | 95 |
| 30:10, | 147 | 10:4, 5 | 85 n. 1 |
| 40:2, | 85 | 11:1, | 105 |
| | | 11:43, | 105 n. 18 |

**Leviticus**

| | | | |
|---|---|---|---|
| 1:2, | 65 | 12:2, | 70, 115 n. 7, 183 |
| 1:4, | 199 | | |
| 1:15, | 60 | 13:2, | 108 n. 2, 128 |
| | | 13:5, | 123, 126 |
| 4:5, | 56 | 13:12, | 119 n. 11 |
| 4:19, | 56 | 13:37, | 126 |
| 4:26, | 56 | 13:58, | 126 n. 18 |
| 4:32, | 130 | | |
| | | 14:2, | 116 |
| ch. 5 | 172 | 14:4-7, | 109 |
| 5:4, | 57 | 14:16, | 53 |
| 5:8, | 43 | 14:31, | 109 |
| 5:9, | 43 | 14:37, | 116 |
| 5:11, | 51 | 14:46, | 135 |
| 5:15, | 50 | 15:2-15, | 137 n. 6 |

# Shadal on Leviticus

# Shadal on Leviticus

# SUBJECT-AUTHOR INDEX

# Shadal on Leviticus

# Shadal on Leviticus

# Shadal on Leviticus